AFRICAN POLITICAL FACTS
SINCE 1945

AFRICAN POLITICAL FACTS SINCE 1945

Second Edition

Chris Cook and David Killingray

MACMILLAN

First edition 1983
Reprinted 1986
Second edition 1991

Printed in Great Britain by
Billing & Sons Ltd, Worcester

Published by
MACMILLAN ACADEMIC AND PROFESSIONAL LTD.
Houndmills, Basingstoke, Hampshire RG21 2XS
and London
Companies and representatives
throughout the world

British Library Cataloguing in Publication Data

Cook, Chris *1945–*
African political facts since 1945.–2nd. ed.
1. Africa, 1945–
I. Title   II. Killingray, David *1959–*
940.32

ISBN 0–333–43985–6

CONTENTS

Preface and Acknowledgements   vii

1 Chronology of Major Events   1
2 Governors and Heads of State   12
3 Major Ministerial Appointments   44
4 Constitutions and Parliaments   103
5 Political Parties   155
6 Conflicts, Armed Forces and Coups   193
7 Foreign Affairs and Treaties   212
8 Population and Ethnic Groups   221
9 Biographies   244

Bibliography   273

Index   275

PREFACE AND ACKNOWLEDGEMENTS

The aim of this second edition of *African Political Facts since 1945* has been to provide as many of the important facts and figures as possible, within a single volume, for the student and teacher of modern African history and politics. The book covers the history of Africa from 1945 to the birth of independent Namibia in 1990. The whole of Africa – from Egypt to Zimbabwe, from Mauritania to Madagascar – has been included. Inevitably, no medium-sized reference work can be entirely comprehensive. The compilers would welcome suggestions for material to be included in future editions of this book.

Among the people we must thank in the compilation of this book are Stephen Brooks and Sheila Fairfield for their help with research, and Linda Hollingworth for her secretarial assistance. In addition, our thanks go to Tim Farmiloe at our publisher's for his encouragement (and patience) in the publication of this second edition.

January 1990

CHRIS COOK
DAVID KILLINGRAY

1 CHRONOLOGY OF MAJOR EVENTS

1945　End of war in Europe
　　　Algerian nationalist demonstration at Sétif leads to riots; large num-
　　　　bers of people killed by French authorities
　　　African representatives elected to French Constituent Assembly in Paris
　　　United Nations formed; Egypt, Liberia, Ethiopia and South Africa
　　　　founder-members
　　　Fifth Pan-African Congress held at Manchester
　　　Arab League founded in Cairo

1946　Mouvement pour le Triomphe des Libertés Démocratiques founded in
　　　　Algeria by Messali Hadj
　　　New constitution for the Gold Coast, which becomes the first British
　　　　colony to have an African majority in the legislative council
　　　Rassemblement Démocratique Africain (RDA) founded by Houp-
　　　　houët-Boigny
　　　Fonds d'Investissement pour le Développement Économique et Social
　　　　(FIDES) set up by France for colonial development
　　　French abolish forced labour in colonies; by Loi Lamine Gueye French
　　　　citizenship extended to all inhabitants of overseas territories

1947　New constitution for Nigeria with African majority on the legislature
　　　Groundnut scheme begun in Tanganyika
　　　Nationalist revolt in Madagascar against French rule
　　　United Gold Coast Convention founded by Dr J. B. Danquah
　　　East African High Commission formed

1948　Ibadan University College opened in Nigeria
　　　Boycott of European goods and riots in Gold Coast
　　　Union des Populations du Cameroun (UPC) formed
　　　Egypt at war with Israel (1948–9)
　　　National Party wins South African general election and begins to
　　　　implement policy of apartheid
　　　Ethiopia reoccupies Ogaden
　　　Bloc Démocratique Sénégalais founded by Léopold Senghor

1

General strike in Zanzibar
African–Indian riots in Durban

1949   University of Louvanium established in Belgian Congo
Convention People's Party (CPP) founded in Gold Coast by Kwame
    Nkrumah
Victoria Falls Conference in favour of federation of Rhodesia and
    Nyasaland; African opposition to proposed federation
Industrial disturbances at Enugu colliery and riots in southern Nigeria
Makarere becomes a university college

1950   Britain returns Somalia to Italy as a United Nations trust territory for
    10 years
Apartheid laws passed in South Africa: Immorality Act, Population
    Registration Act, Suppression of Communism Act, Group Areas
    Act
International Court rules that South West Africa still under United
    Nations trusteeship
Association des Bakongos (Abako) formed in Belgian Congo
Action Group formed in Nigeria
Sierra Leone People's Party (SLPP) founded by Milton Margai

1951   New constitutions for Nigeria and Gambia
CPP wins general election in Gold Coast and Nkrumah becomes
    'leader of government business'
Increased Egyptian pressure to force Britain to leave occupied Canal
    Zone
British Government accepts idea of a federation of Rhodesia and
    Nyasaland
Libya becomes an independent kingdom

1952   Kwame Nkrumah becomes Prime Minister of the Gold Coast
Increased opposition to French in Maghrib
Army coup in Egypt: committee of 'Free Officers' forces King Farouk
    to abdicate; Gen. Neguib in power
Eritrea federated with Ethiopia
'Mau Mau' rising begins in Kenya; emergency proclaimed (to 1960)
All non-whites compelled to carry passes in South Africa; non-white
    political organisations launch 'passive resistance' campaign against
    apartheid

1953   Emergency powers introduced by the South African government
    against passive resistance; new racial laws introduced: Reservation
    of Separate Amenities Act, Public Safety Act, Criminal Law
    Amendment Act, Bantu Education Act

Egypt becomes a republic; Rally of National Liberation under Neguib as Egypt's sole political party

Jomo Kenyatta and five others convicted of managing 'Mau Mau' in Kenya

Albert Margai becomes Chief Minister of Sierra Leone

Julius Nyerere elected President of Tanganyika African Association

Central African Federation of Rhodesia and Nyasaland created (lasts till 1963)

France deposes the Sultan of Morocco

1954   Colonel Nasser seizes power in Egypt

Federal system of government formalised by Lyttleton constitution in Nigeria

CPP wins general election in Gold Coast and Britain promises independence

Start of Algerian war of independence (to 1962) led by the Front Libération Nationale (FLN)

British-Egyptian agreement on the evacuation of Suez Canal Zone

Tanganyika African National Union (TANU) formed with Julius Nyerere as President

1955   Bandung Conference in Indonesia attended by representatives of many African nationalist parties

State of emergency throughout Algeria

Moroccan 'Army of Liberation' attacks French posts in West Algeria

King Mohamed of Morocco restored to throne by French

Start of armed rebellion in South Sudan (to 1972)

UPC banned in Cameroon

South African Congress of the People adopts Freedom Charter

1956   Sudan becomes an independent republic

Oil discovered in southern Nigeria

Morocco and Tunisia become independent

Loi cadre in French overseas territories provides for local autonomy

Egypt nationalises the Suez Canal; Egypt–Israel war and British and French invasion of Egypt

African miners strike in Northern Rhodesian copperbelt; state of emergency declared

End of Cape Coloured voting rights in South Africa

Oil found in Algeria

Start of the Treason Trial in South Africa (lasts till 1961)

African Party for the Independence of Guinea and Cape Verde (PAIGC) and the Popular Movement for the Liberation of Angola (MPLA) founded

1957   Gold Coast becomes independent as Ghana
       Houphouët-Boigny President of Grand Council of French West Africa
       Eastern and Western regions of Nigeria become self-governing
       SLPP wins general election in Sierra Leone
       In South Africa laws passed to ban Africans from worshipping in
           'white' churches
       Bey of Tunis deposed; Tunisia becomes a republic
       Afro-Asian Solidarity Conference in Cairo

1958   French military raids into Tunisia
       Togo becomes independent
       Dr Hastings Banda returns to Nyasaland
       General de Gaulle advocates a federation with internal autonomy for
           French overseas territories as the French Community; at Brazzaville
           he announces independence for French Africa
       Algerian provisional government set up in Cairo
       Guinea becomes independent with Sekou Touré as President; all other
           French African territories remain within French Community
       Military coup led by Gen. Abboud overthrows Sudanese government

1959   State of Emergency declared in Nyasaland; Dr Banda imprisoned
       Oil discovered in Libya
       Northern Region of Nigeria becomes self-governing
       Saniquelle Meeting of Presidents Nkrumah, Tubman and Touré to
           plan union of free African states
       Riots in Belgian Congo
       United Nations condemns apartheid
       Senegal and Sudan demand independence and bring about the end of
           the French Community

1960   Harold Macmillan's 'wind of change' speech in Cape Town
       French atomic device exploded in the Sahara
       Pan-African Congress organises demonstration at Sharpeville, fired on
           by South African police; 67 Africans killed
       African heads of state meet at Monrovia
       Belgian Congo becomes independent; *Force publique* mutinies;
           United Nations troops sent into Congo
       Somalia becomes independent
       Most member states of the French Community become independent
       TANU wins election in Tanganyika and Julius Nyerere becomes Chief
           Minister
       Nigeria becomes an independent state within the Commonwealth

1961   Armed forces announce that they have taken over control of Algeria;
           OAS terrorism begins
       Patrice Lumumba murdered in Katanga
       Algerian peace-talks begin in Evian, Switzerland

Rebellion begins in Angola against the Portuguese
Sierra Leone becomes an independent state within the Commonwealth
South Africa becomes a republic and leaves the Commonwealth
Tanganyika becomes an independent state within the Commonwealth
Rhodesia Front party formed

1962 Rwanda and Burundi become independent
Plots against President Nkrumah's life in Ghana
Uganda becomes an independent state within the Commonwealth
Algerian independence agreed to at end of Evian peace-talks
First African government formed in Northern Rhodesia
Frelimo headquarters set up in Dar es Salaam, Tanganyika

1963 End of Katanga secession in Congo
President Olympio killed in Togo coup
General Law Amendment Act passed to give South African govern-
    ment wide powers of arrest
Organisation of African Unity (OAU) formed in Addis Ababa by
    thirty heads of state
End of the Federation of Rhodesia and Nyasaland
Jomo Kenyatta becomes Prime Minister of Kenya
Zanzibar becomes an independent state within the Commonwealth
French evacuate the naval base at Bizerta, Tunisia
Kenya becomes an independent state within the Commonwealth

1964 Massacre of Tutsi in Rwanda
Revolution in Zanzibar; Sultan overthrown and Karume becomes
    President
Army mutinies in Kenya, Tanganyika and Uganda; British troops
    called in to help restore order
Union of Tanganyika and Zanzibar as Tanzania
Rivonia trial in South Africa; Nelson Mandela sentenced to life-
    imprisonment
Tshombe becomes President of Congo; revolts in Congo provinces and
    Belgian parachutists land at Stanleyville and elsewhere to rescue
    Europeans
Malawi and Zambia become independent states within the Common-
    wealth
Frelimo begins armed struggle against Portuguese in Mozambique

1965 Organisation Commune Africaine et Malagache (OCAM) formed at
    conference of French-speaking heads of state at Novakchott
Chou En-lai, the Chinese premier, visits Tanzania
One-party state adopted in Tanzania
Rhodesia Front Party wins general election in Southern Rhodesia; Ian
    Smith declares Rhodesia's 'unilateral declaration of independence'
    (UDI); UN Security Council embargo placed on Rhodesia

Gen. Mobutu takes over complete power in Congo

1966   Commonwealth Conference at Lagos
First military coup in Nigeria led by Igbo officers; a counter-coup
    follows six months later
President Nkrumah deposed by military and police coup in Ghana
Milton Obote seizes the Kabaka's palace in Kampala and makes
    Uganda into a centralised state
Botswana becomes an independent state within the Commonwealth
Union Minière du Haut-Katanga taken over by Congo government

1967   Arusha Declaration issued in Tanzania
Two army coups in Sierra Leone
Arab–Israeli 'Six-Day War'; Israelis occupy Sinai
Uprising in eastern and northern Congo ended by foreign mercenaries
    employed by Gen. Mobutu's central government
East African Community established by Kenya, Tanzania and Uganda
Secession of Eastern Region as independent state of Biafra and start of
    civil war in Nigeria (to 1970)

1968   Malawi establishes diplomatic relations with South Africa
Start of guerrilla war in Rhodesia
Tanzania, Ivory Coast and two other African states recognise Biafran
    independence
Equatorial Guinea becomes independent of Spain
Military coup in Mali
Swaziland becomes an independent state within the Commonwealth

1969   King Idris deposed by a military coup in Libya; Col. Gaddafi comes to
    power
General election in Ghana returns Dr Busia as Prime Minister
Serious political disturbances in western Kenya
Ghana expels thousands of aliens

1970   End of Nigerian civil war
British withdrawal from military bases in Libya
President Obote's 'Common Man's Charter' introduced in Uganda
Chinese offer aid to Tanzania to build railway from Dar es Salaam to
    the Zambian copperbelt
Aswan High Dam in Egypt comes into operation

1971   Gen. Amin leads military coup which overthrows President Obote of
    Uganda
Central African Republic recognises South Africa and receives econ-
    omic aid from it
Congo renamed Zaïre
President Banda of Malawi on state visit to South Africa and Mozam-
    bique; Ivory Coast delegation to South Africa

Declaration of Mogadishu issued by eastern and central African states stating their intention to continue the armed struggle to liberate South Africa

African National Council (ANC) formed in Rhodesia by Bishop Muzorewa

1972 'African authenticity' campaign launched by President Mobutu in Zaïre

Army coup in Ghana: Gen. Acheampong overthrows Busia government

Pearce Commission in Rhodesia reports an overwhelming 'no' by African population to settlement proposals

President Amin begins to expel Asians from Uganda

Agreement in Sudan on 'southern problem'; regional autonomy granted to the south

Hutu rising in Burundi suppressed with great loss of life

Serious drought in Sahelian region

Military coup in Madagascar

1973 Zambia–Rhodesia border closed by President Kaunda

Serious strikes by black workers in South Africa

African Games at Lagos

Prime Minister Smith of Rhodesia begins talks with African nationalists in an attempt to find some form of internal settlement

Israel–Egypt war; Egyptian troops retake part of Sinai

Oil crisis brings great increase in prices for African states

Widespread drought in Ethiopia

1974 Emperor Haile Selassie overthrown by a military coup; Dergue established to rule the country

Coup in Lisbon by army officers disillusioned with the African wars brings down the Caetano regime and begins the process of decolonisation in the Portuguese empire in Africa

Guinea-Bissau becomes independent

1975 Lomé Agreement signed between EEC and 37 African states

Economic Community of West African States (Ecowas) Treaty signed by 15 states

Portugal's withdrawal from Africa: independence for Cape Verde Islands, São Tomé and Príncipe, Mozambique (June), and Angola (Nov). Civil war in Angola

Tanzam railway officially opened between Zambia and Tanzania

Four 'front-line' presidents at Quilemane pledge support for the Zimbabwe National Liberation Army

Gen. Murtala Mohamed, President of Nigeria, assassinated in Lagos

South African troops invade Angola in support of UNITA forces

1976 Soweto riots in South Africa

Spain withdraws from Western Sahara; territory partitioned between

Morocco and Mauritania. Proclamation of Sahara Arab Democratic Republic, which through its armed Polisario Front wages a guerrilla war against both occupying states

South Africa declares Transkei independent

'Palace coup' in Addis Ababa

1977 Djibouti became an independent state; final withdrawal of France from African territory

Invasion of Shaba province, Zaïre, by Katangese rebels

Somali-supported forces invade Ogaden; serious fighting in the region. Cuban aid to Ethiopia in the war

Central African Empire proclaimed by Bokassa

Widespread purge in Ethiopia by the Dergue

Constituent Assembly meets in Nigeria in preparation for a return to civilian government

1978 Serious strikes in Tunisia

Internal agreement in Rhodesia: transitional government formed

Somali forces defeated by Ethiopia in Ogaden war; Ethiopia steps up its attacks on Eritrean nationalist forces

Reconciliation of Guinea with France

Uganda invades Kagera salient in north-west Tanzania

'Muldergate' scandal in South Africa

Gen. Acheampong deposed in Ghana

1979 Tanzania supports Ugandan Liberation Front in invasion of Uganda; President Amin overthrown

Emperor Bokassa overthrown and Central African Republic re-established

President Macia Nguema of Equatorial Guinea overthrown

Junior officers coup in Ghana led by Flight-Lt Rawlings; three former heads of state executed

Elections in Ghana and Nigeria return both countries to civilian rule

Lancaster House talks in London on a settlement for Rhodesia; the country reverts to British rule for a transitional period

1980 Ceasefire in Rhodesia brings end to the civil war

Robert Mugabe's ZANU (PF) party won 57 of the 80 contested seats in the Rhodesian election

Egypt and Israel exchange ambassadors

Military coup in Liberia led by Sergeant Doe overthrows and kills President Tolbert

Southern African Development Coordination Conference (SADCC) formally established to counter South Africa's destabilisation of the frontline states

Zimbabwe, formerly Rhodesia, becomes independent

President Binaisa stripped of power and Milton Obote returns to Uganda

Police violence against strikers in the Cape, South Africa
South African Defence Force operations in southern Angola
Presidential Council established in South Africa
Coup in Guinea-Bissau overthrows government of Luis Cabral
Milton Obote's Uganda People's Party won Uganda election. Obote
    became president. National Resistance Army launched guerrilla
    campaign against the Obote government
President Senghor of Senegal resigns

1981   Organisation of African Unity demand that Libya withdraw troops
        from Chad
      Serious fighting in Zimbabwe between ZANLU and ZIPRA guerrillas
      President Kaunda of Zambia and South African Prime Minister Botha
        meet on Botswana–South African border
      President Sadat of Egypt and Prime Minister Begin of Israel meet in
        Sinai
      Kenya became an official one-party state
      Attempted coup in The Gambia suppressed with help of troops from
        Senegal
      Libyan jets shot down by United States aircraft in Gulf of Sidra
      South African troops and armour advance into southern Angola
        against SWAPO guerrillas
      President Sadat of Egypt assassinated in Cairo
      Mercenaries from South Africa attempt a coup in the Seychelles
      Organisation of African Unity forces sent to Chad
      Fl.-Lt Rawlings seized power in Ghana

1982   Polisario (Western Sahara) admitted to the Organisation of African Unity
      Split in ruling National Party in South Africa as Treurnicht opposes
        Botha's proposals for constitutional change
      South African raids on ANC bases in Mozambique
      Fighting between Ethiopian and Somalian troops
      Religion-motivated riots in northern Nigeria

1983   Nigeria expels up to two million other West Africans
      Ethiopian drought results in large numbers of refugees
      New Constitutional Bill in South Africa
      French troops intervene in Chad civil war to counter aid from Libya
      Captain Sankara seizes power in Upper Volta to initiate a radical
        reform of the country
      Talks begin between South Africa and the United Nations over the
        future of Namibia
      Referendum in South Africa over new constitution
      Death of President Somara Machel in aircrash; Mozambique blamed
        South Africa
      Shagari government overthrown in Nigeria by military

Rioting in Tunisia over the price of bread

1984   Nkomati Accord, a non-aggression pact, signed by South Africa and Mozambique

Religious riots in Yola, Nigeria, result in many deaths

Report by Roman Catholic church on violent action by Zimbabwean troops in southern Matabeleland

Coup in Guinea following death of President Sekou Touré

Morocco sealed border with Algeria in attempt to end aid to Polisario forces in the Western Sahara

Continuing violence in Uganda

P. W. Botha becomes President of South Africa

Libyan and French troops withdraw from Chad

Morocco left Organisation of African Unity over admission of Polisario

Continuing war in Ethiopia against Eritrean secessionist forces

Lomé III treaty signed to govern trade relations between European Community and African states

1985   South African police fire on African crowds attending funeral at Uitenhage; official report later blamed the police

Military coup in the Sudan

South African troops withdraw from Angola

Transitional government set up in Namibia

General election in Zimbabwe in which ZANU (PF) won 69 of the 73 contested seats

Bloodless coup in Nigeria

Escalation of confrontation in South Africa between black opposition and the white regime

President Nyerere of Tanzania resigns office

President Obote overthrown by army coup in Uganda; Major-General Okello sworn in as country's new leader

1986   Yoweri Museveni, backed by the National Resistance Army, overthrows President Okello in Uganda

South-African-backed coup in Lesotho; South African raids into Zambia, Zimbabwe and Botswana

Widespread boycotts and violence leads to declaration of a state of emergency in South Africa; hundreds killed by Government forces and in communal violence; over eight thousand detained. US applies trade sanctions and disinvestment by US companies begins

President Machel of Mozambique killed in plane crash; succeeded by Joachim Chissano

US air attack on Libya for complicity with terrorism

1987   Conservative Party becomes official opposition following whites-only elections in South Africa

Meeting in Dakar between ANC leaders and dissident white Afrikaners
Chad troops capture Aozou strip and defeat Libyan invaders
Army coup in the South African 'bantustan' of Transkei
Military coup in Burkina Faso and President Sankara overthrown
President Bourguiba of Tunisia removed from office

1988 Talks in London, New York, Geneva and Brazzaville lead to agreement for Cuban withdrawal from Angola and to independence for Namibia
African-led strikes in South Africa against government anti-strike laws
Nelson Mandela, the ANC leader, moved from prison to hospital and later to a house in prison grounds
Civil War in Somalia
Meeting in Mocambique between President Botha of South Africa and President Chissano of Mocambique; Botha agrees to end South African aid to rebels in Mocambique. Botha also visits Malawi, Zaïre and Ivory Coast
Riots in Algiers over declining standards of living; President Benjedid promises 'democratisation of political activity'

1989 Cuban troops withdraw from Angola
Arab Maghreb Union common market set-up by Algeria, Tunisia, Libya and Mauritania
Parliamentary elections in Tunisia
Dispute over grazing rights on Senegal-Mauritania border
Truce agreed between Angola government and UNITA rebels
Military coup in Sudan
President P W Botha in secret talks with Nelson Mandela the imprisoned ANC leader
President Botha of South Africa resigns and is succeeded by F W de Klerk
South African elections: ruling National Party falls from 123 seats to 93, Conservative opposition increases from 22 to 39 seats. President de Klerk announces programme of reform to apartheid system
Walter Sisulu of the ANC released from a South African prison

1990 Continuing attempt to overthrow Liberian government turns into civil war
Release of Nelson Mandela from prison in South Africa; the ANC, PAC and the South African Communist Party un-banned
Independence for Namibia
Several African states (Benin, Zaïre, Ivory Coast) declare intention to move towards freer political institutions
Attempted coup in Nigeria
South African government introduces further measures to end apartheid
Attempted military coup in Zambia

2 GOVERNORS AND HEADS OF STATE*

ALGERIA

Ruled by France to 1962, when it became an independent republic.

GOVERNORS-GENERAL
1944–8	Yves Chataigneau
1948–51	Marcel Édmond Naegelen
1951–5	Roger Étienne Joseph Leonard
1955–6	Jacques Émile Soustelle

MINISTERS-RESIDENT
1956	Georges Albert Julien Catroux
1956–8	Robert Lacoste

DELEGATES-GENERAL
1958	Raoul Salan
1958–60	Paul Albert Louis Delouvrier
1960–2	Jean Morin
1962	Christian Fouchet

PRESIDENTS
1962–3	Ferhat Abbas
1963–5	Ahmed Ben Bella
1965–79	Houari Boumédienne
1979–	Chadli Benjedid

ANGOLA

A Portuguese colony to 1975, when it became a republic.

* In compiling this chapter, the authors are deeply indebted to two published sources – David Henige's indispensable *Colonial Governors from the Fifteenth Century to the Present* (University of Wisconsin Press, 1971) and *The Statesman's Yearbook* (edited by Dr John Paxton).

GOVERNORS-GENERAL

1943–7	Vasco Lopes Alves
1947	Fernando Falcão Pacheco Mena
1947–55	José Agapito da Silva Carvalho
1956–9	Horácio de Sá Viana Rebelo
1960–1	Álvaro Rodrigues da Silva Tavares
1961–2	Venâncio Augusto Deslandes
1962–6	Jaime Silvério Marquês
1966–72	Camilo Augusto de Miranda Rebocho Vaz
1972–4	Fernando Augusto Santos E. Castro

HIGH COMMISSIONER

| 1974–5 | Antonio Alba Rosa Coutinho |

PRESIDENTS

1975–9	Antonio Agostinho Neto
1979–	José Eduardo dos Santos
	(Re-elected 1985)

BENIN

The French colonial territory of Dahomey to 1960, when it became an independent republic under the same name; the People's Republic of Benin was proclaimed in 1975.

GOVERNORS

1943–5	Charles André Maurice Assier de Pompignan
1945–6	Marc Antoine Christian Laurent de Villedeuil
1946–8	Robert Legendre
1948	Jean Georges Chambon
1948–9	Jacques Alphonse Boissier
1949–51	Claude Valluy
1951–5	Charles Henri Bonfils
1955–8	Casimir Marc Biros

HIGH COMMISSIONER

| 1959–60 | René Tirant |

PRESIDENTS

1960–3	Hubert Maga
1963–4	Christophe Soglo
1964–5	Sourou Migan Apithy
1965–7	Christophe Soglo

1967–8	Maurice Kouandeté
1968–9	Émile Derlin Zinsou
1969–70	[Presidency suspended: presidential council of three]
1970–2	Hubert Maga
1972 (May–Oct)	Justin Ahomadégbé
1972–	Mathieu Kerekou (Re-elected 1984)

BOTSWANA

The British High Commission territory of Bechuanaland until 1966, when it became a republic.

HIGH COMMISSIONERS
[also for Basutoland (Lesotho, q.v.) and Swaziland (q.v.)]

1944–51	Evelyn Baring
1951–5	J. le Rougetel
1955–8	Percivale Liesching
1959–63	R. R. Ratcliffe Maud
1963–4	H. S. Stephenson
1964	[post abolished]

COMMISSIONERS

1946–50	A. Sillery
1950–3	E. B. Beetham
1953–5	W. F. MacKenzie
1955–9	M. O. Wray
1965–6	H. S. Norman-Walker

PRESIDENTS

1966–80	Sir Seretse Khama
1980–	Quett K. J. Masire

BURKINA FASO

The French colonial territory of Upper Volta, separated from the Ivory Coast in 1947, and proclaimed an independent republic in 1960. Upper Volta was renamed Burkina Faso ('Land of the Incorruptible Men') in August 1984.

GOVERNORS

1947–8	Gaston Mourgies

1948–52	Albert Jean Mouragues
1952–3	Roland Joanes Louis Pré
1953–6	Salvador Jean Étcheber
1956–8	Yvon Bourges

HIGH COMMISSIONER
1959–60	Paul Jean Marie Masson

PRESIDENTS
1960–6	Maurice Yameogo
1966–80	Sangoulé Lamizana
1980–2	Saye Zerbo
1982–3	Jean-Baptiste Ouedraogo
1983–7	Thomas Sankara
1987–	Blaise Campaore

BURUNDI

A Belgian-mandated territory; an independent kingdom in 1962 and a republic from 1966. (For governors see under Ruanda-Urundi.)

HIGH REPRESENTATIVE
1962	E. Hennequiau

KINGS
1961–6	Mwambutsa IV
1966	Ntare V

PRESIDENTS
1966–76	Michel Micombero
1976–87	Jean-Baptiste Bagaza
1987–	Pierre Buyoya

CAMEROON

A trust territory divided between France and the United Kingdom, Cameroon achieved independence in 1960.

HIGH COMMISSIONERS
1944–6	Henri Pierre Nicolas
1946–7	Robert Louis Delavignette
1947–9	René Hoffherr

1949–54	Jean Louis Maurice André Soucadaux
1954–6	Roland Joanes Louis Pré
1956–7	Pierre Auguste Joseph Messmer
1958	Jean Paul Ramadier
1958–60	Xavier Antoine Torré

PRESIDENTS

1960–82	Ahmadou Ahidjo
1982–	Paul Biya

CAPE VERDE ISLANDS

A Portuguese colony from the fifteenth century until 1975, when a republic was formed.

GOVERNORS

1943–9	João de Figueiredo
1949–53	Carlos Alberto Garcia Alves Roçadas
1953–7	Manuel Marques de Abrantes Amaral
1957–8	António Augusto Peixoto Correia
1958–63	Silvino Silvério Marques
1963–73	Leão Maria de Tavares Rosado do Sacramento Monteiro
1973–4	António Lopes dos Santos
1974–5	Henrique da Silva Horta

PRESIDENT

1975–	Aristides Maria Pereira

CENTRAL AFRICAN REPUBLIC

The French colonial territory of Ubangi-Chari to 1960, when it became a republic. From 1976 to 1979 it was known as the Central African Empire.

LIEUTENANT GOVERNOR

1942–6	Henri Camille Sautot

GOVERNORS

1946–8	Jean Victor Louis Joseph Chalvet
1949–50	Pierre Jean Marie Delteil
1950–1	Ignace Jean Aristide Colombani
1951–4	Aimé Marius Louis Grimald
1954–8	Louis Marius Pascal Sanmarco

1958   Paul Camille Bordier

HIGH COMMISSIONER
1959–60   Paul Camille Bordier

PRESIDENTS
1960–6   David Dacko
1966–76   Jean Bédel Bokassa

EMPEROR
1976–9   Jean Bédel Bokassa

PRESIDENTS
1979–81   David Dacko
1982–   André Kolingba

CHAD

A French colonial territory to 1960, when it became a republic.

LIEUTENANT GOVERNORS
1944–6   Jacques Camille Marie Roqué

GOVERNORS
1946–9   Jacques Camille Marie Rogué
1949   Paul Hippolyte Julien Marie le Layec
1950–1   Henri Jean Marie de Mauduit
1951   Charles Émile Hanin
1951–6   Ignace Jean Aristide Colombani
1956–8   Jean René Troadec

HIGH COMMISSIONER
1959–60   Daniel Marius Doustin

PRESIDENTS (AND MILITARY RULERS)
1960–75   François (later N'Garta) Tombalbaye
1975–9   Félix Malloum
1979 (Mar–
   Apr)   Goukouni Oueddei   ⎫ Period
1979 (Apr–   ⎬ of civil war
   Aug)–   Lol Mohamed Shawa   ⎪ and Libyan
1979–82   Goukouni Oueddei   ⎭ armed intervention
1982–   Hissene Habré

COMORO ISLANDS

A French protectorate to 1975, when a republic was proclaimed in three islands while Mayotte remained French. The Comoros claims Mayotte and has the title 'The Federal and Islamic Republic of the Comoros'.

GOVERNORS
1947–9	Eugène Alain Charles Louis Alaniou
1949–50	Marie Emmanuel Adolphe Roger Remy
1950–7	Pierre Léonard Alphonse Coudert
1957–60	Georges Arnaud
1961	Louis Joseph Édouard Saget

HIGH COMMISSIONERS
1961–3	Louis Joseph Édouard Saget
1963–7	Henri Joseph Marie Bernard
1967–71	Antoine Padouan Columbani
1971–3	Jacques Mouradian

DELEGATES-GENERAL
1973–4	Georges Poulet
1974–5	Henri Beaux

PRESIDENTS
1975	Ahmed Abdallah
1975–6	Said Mohamed Jaffar
1976–8	Ali Soilih
1978	Said Alloumani
1978–9	Ahmed Abdallah and Mohamed Ahmed (co-pres.)
1979–89	Ahmed Abdallah (re-elected September 1984)

THE CONGO

The French colonial territory of Middle Congo to 1960, when it became a republic.

LIEUTENANT GOVERNORS
1944–6	Ange Marie Charles André Bayardelle
1946	. Christian Robert Roger Laigret
1946–7	Numa Henri François Sadoul
1947–50	Jacques Georges Fourneau
1950–2	Paul Hippolyte Julien Marie Le Layec

1952–3	Jean Jacques Chambon
1953–6	Ernest Eugène Rouys
1956–8	Jean Michel Soupault
1958	Paul Charles Dériaud

HIGH COMMISSIONER
| 1959–60 | Gui Noël Georgy |

PRESIDENTS
1960–3	Abbé Fulbert Youlou
1963–8	Alphonse Massemba-Débat
1968–9	Alfred Raoul
1968–77	Marien N'Gouabi
1977–9	Joachim Yhombi-Opango
1979–	Denis Sassou-Nguesso

CONGO (ex-Belgian): see ZAÏRE

DAHOMEY: see BENIN

DJIBOUTI

Formerly French Somaliland; in 1967 it became the French territory of the Afars and Issas, and in 1977 an independent republic.

GOVERNORS
1946–50	Paul Henri Siriex
1950–4	Numa Henri François Sadoul
1954	Roland Joanes Louis Pré
1954–7	Jean Albert René Petitbon
1957–8	Maurice Meker
1958–62	Jacques Marie Julien Campain
1962–6	René Tirant
1966–7	Louis Joseph Édouard Saget

HIGH COMMISSIONERS
1967–9	Louis Joseph Édouard Saget
1969–72	Dominique Ponchardier
1972–7	Georges Thiercy

PRESIDENTS
| 1977– | Hassan Gouled Aptidon |

EGYPT

An independent monarchy from 1922 until 1953, when a republic was established.

KINGS
1936–52   Farouk I
1952–3   Fuad II

PRESIDENTS
1953–4   Mohamed Neguib
1954–70   Gamal Abdul Nasser
1970–81   Mohamed Anwar El Sadat
1981–   Hosni Mubarak

EQUATORIAL GUINEA

Rio Muni and the island of Fernando Po were Spanish territories until 1968, when they were merged to form an independent republic.

GOVERNORS
1943–9   Juan Marian Bonelli Rubío
1949–62   Faustino Ruíz González
1962–3   Francisco Núñez Rodríguez

HIGH COMMISSIONERS
1963–4   Francisco Núñez Rodríguez
1964–6   Pedro Latorre Alcubierre
1966–8   Victor Suances Díaz del Río

PRESIDENTS
1968–79   Francisco Macias Nguema
1979–   Teodoro Obiang Nguema Mbasogo

ERITREA

An Italian colony until 1942, when it was conquered by the British. Under British administration until 1952, when it was incorporated into Ethiopia.

CHIEF ADMINISTRATORS
1944–5   C. D. McCarthy
1945–6   John Meredith Benoy

1946–51	Francis Greville Drew
1951–2	Duncan Cameron Cumming

ETHIOPIA

An independent kingdom which was ended in 1975, when a republic was proclaimed.

EMPEROR
1930–74	Haile Selassie (in exile 1936–41)

HEADS OF GOVERNMENT
1974	Aman Mikhail Andom
1974–5	Teferi Benti
1976–	Mengistu Haile Mariam

FRENCH EQUATORIAL AFRICA

The four French colonial territories of Chad, Ubangi-Chari, Middle Congo and Gabon, which were administered as a federal unit to 1958.

GOVERNORS-GENERAL
1944–7	Ange Marie Charles André Bayardelle
1947	Charles Jean Luizet

HIGH COMMISSIONERS
1947–51	Bernard Cornut-Gentille
1951–8	Paul Louis Gabriel Chauvet
1958	Pierre Auguste Joseph Messmer
1958	Yvon Bourges

HIGH COMMISSIONER-GENERAL
1959–60	Yvon Bourges

FRENCH WEST AFRICA

The French colonial territories of West Africa were administered as a federal unit until 1958.

HIGH COMMISSIONERS
1943–6	Pierre Charles Albert Cournarie

1946–8	René Victor Marie Barthes
1948–51	Paul Léon Albin Bechard
1951–6	Bernard Cornut-Gentille
1956–8	Gaston Cusin

HIGH COMMISSIONER-GENERAL
1958–9   Pierre Auguste Joseph Messmer

GABON

A French colonial territory to 1960, when it became a republic.

LIEUTENANT GOVERNORS

1944–6	Numa François Henri Sadoul
1946–7	Roland Joanes Louis Pré
1947–9	Numa François Henri Sadoul
1949–51	Pierre François Pelieu
1951–2	Charles Émile Hanin
1952–8	Yves Jean Digo
1958	Louis Marius Pascal Sanmarco

HIGH COMMISSIONER
1959–60   Jean Risterucci

PRESIDENTS

| 1960–7 | Léon M'Ba |
| 1967– | Albert Bernard (later El Hadj Omar) Bongo |

THE GAMBIA

A British colony to 1965, when it was proclaimed an independent dominion. In 1970 the Gambia became a republic within the Commonwealth.

GOVERNORS

1942–7	H. R. Blood
1947–9	A. B. Wright
1949–58	P. Wyn-Harris
1958–62	E. H. Windley
1962–5	J. W. Paul

GOVERNORS-GENERAL

| 1965–6 | J. W. Paul |
| 1966–70 | F. M. Singhateh |

PRESIDENT
1970–   Sir Dawda Kairaba Jawara

GHANA

Britain's Gold Coast colony became the dominion of Ghana in 1957 and a republic in 1960.

GOVERNORS
1941–8   A. C. M. Burns
1948–9   G. H. Creasy
1949–57   C. N. Arden-Clarke

ASHANTI: CHIEF COMMISSIONERS
1941–6   E. G. Hawkesworth
1946–51   C. O. Butler
1951–2   W. H. Beaton

ASHANTI: REGIONAL OFFICERS
1952–4   W. H. Beaton
1954–5   A. J. Loveridge
1955–7   A. C. Russell

GOLD COAST COLONY: CHIEF COMMISSIONERS
1945–50   T. R. O. Mangin
1950–3   A. J. Loveridge

NORTHERN TERRITORIES: CHIEF COMMISSIONERS
1942–6   W. H. Ingrams
1948–50   E. N. Jones
1950–3   G. N. Burden

NORTHERN TERRITORIES: REGIONAL OFFICERS
1953–4   A. J. Loveridge
1954–7   S. McDonald-Smith

GOVERNOR-GENERAL
1957–60   W. F. Hare, Earl of Listowel

PRESIDENTS (AND MILITARY RULERS)
1960–6   Kwame Nkrumah
1966–9   Joseph Arthur Ankrah
1969–70   Akwasi A. Afrifa
1970–2   Edward Akufo-Addo

1972–8	Ignatius Kutu Acheampong
1978–9	Frederick W. K. Akuffo
1979	Jerry John Rawlings
1979–81	Hilla Limann
1982–	Jerry John Rawlings

GUINEA

A French colonial territory to 1958, when it became a republic.

GOVERNORS

1944–6	Jacques Georges Fourneau
1946–8	Édouard Louis Barthélemy Marie Joseph Terrac
1948–50	Roland Joanes Louis Pré
1950–3	Paul Henri Siriex
1953–5	Jean Paul Parisot
1955–6	Charles Henri Bonfils
1956–7	Jean Paul Ramadier
1958	Jean Mauberna

PRESIDENT

| 1958–84 | Ahmed Sekou Touré (1966–72 Kwame Nkrumah as titular co-president) |
| 1984– | Lansana Conté |

GUINEA-BISSAU

A Portuguese colony until 1974, when it became a republic.

GOVERNORS

1949–53	Raimundo António Rodrigues Serrão
1953–6	Diogo António José Leite Pereira de Melo e Alvim
1956–8	Álvaro Rodrigues da Silva Tavares
1958–62	António Augusto Peixoto Correia
1962–5	Vasco António Marints Rodrigues
1965–8	Arnaldo Schultz
1968–73	António Sebastião Ribeiro de Spínola
1974	Arnaldo Schultz

PRESIDENT

| 1974–80 | Luiz Cabral |
| 1980– | João Bernardo Vieira |

IVORY COAST

A French colonial territory to 1960, when it became a republic.

GOVERNORS

1943–7	André Jean Gaston Latrille
1947–8	Oswald Marcellin Maurice Marius Durand
1948	Georges Louis Joseph Orselli
1948–51	Laurent Élisée Pecheux
1951–2	Pierre François Pelieu
1952–4	Camille Victor Bailly
1954–6	Pierre Joseph Auguste Messmer
1956–7	Pierre Auguste Michel Marie Lami
1957–8	Ernest de Nattes

HIGH COMMISSIONERS

1959	Ernest de Nattes
1959–60	Yves René Henri Guena

PRESIDENT

1960–	Félix Houphouët-Boigny

KENYA

A British colony from 1920 to 1963, when it became an independent dominion; a republic was proclaimed in 1964.

GOVERNORS

1944–52	P. E. Mitchell
1952–7	E. Baring
1957–9	F. Crawford
1959–63	P. M. Renison
1963–4	M. J. MacDonald

PRESIDENTS

1964–78	Jomo Kenyatta
1978–	Daniel T. Arap Moi

LESOTHO

The British High Commission territory of Basutoland until 1966, when it became an independent kingdom.

RESIDENT COMMISSIONERS
1942–6	C. N. Arden-Clarke
1947–51	A. D. F. Thompson
1951–5	E. P. Arrowsmith
1955–61	A. G. T. Chaplin
1961–6	A. F. Giles

KING
1966–	Moshoeshoe II

LIBERIA

An independent republic since 1847.

PRESIDENTS
1944–71	William V. S. Tubman
1971–80	William Richard Tolbert
1980–	Samuel K. Doe

LIBYA

An Italian colony from 1912 to 1942, when it came under British administration. In 1951 it was created an independent kingdom by the United Nations. Libya was proclaimed a republic in 1969.

CYRENAICA: CHIEF ADMINISTRATORS
1942–5	D. C. Cumming
1945–6	P. B. E. Acland
1946–8	J. W. N. Haugh
1948–51	E. A. V. de Candole

TRIPOLITANIA: CHIEF ADMINISTRATOR
1943–51	T. R. Blackley

KING
1951–69	Idris I

PRESIDENT (REVOLUTIONARY LEADER)
1969–	Mu'ammar Mohamed al-Gaddafi

MADAGASCAR (MALAGASY REPUBLIC)

A French colony to 1960, when it became a republic.

GOVERNOR-GENERAL
1944–6   Paul de Saint-Mart

HIGH COMMISSIONERS
1946–8   Jules Marcel de Coppet
1948–50   Pierre de Chevigné
1950–4   Isaac Robert Bargues
1954–60   Jean Louis Maurice André Soucadaux

PRESIDENTS (AND MILITARY RULERS)
1960–72   Philibert Tsirinana
1972–5   Gabriel Ramanantsoa
1975 (Feb)   Richard Ratsimandrara
1975 (Feb–   Gilles Andriamahazo
  June)
1975 (June)   Didier Ratsiraka (re-elected November 1982)

MALAWI

The British colony of Nyasaland became part of the Central African Federation from 1953 to 1963. It was proclaimed an independent dominion in 1964 and a republic in 1966.

GOVERNORS
1942–7   E. C. S. Richards
1948–56   G. F. T. Colby
1956–61   R. P. Armitage
1961–6   G. S. Jones

PRESIDENT
1966–   Hastings Kamuzu Banda

MALI

The French colonial territory of Soudan joined Senegal in the Mali Federation in 1960 (June–Aug) and then became the republic of Mali.

GOVERNORS
1942–6   Auguste Maurice Léon Calvel

1946–52	Edmond Jean Louveau
1952	Camille Victor Bailly
1952–3	Salvador Jean Etcheber
1953	Albert Jean Mouragues
1953–6	Lucien Eugène Geay
1956–8	Henri Marie Joseph Gipoulon

HIGH COMMISSIONER
1959–60	Jean Charles Sicurani

PRESIDENTS
1960–8	Mobido Keita
1968–	Moussa Traoré

MAURITANIA

A French colonial territory to 1960, when it became a republic.

GOVERNORS
1944–6	Christian Robert Roger Laigret
1947–8	Lucien Eugène Geay
1948–9	Henri Jean Marie de Mauduit
1949–50	Édouard Louis Barthélemy Marie Joseph Terrac
1950–1	Jacques Camille Marie Rogué
1951–4	Pierre Auguste Joseph Messmer
1954–5	Albert Jean Mouragues
1955–6	Jean Paul Parisot
1956–8	Albert Jean Mouragues

HIGH COMMISSIONER
1959–60	Pierre Amédée Joseph Émile Jean Anthonioz

PRESIDENTS
1960–78	Mokhtar Ould Daddah
1978–9	Mustapha Ould Mohamed Salek
1979–80	Mohamed Ould Ahmed Louly
1980–4	Mohamed Khouna Ould Haidalla
1984–	Maawiya Ould Sid'Ahmed Taya

MAURITIUS

The island was ruled by Britain from 1810 to 1968, when an independent dominion was established.

GOVERNORS
1942–9	H. C. D. C. MacKenzie-Kennedy
1949–53	H. R. R. Blood
1953–9	R. Scott
1959–62	C. M. Deverell
1962–8	J. S. Rennie

GOVERNORS-GENERAL
1968	J. S. Rennie
1968–72	A. L. Williams
1972–8	Sir Rainan Osman
1978–84	Sir D. Burrenchobay
1984–6	Sir Seewoosagur Ramgoolam
1986–	Sir Veerasamy Ringadoo

MOROCCO

From 1912 to 1956 the sultanate of Morocco was divided into French and Spanish protectorates and an internationally administered area around Tangier.

RESIDENTS-GENERAL
1943–6	Gabriel Puaux
1946–7	Eirik Labonne
1947–51	Alphonse Pierre Juin
1951–4	Augustin Léon Guillaume
1954–5	François Lacoste
1955	Gilbert Yves Édmond Grandval
1955	Pierre Boyer de la Tourdu Moulin
1955–6	André Louis Dubois

SULTAN
1927–56	Mohamed V

KINGS
1956–61	Mohamed V (Sultan 1927–56; deposed by French 1953–5)
1961–	Hassan II

MOZAMBIQUE

A Portuguese colony to 1975, when it became a republic.

GOVERNORS-GENERAL
1940–7	José Tritão de Bettencourt
1947–58	Gabriel Maurício Teixeira
1958–61	Pedro Correia de Barros
1961–4	Manuel Maria Sarmento Rodrigues
1964–8	José Augusto da Costa
1968–70	Baltasar Rebêlo de Sousa Almeida
1970–1	Eduardo de Arantes de Oliveira
1971–4	Manuel Pimental dos Santos

HIGH COMMISSIONER
1974–5	Vitor Crespo

PRESIDENTS
1975–86	Samora M. Machel
1986–	Joachim Alberto Chissano

NAMIBIA

Former German colony administered by South Africa as a mandated territory. South Africa's control of the country was contested by the United Nations and independence was finally achieved in 1990.

ADMINISTRATORS
1943–51	P. I. Hougenhout
1951–3	A. J. R. van Rhijn
1953–63	D. T. du P. Viljoen
1963–8	W. C. du Plessis
1968–71	J. G. H. van der Wath
1971–5	B. J. van der Walt

ADMINISTRATORS-GENERAL
1977–9	M. T. Steyn
1979–85	G. Viljoen
1985–90	Louis Pienaar

PRESIDENT
1990–	Sam Nujoma

NIGER

A French colonial territory to 1960, when it became a republic.

GOVERNORS
1942–54	Jean François Toby
1955–6	Jean Paul Ramadier
1956–8	Paul Camille Bordier
1958	Louis Félix Rollet
1958–9	Don Jean Colombani

HIGH COMMISSIONER
1959–60	Don Jean Colombani

PRESIDENTS
1960–74	Hamani Diori
1974–87	Seyni Kountché
1987–	Col. Ali Saibou

NIGERIA

A British colony which became an independent dominion in 1960 and a republic in 1963.

GOVERNORS
1943–8	A. F. Richards
1948–54	J. S. Macpherson

GOVERNORS-GENERAL
1954–5	J. S. Macpherson
1955–60	J. Robertson
1960–3	B. M. Azikiwe

NORTHERN REGION: CHIEF COMMISSIONERS
1943–7	J. R. Patterson
1947–51	E. W. Thompstone

NORTHERN REGION: LIEUTENANT GOVERNORS
1951–2	E. W. Thompstone
1952–4	B. E. Sharwood-Smith

NORTHERN REGION: GOVERNORS
1954–7	B. E. Sharwood-Smith

1957–62   G. W. Bell

EASTERN REGION: CHIEF COMMISSIONERS
1943–8   F. B. Carr
1948–51   J. G. Pyke-Nott

EASTERN REGION: LIEUTENANT GOVERNORS
1951–2   J. G. Pyke-Nott
1952–4   C. J. Pleass

EASTERN REGION: GOVERNORS
1954–6   C. J. Pleass
1956–60   R. de S. Stapledon

WESTERN REGION: CHIEF COMMISSIONERS
1939–46   G. C. Whiteley
1946–51   T. C. Hoskyns-Abrahall

WESTERN REGION: LIEUTENANT GOVERNORS
1951   T. C. Hoskyns-Abrahall
1951–4   H. F. Marshall

WESTERN REGION: GOVERNOR
1954–60   J. D. Rankine

PRESIDENTS (AND MILITARY RULERS)
1963–6   Benjamin Mhamdi Azikiwe
1966 (Jan)   Nwafoi Orzu
1966 (Jan–   Johnson Aguiyi-Ironsi
  Aug)
1966–75   Yakubu Gowon
1975–6   Murtala Ramal Mohamed
1976–9   Olusegun Obasanjo
1979–83   Alhaji Shehu Usman A. Shagari
1984–5   Muhammadu Buhari
1985–   Ibrahim Babangida

RHODESIA: see ZIMBABWE

RHODESIA AND NYASALAND

The Federation of Northern and Southern Rhodesia and Nyasaland came into
being in 1953 and lasted until 1963.

GOVERNORS-GENERAL
1953–7   J. J. Llewellin, Baron Llewellin
1957–63   S. Ramsey, Earl of Dalhousie

RUANDA-URUNDI

A Belgian mandated territory which in 1962 became the independent republic of Rwanda (q.v.) and the kingdom of Burundi (q.v.).

GOVERNORS
1932–46   Eugène Jacques Pierre Louis Jungers
1946–52   Léon Antonin Marie Pétillon
1952–5   Alfred Maria Josephus Ghislencus Claeys-Bouuaert
1955–62   Jean Paul Harroy

HIGH REPRESENTATIVE
1962   Édouard Hennequiau

RWANDA

A Belgian territory which became an independent republic in 1962.

PRESIDENTS
1962–73   Grégoire Kayibanda
1973–   Juvénal Habyarimana

SAINT HELENA, ASCENSION ISLAND AND TRISTAN DA CUNHA

A British dependency in the South Atlantic.

GOVERNORS
1941–7   W. B. Gray
1947–54   G. A. Joy
1954–8   J. D. Harford
1958–62   R. E. Alford
1962–8   J. O. Field
1968–74   D. A. P. Murphy
1974–8   T. Oates
1978–80   G. C. Guy
1980–4   J. D. Massingham
1984–   F. E. Baker

SÃO TOMÉ AND PRÍNCIPE

A Portuguese colony from 1483, the islands formed a republic in 1975.

GOVERNORS

1941–5	Amadeu Gomes de Figueiredo
1945–53	Carlos de Sousa Gorgulho
1953–7	Francisco António Pires Barata
1957–63	Manuel Marques de Abrantes Amaral
1963–71	António Jorge da Silva Sebastião
1972–4	João Cecilio Goncalves
1974–5	António E. C. Peres Veloso

PRESIDENT

1975–	Manuel Pinto da Costa

SENEGAL

A French colonial territory to 1960, when Senegal became independent within the Federation of Mali. The Federation split after a few months and Senegal was proclaimed a separate republic.

GOVERNORS

1945–6	Pierre Louis Maestracci
1946–7	Oswald Marcellin Maurice Durand
1947–50	Laurent Marcel Wiltord
1950–2	Camille Victor Bailly
1952–3	Lucien Eugène Geay
1953–4	Daniel Henri Marie Goujon
1954–5	Maxime Marie Antoine Jourdain
1955–7	Don Jean Colombani
1957–8	Pierre Auguste Michel Marie Lami

HIGH COMMISSIONER

1959–60	Pierre Auguste Michel Marie Lami

PRESIDENT

1960–81	Léopold Sédar Senghor
1981–	Abdou Diouf

SEYCHELLES

A British colony which became an independent republic in 1976.

GOVERNORS

1942–7	W. M. Logan
1947–51	P. S. Selwyn-Clarke
1951–3	F. Crawford
1953–8	W. Addis
1958–61	J. K. Thorp
1961–7	J. E. Asquith, Earl of Oxford and Asquith
1967–9	H. S. Norman-Walker
1969–74	B. Greatbatch
1974–6	C. H. Allan

PRESIDENTS

| 1976–7 | James Richard Mancham |
| 1977– | France Albert René |

SIERRA LEONE

A British colony which became an independent dominion in 1961 and a republic in 1971.

GOVERNORS

1941–8	H. C. Stevenson
1948–53	G. B. Stooke
1953–6	R. D. Hall
1956–61	M. H. Dorman

GOVERNORS-GENERAL

1961–2	M. H. Dorman
1962–8	H. J. L. Boston
1968–71	B. Tejan-Sie

PRESIDENTS

| 1971–85 | Siaka Probyn Stevens |
| 1985– | Joseph Saidu Momoh |

SOMALIA

The republic was created in 1960, incorporating British Somaliland, a former colony, and Italian Somaliland, which was a United Nations trust territory from 1945.

BRITISH SOMALILAND: GOVERNORS

| 1943–8 | G. T. Fisher |

1948–54	G. Reece
1954–9	T. O. Pike
1959–60	D. B. Hall

ITALIAN SOMALILAND: GOVERNORS
(under United Kingdom)

1943–8	D. H. Wickham
1948	E. A. V. de Candole
1948–50	G. M. Gamble

(under Italy)

1950–3	G. Fornari
1953–5	E. Martino
1955–8	E. Anzilotti
1958–60	M. di Stefani

PRESIDENTS

1960–7	Adan Abdullah Osman
1967–9	Abdelrashid Ali Shermarke
1969–	Mohamed Siyad Barre

SOUTH AFRICA

The Union of South Africa was created in 1910. South Africa became a republic in 1961 and left the Commonwealth.

GOVERNORS-GENERAL

1943–6	N. J. de Wet
1946–51	G. B. van Zyl
1951–9	E. Jansen
1959–61	C. R. Swart

STATE PRESIDENTS

1961–7	C. R. Swart
1967	T. E. Dönges (never assumed office, owing to illness; J. F. T. Naude was acting president)
1968–75	J. J. Fouché
1975–8	N. Diederichs
1978–9	B. J. Vorster
1979–84	M. Viljoen
1984–9	Pieter Willem Botha
1989–	F. de Klerk

Under the policy of apartheid four homelands, or 'bantustans', have been declared republics by the South African government: Transkei in 1976, Bophuthatswana in 1977, Venda in 1979, and

Ciskei in 1981. None of these 'independent' states has received any international recognition.

TRANSKEI: PRESIDENTS

1976–9	Chief Botha Sigcau
1979–86	Chief Kaiser Matanzima
1986–87	Paramount Chief Tutor Nyangelizwe Vulinolela Ndamase
1987–	Bantu Holomisa

BOPHUTHATSWANA: PRESIDENT

1977–	Chief Lucas L. M. Mangope

VENDA: PRESIDENT

1979–87	Chief Patrick Mphephu
1987–	Frank Ravhele

CISKEI: PRESIDENT

1981–90	Chief Lennox L. Sebe
1990–	Joshua Oupa Gqozo

SOUTH WEST AFRICA: see NAMIBIA

SPANISH WEST AFRICA (WESTERN SAHARA)

The Spanish territories of West Africa were administered as a single unit until 1958, when they were divided into two provinces. Spain handed over Ifni to Morocco in 1969. In 1976 Spain withdrew from Spanish Sahara and the territory was divided between Morocco and Mauritania. The Polisario Front then declared the region an independent republic in 1976, a position recognised by many African states although Morocco claimed Western Sahara.

GOVERNORS

1939–49	J. B. Lopez
1949–52	F. R. Burguet
1952–4	V. T. Gil
1954–7	R. P. de Santallana
1957–8	E. G. Z. Quirce

SPANISH SAHARA: GOVERNORS

1958	Jose Hector Vázquez
1958–61	Mariano Alonso Alonso
1961–4	Pedro Latorre Alcubierre
1964–5	Joaquín Agulla Jiménez Coronado
1965–7	Angel Enríquez Larrondo

1967–71   José María Pérez de Lema Tejero
1971–4   Don Fernando de Santiago y Diaz de Mendevil
1974–6   Federico Gomez de Salazar y Nieto

IFNI: GOVERNORS
1958–9   M. G. Z. Quirce
1959–61   P. L. Alcubierre
1961–3   J. A. J. Coronado
1963–5   A. A. Campos
1965–7   M. T. Larrasquito
1967–9   J. M. V. Rodríguez

SUDAN

The territory, which formed the Anglo-Egyptian condominium from 1899, became an independent republic in 1956.

GOVERNORS-GENERAL
1940–7   H. J. Huddleston
1947–54   R. G. Rowe
1954–5   A. K. Helm

HEADS OF GOVERNMENT, PRIME MINISTERS
1956–8   [Presidential Council]
1958–64   Ferik Ibrahim Abboud
1964–5   [Supreme Council of State]
1965–9   Ismail al-Azhari
1969–85   Jaafar Mohamed al-Nimeri
1985–6   Abdel Rahman Swar ad-Dahab (Transitional Military Council)
1986–90   Ahmed Ali al-Mirghani (head of six member Supreme Military
           Council)
1990–   Omar Hassan Ahmed al-Bashir

SWAZILAND

A British protectorate from 1906, Swaziland became an independent kingdom within the Commonwealth in 1968.

RESIDENT COMMISSIONERS
1946–50   E. B. Beetham
1950–6   D. L. Morgan
1956–63   B. A. Marwick
1963–8   F. A. Loyd

KINGS

1921–82	Sobhuza II
1982–5	Regency
1986–	Mswati III

TANGANYIKA/TANZANIA

The United Republic of Tanzania was formed in 1964 from the Republic of Tanganyika, a British trust territory until 1961, and Zanzibar, which had become an independent sultanate in 1963 and a republic in 1964.

GOVERNORS OF TANGANYIKA

1942–5	W. E. Jackson
1945–9	W. D. Battershill
1949–58	E. F. Twining
1958–61	R. G. Turnbull

PRESIDENTS

1961–85	Julius K. Nyerere
1985–	Ali Hassan Mwinyi

TOGO

A French trust territory which became an independent republic in 1960.

HIGH COMMISSIONERS

1944–8	Jean Noutary
1948–51	Jean Henri Arsène Cédile
1951–2	Yves Jean Digo
1952–4	Laurent Elisée Péchoux
1955–7	Jean Louis Philippe Bérard
1957–60	Georges Léon Spénale

PRESIDENTS

1960–3	Sylvanus Olympio
1963–7	Nicolas Grunitzky
1967	Kléber Dadjo
1967–	Étienne (later Gnassingbe) Eyadéma

TUNISIA

Under French rule from 1881 to 1956, when Tunisia became an independent monarchy. A republic was proclaimed in 1957.

BEYS
1943–56	Mohamed al-Amin
1956–7	Sidi Lamine

RESIDENTS-GENERAL
1946–50	Jean Mons
1950–2	Louis Marcelin Marie Perillier
1952–3	Jean de Hauteclocque
1953–4	Pierre Voizard
1954–5	Pierre Georges Jacques Marie Boyer de la Tour du Moulin

HIGH COMMISSIONER
1955–6	Roger Seydoux Fornier de Clausonne

PRESIDENTS
1957–87	Habib Ben Ali Bourguiba
1987–	Zine el-Abidine Ben Ali

UGANDA

A British colony which became an independent dominion in 1962 and a republic in 1967.

GOVERNORS
1944–52	J. H. Hall
1952–7	A. B. Cohen
1957–61	F. Crawford
1961–2	W. F. Coutts

GOVERNOR-GENERAL
1962–3	W. F. Coutts

PRESIDENTS
1962–6	Mutesa II, Kabaka of Buganda
1966–71	A. Milton Obote
1971–9	Idi Amin

1979 (Apr-June)	Yusaf Lule
1979–80 (Dec)	Godfrey Binaisa
1980–5	A. Milton Obote
1985–6	Tito Okello
1986–	Yoweri Museveni

UPPER VOLTA: see BURKINA FASO

ZAÏRE

The Belgian Congo, which achieved independence as the Republic of Congo in 1960. The name Zaïre was adopted in 1971.

GOVERNORS

1934–46	Pierre Marie Joseph Ryckmans
1946–52	Eugène Jacques Pierre Louis Jungers
1952–8	Léon Antonin Marie Pétillon
1958–60	Henri Arthur Adolf Antoon Marie Christophe Cornelis

PRESIDENTS

1960–5	Joseph Ileo Kasavubu
1965–	(Joseph Désiré) Mobutu Sese Seko

ZAMBIA

The British colony of Northern Rhodesia, which became an independent republic in 1964.

GOVERNORS

1941–7	E. J. Waddington
1948–54	G. M. Rennie
1954–8	A. E. T. Benson
1958–64	E. D. Hone

PRESIDENT

1964–	Kenneth David Kaunda

ZANZIBAR

A British territory which became an independent sultanate in 1963 and a republic in 1964. In the same year Zanzibar joined Tanganyika to form a united republic, now Tanzania.

SULTANS
1911–60	Seyyid Sir Khalifa bin Harub
1960–3	Seyyid Abdullah
1963–4	Seyyid Jamshid

RESIDENTS
1941–46	H. G. Pilling
1946–51	V. G. Glenday
1952–4	J. D. Rankine
1954–60	H. S. Potter
1960–3	G. R. Mooring

PRESIDENT
1964–5	Sheikh Abeid Karume

ZIMBABWE (formerly RHODESIA)

The British territory of Southern Rhodesia became self-governing in 1923. In 1965 the white minority government unilaterally declared the country an independent state as Rhodesia. A republic was proclaimed in 1970 but it failed to gain international recognition. By 1978 agreement had been reached between the regime and African nationalists within the country to form a more representative government for the state of Zimbabwe–Rhodesia. A provisional government was established, but continuing guerrilla warfare forced that government to return the territory temporarily to British supervision. Zimbabwe became an independent republic in 1980.

GOVERNORS
1944–6	W. C. Tait
1947–53	J. N. Kennedy
1954–9	P. B. R. W. William-Powlett
1959–69	H. V. Gibbs

PRESIDENTS
1970–5	C. Dupont
1975–8	J. J. Wrathall
1979	J. Gumede

GOVERNOR
1980 Christopher Soames, Lord Soames

PRESIDENT
1980–87 Canaan Banana

EXECUTIVE PRESIDENT
1987– Robert Mugabe

3 MAJOR MINISTERIAL APPOINTMENTS

ALGERIA

1 July 62	Independence granted; first effective government formed after elections of Sep 63 – before that, wrangling factions shoved each other in and out
18 Sep 63	*Pres/PM* Ahmed Ben Bella *FA* Abdul Aziz Bouteflika *National Economy* (incorporating Finance, Commerce and Industry) Bachir Boumaza
28 Sep 63	*FA* Mohamed Khemisti *Fin* Ahmed Francis
19 June 65	Coup under Col. Boumédienne; Revolutionary Council assumes power
10 July 65	Boumédienne forms a cabinet *PM* Col. Houari Boumédienne *FA* Abdul Aziz Bouteflika *Fin* Ahmed Kaïd
10 Dec 67	*Fin* (acting; later confirmed) Ahmed Medhegri
28 July 70	*Fin* Ismaïl Mahroug
16 Feb 76	*Fin* Abdelmalek Temam
21–27 Apr 77	Cabinet reshuffle *Fin* Mohamed Seddik Benyahia

| 9 Feb 79 | *President of the Republic, Council of Revolution, Council of Ministers* Col. Benjeddid Chadli |

8 Mar 79	*PM*	Mohamed Ben Ahmed Abdelghani
	FA	Mohamed Seddik Benyahia
	Fin	Mohamed Hadj Yalla

| 12 Jan 82 | *Fin* | Boualem Ben Hamouda |

| 8 May 82 | *FA* | Ahmed Talib Ibrahimi |

| 22 Jan 84 | *PM* | Abdelhamid Brahimi |

| Feb 86 | *Fin* | Abdelaziz Khallaf |

| 5 Nov 88 | *PM* | Col. Kaski Merbah |

| 11 Sep 89 | *PM* | Mouloud Hamroche |

ANGOLA

| 11 Nov 75 | Independence |

| 14 Nov 75 | Neto's government sworn in: |

PM Lopo do Nascimento
FA José Eduardo dos Santos
Fin none; Carlos Rocha is Minister for Planning and Economic Co-ordination

| 23 Nov 75 | Roberto government: |

PM Johnny Eduardo/José N'dale (coalition of FNLA/ UNITA, joint premiership)
FA Hendrik Vaal Neto
Fin Craca Tavares

26 Nov 76	*PM*	Lopo do Nascimento
	FA	Paulo Teixeira Jorge
	Fin	Saidi Vieira Dias Mingas

| 27 May 77 | Mingas killed in an attempted coup |

| 31 Aug 77 | *Fin* | Ismael Gaspar Martins |

| Dec 78 | Post of PM abolished |

| 17 Jan 79 | Death of Neto |
| | *Pres* José Eduardo dos Santos |

| 12 July 80 | *FA* | Paulo Teixeira Jorge |
| | *Fin* | Ismael Gaspar Martins |

| 15 Aug 82 | *Fin* | Augusto Teixeira de Matos |

| 21 Oct 84 | *FA* | President Santos (interim) |

| 8 Mar 85 | *FA* | Alfonso van Dunem |

BENIN (formerly DAHOMEY)

| 4 Dec 58 | Independence as Dahomey, an autonomous republic within the French Community |
| | *PM* Sourou Migan Apithy |

| 22 May 59 | *PM* Hubert Maga |
| | *FA* Émile Derlin Zinsou |

| 1 Aug 60 | Full independence |

| 2 Nov 60 | *Fin* Sourou Migan Apithy |

| 12 Dec 60 | *FA* Oké Assaba |

| Feb 62 | *FA* Émile Derlin Zinsou |

| July 62 | Reference to Borna Bertin as Fin Minister |

| 28 Oct 63 | Army coup |

29 Oct 63	*Pres/PM* Col. Christophe Soglo
	FA Hubert Maga
	Fin Sourou Migan Apithy

25 Jan 64	*PM* Justin Ahomadegbé
	FA Gabriel Lozès
	Fin François Aplogan

| 29 Nov 65 | Ahomadegbé resigns as PM |

| 1 Dec 65 | *PM/FA* Tahirou Congacou |
| | *Fin* Antoine Boya |

23 Dec 65	*Pres/PM* Christophe Soglo
	FA Émile Derlin Zinsou
	Fin Nicéphore Soglo

| Dec 66 | *Fin* Bertin Borna |

| 17 Dec 67 | Army coup |

| 18 Dec 67 | *Pres/PM* Maj. Maurice Kouandeté |

	FA Émile Derlin Zinsou
	Fin Pascal Tchabi Kao
17 July 68	Zinsou elected President, and asked to form a government, which he does on 31 July 68:
	Pres/PM Émile Derlin Zinsou
	FA Daouda Badarou
	Fin Stanislas Kpognon
10 Dec 69	Army coup
12 Dec 69	Directorate installed under Lt-Col. Émile de Souza; the former Cabinet resigns on 16 Dec 69
	FA Lt-Col. Benoît Sinzogan
	Fin Lt-Col. Maurice Kouandeté
Apr 70	Introduction of presidency by rotation; the President heads the Cabinet during his two-year term
1 May 70	*Pres/PM* Hubert Maga
	FA Daouda Badarou
	Fin Pascal Tchabi Kao
4 Aug 71	*FA* Michel Ahouanmenou
7 May 72	*Pres/PM* Justin Ahomadegbé
26 Oct 72	Army coup
27 Oct 72	*Pres/PM* Maj. Mathieu Kerekou
	FA Maj. Michel Aladaye
	Fin Thomas Lahami
30 Mar 73	*Fin* Janvier Assogba
21 Oct 74	*Fin* Quartermaster Isidore Amoussou
81	*FA* Simon Ifede Okouma
9 Apr 82	*FA* Tiamiou Adjibadé
2 Aug 84	*FA* Frédéric Affo
	Fin Hospice Antonio
13 Feb 87	*FA* Guy Landry Hazoume
	Fin Barnabi Bidouzo

BOTSWANA (formerly BECHUANALAND)

3 Mar 65   *PM*   Seretse Khama (forms a cabinet 4 Mar 65; contains no FA minister)

30 Sep 66   First cabinet on Independence:

             Pres Sir Seretse Khama
             Ext   M. P. K. Nwako
             Fin   B. C. Thema

22 Oct 69   Sir Seretse Khama appointed PM once more; chooses cabinet on 23 Oct 69
             Fin   J. G. Haskins

30 Oct 74   *Fin*   Quett K. J. Masire
             Ext   A. M. Mogwe

18 July 80   *Pres* Quett K. J. Masire
             Fin   Peter S. Mmusi

14 Sep 84   *FA*   Gaositwe K. T. Chiepe

BURKINA FASO (formerly UPPER VOLTA)

5 Aug 60   Independence
             Pres/PM Maurice Yameogo (appointed Oct 58 on the death of PM Ouezzin Coulibaly)

3 Jan 61   *FA*   Lompolo Koné

4 Jan 66   Yameogo overthrown

7 Jan 66   *Pres/PM/FA*   Lt-Col. (later Gen.) Sangoulé Lamizana
             Fin   Tiemoko Marc Garango

6 Apr 67   *FA*   Malick Zomore

13 Feb 71   *PM*   Gérard Kango Ouedraogo

22 Feb 71   *FA*   Joseph Issou Conombo

8 Feb 74   Government dismissed by Pres Lamizana

11 Feb 74   *Pres/PM* Sangoulé Lamizana
             FA   Capt. Seye Zerbo

29 Jan 76   Government dissolved

9 Feb 76   *FA*   Alfred Kabore
             Fin   Sango Mamadou

23 July 76	*Fin*	Capt. Léonard Kalmogo
14 Jan 77	*FA*	Moussa Kargougou
July 78	*PM*	Joseph Issou Conombo
30 Sep 82	*FA*	Michel Kafando
	Fin	Maiga Inoussa
26 Nov 82	*PM*	Capt. Thomas Sankara
	Fin	Pascal Sanou
17 May 83	*PM*	post abolished
		(Sankara arrested; Council dissolved 27 May)
4 Aug 83		Coup: Sankara-led National Revolutionary Council installed
24 Aug 83	*Chairman*	Capt. Thomas Sankara
	FA	Arba Diallo
	Fin	Justin Damou Barro
31 Aug 84	*FA*	Leandre Bassolet
at 4 Sep 87	*Fin*	T. Eugene Dondasse
15 Oct 87		Coup: Sankara overthrown and killed. Government dissolved by the coup leader Capt. Blaise Campaore.

BURUNDI

1 July 62		Independence
	PM	André Muhirwa
June 63	*PM*	Pierre Ngendandumwe
Apr 64	*PM*	Albin Nyamoya
11 Jan 65	*PM*	Pierre Ngendandumwe (assassinated 15 Jan 65)
23 Jan 65	*PM*	Joseph Bamina
Oct 65	*PM*	Léopold Biha
11 July 66	*PM*	Michel Micombero (he appointed his cabinet on 13 July 66)
	FA	Pie Masumbuku
Sep 66		Masumbuku resigns; replaced by Prime Nyongabo
29 Nov 66		PM Micombero deposes the head of state and becomes Pres as well as PM. He dissolves the government and forms a new one on 6 Dec 66:

	FA	Prime Nyongabo
	Fin	Donatien Bihute
14 Mar 67	*PM*	takes FA portfolio
Aug 68	*FA*	Lazare Ntawurishira
	Fin	André Kabura (imprisoned 8 Oct 69)

29 Apr 72   Pres Micombero dissolves the government and takes full powers till 14 July 72

15 July 72	*PM*	Albin Nyamoya
	FA	Artemon Simbananiye
	Fin	Joseph Hicuburundi

5 June 73   Nyamoya sacked

11 July 74   Constitution comes into force

13 Mar 74	*Fin*	Maj. Samuel Nduwingoma
11 Nov 74	*FA*	Gilles Bimazubute
	Fin	Gabriel Mpozagara
27 Nov 75	*FA*	Melchior Bakwira

1 Nov 76   Pres Micombero overthrown

9 Nov 76	*Pres*	Lt-Col. Jean Baptiste Bagaza
11 Nov 76	*PM*	(office re-created) Lt-Col. Edouard Nzambimana
13 Nov 76	*FA*	Albert Muganga
	Fin	Dominique Shiramanga
13 Oct 78	*PM*	(office abolished)
	FA	E. Nzambimana
	Fin	Astère Girumkwigomba
8 Nov 82	*FA*	Laurent Nzeyimana
	Fin	Edouard Kadigiri
14 Sep 84	*Fin*	Pierre Ngenzi
Apr 86	*FA*	Egide Nkuriyingoma
13 Jan 87	*Fin*	Isaac Budabuda

3 Sep 87   Coup

9 Sep 87   Maj. Pierre Buyoya elected leader of a Military Committee for National Salvation

CAMEROON

1 Jan 60	Independence
	Pres/PM Ahmadou Ahidjo
	FA Charles Okala
Oct 61	*FA* Jean Betayene
1964	*FA* Benoît Balla
May 65	*FA* Simon Nko'o Efoundgou
July 66	*Fin* Simon Nko'o Efoundgou
Jan 68	*FA* Simon Nko'o Efoundgou
13 June 70	*FA* Raymond Ntheppe
25 Jan 71	*FA* Jean Keutcha
June 72	*FA* Vincent Efon
	Fin Charles Ouana Awana
2 June 75	Post of PM recreated, but no date for when it previously lapsed, as Ahidjo was originally PM
30 June 75	*PM* Paul Biya
	FA Jean Keutcha
	Fin Marcel Yondo
8 Nov 79	*Fin* Gilbert Ntang
19 July 80	*FA* Paul Doutsop
6 Nov 82	*PM* Bello Bouba Maigari
12 Apr 83	*FA* Felix Tonye Mbog
	Fin Etienne Ntsama
22 Aug 83	*PM* Luc Ayang
4 Feb 84	*PM* post abolished
7 July 84	*FA* W. Eteki Mboumoua
24 July 85	*Fin* Edouard Koula
21 Nov 86	*Fin* André Boto A Ngon
23 Jan 87	*FA* Philippe Mataga

CAPE VERDE ISLANDS

5 July 75   Independence

         Pres   Aristides Maria Pereira
         PM   Pedro Pires
         FA   Abilio Duarte
         Fin   Amaro da Luz

Dec 80   *FA*   Col. S Manuel da Luz
         Fin   Maj. O Lopes da Silva

16 Jan 86   Maj. Lopes da Silva dismissed, no Finance Minister given, but Arnaldo Vasconcellos Franca is Deputy Minister.

CENTRAL AFRICAN REPUBLIC (formerly UBANGI-CHARI)

Apr 59   PM Barthelemy Boganda killed in an air crash; new PM appointed, David Dacko

12 Aug 60   Independence

         PM   David Dacko
         FA   Maurice Dejean

17 Nov 60   PM Dacko is also elected Pres

1 Jan 66   Pres Dacko imprisoned by Col. Jean Bédel Bokassa

3 Jan 66   *Pres/PM*   Col. Jean Bédel Bokassa
         FA   Antoine Guimali
         Fin   Alexandro Banza

12 Jan 67   *FA*   Jean Arthur Bandio

13 Feb 68   *Fin*   Antoine Guimali

19 Aug 70   *FA*   Nestor Kombot Naguemon

5 Feb 71   *FA*   Clément N'Gai Voueto

4 Aug 71   *FA*   Joseph Potelot

29 Dec 71   *Fin*   Derant Enoch-Lakoué in place of François Gon, but no date for the appointment of Gon

16 Oct 73   *FA*   Louis Alazoula
         Fin   Alphonse Koyamba

15 June 74   *FA*   Joseph Potelot

1 Jan 75   *PM* (newly-created post)   Elisabeth Domitien

23 June 75	*FA*	Antonio Franck
	Fin	Marie Christiane Ghoukou
1976	PM Domitien sacked and replaced by Pres Bokassa	
5 Sep 76	*PM*	Ange Patassé
4 Dec 76	Empire proclaimed, with Bokassa as Emperor	
14 Dec 76	*FA*	Jean Paul Mokodopo
	Fin	Alphonse Koyamba
Oct 77	*FA*	Michel Gbezera-Bria
	Fin	Hugues Dobozeildi
17 July 78	*PM*	Henri Madou
	Fin	François Estrade
24 Sep 79	Restoration of Central African Republic	
	Pres	David Dacko
	PM	Bernard Christian Ayandho
	FA	Sylvestre Bangui
	Fin	Alphonse Koyamba
16 July 80	*Fin*	Padoundji Yadjoua
23 Aug 80	*PM*	dismissed
12 Nov 80	*PM*	Jean-Pierre Lebouder
	FA	resigned
4 Apr 81	*PM*	Simon Narcisse Bozanga
	FA	Jean-Pierre Kombet
	Fin	Barthelémy Kanda
1 Sep 81	Coup, led by Gen André Kolingba who became head of state and head of the government (Military Committee for National Recovery)	
	FA	Lt-Col. J.-L. Gervil Yambala
	Fin	Quartermaster T Marloua
4 Mar 82	*Fin*	Quartermaster Alphonse Kongola
27 May 83	*FA*	Lt Michel Salle
23 Jan 84	*Fin*	Lt-Col. J.-L. Gervil Yambala
	FA	2nd Lieut. C. M. N'Gai Voueto
21 Sep 85	*FA*	J.-L. Psimhis
8 Dec 86	*Fin*	Dieudonné Wazoua

CHAD

28 Nov 58	Autonomous republic within the French Community *PM* Gabriel Lisette (defeated 10 Feb 59)
10 Feb 59	*PM* Goutchomo Sahoulba (resigns 13 Mar 59)
13 Mar 59	*PM* Ahmed Koulamallah (resigns 24 Mar 59)
24 Mar 59	*PM* François Tombalbaye *Fin* Ahmed Kotoko
11 Aug 60	Independence
Dec 60	*Pres/PM* François Tombalbaye *Fin* Djibrine Kherallah
22 Aug 61	*FA* Djibrine Kherallah *Fin* Michel Djidingar
6 Mar 63	*FA* Maurice Ngantar
24 Nov 64	*FA* Jacques Baroum
20 Apr 66	*Fin* Abakar Sanga Traore
15 Oct 68	*Fin* Abdoulaye Lamana
23 May 71	*FA* Baba Hassane *Fin* Djibrine Kherallah Qui (mention of another FA minister, Élie Romba, 26 Dec 71–9 Mar 73)
1 Oct 73	*FA* Djiriabaye Doralta
30 Aug 73	Pres Tombalbaye changes his forename to N'Garta, Christian names having been abolished by decree, 27 Aug 73
13 Apr 75	Military coup; Tombalbaye assassinated
12 May 75	Provisional government: *PM* Brig.-Gen. Félix Malloum *FA* Sq.-Ldr Wadal Abdelkader Kamoungue *Fin* Brig.-Gen. Negue Djogo
29 Aug 78	*PM* Hissène Habré (resigns Mar 1979) *FA* Kotigua Guerina *Fin* Elie Romba
23 Mar 79	Formation of Provisional State Council: *Chairman* (i.e. *de facto* head of state) Goukouni Oueddei *FA* Barma Ramadan Omer *Fin* Mahamat Saleh Ahmat

29 Apr 79	Provisional government formed	
	Pres	Lol Mohamed Shawwa
	FA	Koumbamba Dering
10 Nov 79	*Pres*	Goukouni Oueddei
	FA	Acyl Ahmat
	Fin	Mahamat Saleh Ahmat
16 Mar 80	Beginning of civil war	
25 Apr 80	*Fin*	President Oueddei (Ahmat dismissed as a rebel)
29 May 82	*PM*	Djidingar Dono Ngardoum
2 June 82	*FA*	M. N. Adem Barka
19 June 82	President Hissène Habré head of government with a new Council	
	FA	Idriss Miskine
	Fin	Elie Romba
8 Jan 84	*FA*	Korom Ahmed
24 July 84	*FA*	Capt. Gouara Lassou
23 Mar 86	*Fin*	M. Bana Ngarnayal

COMORO ISLANDS

26 Dec 72	Government elected to work for independence	
	PM	Ahmed Abdallah
6 July 75	Unilateral declaration of independence from France; the Mayotte islanders refuse to support it. Comoros apart from Mayotte instal a government on 24 July 75	
	Pres/PM	Ahmed Abdallah
	FA	Ali Mroudjae
3 Aug 75	Coup by Front National Uni	
4 Aug 75	Revolutionary Council headed by Prince Said Mohamed Jaffar	
6 Jan 76	*PM*	Abdellahi Mohamed
	FA	Mouzaoir Abdallah
	Fin	Tadjidine Massoundi
12 May 78	Coup	

15 May 78	*PM* Abdellahi Mohamed
	Minister of State Abbas Djoussouf

23 May 78	*Co-Pres* Ahmed Abdallah and Mohamed Ahmed

24 May 78   New name: Federal and Islamic Republic of the Comoros

	PM	Abdellahi Mohamed
	FA	Ali Mroudjae
	Fin	Said Kafe

22 Dec 79	*Pres*	Ahmed Abdallah
	PM	Salim Ben Ali
	FA	Ali Mroudjae

15 Feb 82	*PM*	Ali Mroudjae
	FA	Saïd Kafe
	Fin	Ali Nassor

1 Jan 85	*PM* post abolished

21 Sep 85	*PM*	President A. Abdallah Abderrharyan
	Fin	S Ahmed Saïd Ali

CONGO (formerly MIDDLE CONGO)

28 Nov 58   Independence as an autonomous republic within the French
Community

   PM   Abbé Fulbert Youlou

14 Aug 60   Full independence

   FA   Stéphane Tchichelle

15 Aug 63   Youlou, Pres/PM, overthrown

16 Aug 63	*Pres/PM* Alphonse Massemba-Débat
	FA Charles Ganao
	Fin Edouard Babackas

24 Dec 63	*PM* Pascal Lissouba
	FA Charles Ganao
	Fin Edouard Babackas

26 Apr 66   PM Lissouba resigns

6 May 66   *PM*   Ambroise Noumazalay

12 Jan 68   *FA*   Nicolas Mondjo

1 Aug 68	Pres Massemba-Débat announces dissolution of National Assembly; he will rule himself by decree
3 Aug 68	Pres deposed by the army
4 Aug 68	Pres recalled. Cabinet resigns
5 Aug 68	New cabinet:

Pres/PM Alphonse Massemba-Débat
FA Nicolas Mondjo
Fin Edouard Babackas

22 Aug 68	*Pres/PM* Capt. Alfred Raoul
6 Sep 68	*Fin* Pierre-Félicien Koua
21 June 69	*FA* Charles Assemekeng
3 Jan 70	Cabinet resigns
4 Jan 70	New cabinet:

Pres/PM Maj. Marien N'Gouabi
FA Auxence Ikonga
Fin Edouard Madingou

13 June 71	Keesing's gives a new Fin Minister, Edouard Ange Poungui, and says he replaced Boniface Matingou. Probably a confusion of names
16 Dec 71	*FA* Henri Lopes
8 Jan 73	*FA* David Charles Ganao
	Fin Saturnin Okabe
9 Nov 74	*PM* (post separated from presidency) Henri Lopes
12 Dec 75	Lopes resigns
18 Dec 75	*PM* Louis Sylvain Goma
	FA Théophile Obenga
	Fin Alphonse Poaty
18 Mar 77	Pres N'Gouabi assassinated
3 Apr 77	*Pres* Col. Joachim Yhombi-Opango
5 Apr 77	New council of ministers appointed by new Pres:

PM and *FA* as before
Fin Henri Lopes

4 Apr 79	*Pres* Denis Sassou Nguessou

	V Pres	Jean-Pierre Thystère Tchicaya
	PM	Louis Sylvain Goma
	FA	Pierre Nze
	Fin	Henri Lopes

at May 83   *Fin*   J Lekoundzou Ithi Ossetoumba

7 Aug 84   *PM*   Ange Edouard Poungui
              FA   Antoine Ndinga Oba

21 Aug 87   *Fin*   Pierre Moussa

DJIBOUTI (formerly FRENCH SOMALILAND, then TERRITORY OF THE AFARS AND ISSAS)

26 June 77   Independence
              Pres/PM   Hassan Gouled Aptidon

12 July 77   *PM*   Ahmed Dini Ahmed

15 July 77   *Fin*   Ibrahim Harbi Farah (dies 22 Nov 77; replacement unknown)
              FA   Abdallah Mohamed Kamil

17 Dec 77   PM Ahmed resigns; Pres Aptidon takes on post of PM

2 Oct 78   *PM*   Barkat Gourad Hamadou
              FA   Moumin Bahdon Farah
              Fin   Ibrahim Soultan

2 Oct 86   *Fin*   Mohammed Djama Elabe

EGYPT

9 Oct 44   *PM*   Ahmed Maher
              FA   Mahmoud Fahmy al-Noukrachy
              Fin   Makram Ebeid

24 Feb 45   PM assassinated

25 Feb 45   *PM/FA*   Mahmoud Fahmy al-Noukrachy

7 Mar 45   *FA*   Abdul Hamid Badawy

15 Feb 46   PM resigns; Ebeid had resigned as Fin Minister 13 Feb 46

17 Feb 46   *PM/Fin*   Ismail Sidky
              FA   Ahmed Lufty es-Sayed

8 Dec 46	PM Sidky resigns
9 Dec 46	*PM/FA* Mahmoud Fahmy al-Noukrachy *Fin* Ibrahim Abdul Hadi
17 Feb 47	*Fin* Abdul Magid
20 Nov 47	*PM/Fin* Mahmoud Fahmy al-Noukrachy *FA* Khashaba Pasha
28 Dec 48	Noukrachy assassinated *PM/Fin* Ibrahim Abdul Hadi *FA* Ibrahim Dessuky Abaza
27 Feb 49	*FA* Ahmed Mohamed Khashaba
25 July 49	PM Hadi resigns
26 July 49	*PM/FA* Hussein Sirry (leads a caretaker government pending elections in Oct)
3 Nov 49	PM Sirry resigns and forms a new cabinet on the same day: *PM/FA* Hussein Sirry *Fin* Mohamed Zaki Abdul Motaal
3 Jan 50	Fresh elections
12 Jan 50	*PM* Mustapha Nahas *FA* Mohamed Saleh al-Din *Fin* Mohamed Zaki Abdul Motaal
11 Nov 50	*Fin* Fuad Sirag el-Din
26 Jan 52	PM Nahas dismissed
27 Jan 52	*PM/FA* Aly Maher *Fin* Mohamed Zaki Abdul Motaal
1 Mar 52	Maher resigns
2 Mar 52	*PM* Ahmed Naguib Hilaly *FA* Abdul Khalek Hassouna *Fin* Mohamed Zaki Abdul Motaal
30 June 52	Hilaly resigns
2 July 52	*PM/FA* Hussein Sirry *Fin* Naguib Ibrahim
20 July 52	*PM* Sirry resigns
22 July 52	*PM* Ahmed Naguib Hilaly
23 July 52	Coup under Maj.-Gen. Mohamed Neguib; Hilaly resigns

24 July 52   *PM/FA*   Aly Maher
                  Fin   Abdul Gelil al-Emary

7 Sep 52   *PM*   Mohamed Neguib
                  FA   Ahmed Farrag Tayeh

9 Dec 52   *FA*   Mohamed Fawzi

25 Feb 54   Neguib resigns

                  PM   Lt-Col. Gamal Abdul Nasser
                  FA   Mohamed Fawzi
                  Fin   Aly al-Gereitly

8 Mar 54   *PM*   Mohamed Neguib (Nasser having withdrawn and the government having made it up with Neguib)

17 Apr 54   *PM*   Gamal Abdul Nasser
                  Fin   Abdul Hamid al-Sherif

1 Sep 54   *Fin*   Abdul Moneim al-Khaissouny

17 Aug 61   Fin is now the responsibility of three ministers:

                  Abdul Moneim al-Khaissouny
                  Hassan Abbas Zaky
                  Col. Akram Deiry

19 Oct 61   *Fin*   Abdul Latif al-Boghdadi

29 Sep 62   (Nasser now Pres)

                  PM   Wing-Commander Ali Sabry
                  Fin   Abdul Moneim al-Khaissouny

25 Mar 64   *FA*   Mohamed Riad
                  Fin   Nazih Deif

2 Oct 65   *PM*   Zakaria Mohieddin
                  FA   Mohamed Fawzi
                  Fin   Abdul Moneim al-Khaissouny

10 Sep 66   *PM*   Mohamed Sidki Soliman
                  Minister of the Economy   Hassan Abbas Zaky
                  Minister for the Treasury   Nazih Deif

20 Mar 67   *Pres/PM*   Gamal Abdul Nasser
                  Presidential adviser on FA   Mohamed Fawzi
                  FA   Mohamed Riad
                  Fin   Abdul Aziz Mohamed Hegazy

19 June 67   *Fin*   Nazih Ahmed Deif

28 Sep 70	Pres Nasser dies
21 Oct 70	*PM* Mohamed Fawzi
16 Nov 70	Fawzi's cabinet resigns
18 Nov 70	New cabinet:
	PM Mohamed Fawzi *FA* Mohamed Riad *Fin* Abdul Aziz Mohamed Hegazy
16 Jan 72	*PM* Aziz Sidky
17 Jan 72	*FA* Mohamed Murad Ghaleb
8 Sep 72	*FA* Mohamed Hassan al-Zayat
27 Mar 73	*Pres/PM* Mohamed Anwar El Sadat *Vice-Premier for Finance* (new title) Abdul Aziz Mohamed Hegazy
31 Oct 73	*FA* Ismail Fahmy
26 Apr 74	Hegazy promoted to First Vice-Premier, Economy and Commerce, which gives him a supervisory position over new Fin Minister, Abdul Fattah Ibrahim
25 Sep 74	*PM* Abdul Aziz Mohamed Hegazy
13 Apr 75	Government resigns
14 Apr 75	*PM* Mamdouh Mohamed Salem
15 Apr 75	*FA* Ismail Fahmy *Fin* Ahmed Abu Ismail
28 Oct 76–	Elections; government resigns and forms again, 9 Nov 76
4 Nov 76	*Deputy PM for Financial and Economic Affairs* Abdul Moneim al-Khaissouny *FA* Ismail Fahmy *Fin* Mahmoud Sakaheddin Hamid
17 Nov 77	Fahmy resigns; temporarily replaced by Mohamed Riad. He resigns at once and is in turn replaced by Boutros-Ghali
24 Dec 77	*FA* Mohamed Ibrahim Kamel
1 May 78	*FA* Boutros Boutros-Ghali
2 Oct 78	*PM* (of the 'Peace Cabinet') Mustapha Khalil
17 Feb 79	*PM/FA* Mustapha Khalil

19 June 79	*Fin*	Ali Lutfi Mohamed Lutfi
12 May 80	*PM*	Mohamed Anwar El Sadat
	FA	Gen. Kamel Hassan Ali
	Fin	A Abdel Meguid
13 Oct 81	*PM*	Hosni Mubarak (also President)
2 Jan 81	*PM*	Ahmed Fuad Mohieddin
3 Jan 82	*Fin*	M Salaheddin Hamid
5 June 84	*PM*	dies: Gen. Kamel Hassan Ali, acting PM
16 July 84	*PM*	Gen. Kamel Hassan Ali confirmed
	FA	A Abdel Meguid
4 Sep 85	*PM*	Ali Lutfi
9 Nov 86	*PM*	Atef Sidki
10 Nov 86	*Fin*	M Ahmed Al Razaz

EQUATORIAL GUINEA

12 Oct 68	Independence	
	Pres/PM	Francisco Macias Nguema
	FA	Atanasio Ndongo
5 Mar 69	*Pres/PM/FA*	Francisco Macias Nguema
4 Aug 73	New constitution, forming a unitary state out of two formerly autonomous provinces, Fernando Po and Rio Muni. Pres Macias Nguema is made Life Pres	
Dec 78	*V Pres/FA*	Nguema Esono Nchama
3 Aug 79	Pres Macias Nguema overthrown	
25 Aug 79	*Pres of Supreme Military Council*	Teodoro Nguema
	V Pres/FA	Florencio Maye
	Fin	Salvador Ela
7 Dec 81	*FA*	Lt Marcos Mba Obando
	Fin	Andres Nkue
Dec 82	*PM*	Cristino Seriche Bioko
17 Jan 86	*FA*	M. Nguema Onguene
	Fin	F. Inestroca Ikaka

ETHIOPIA

	FA (from 1943) Akilou Habtewold
	Fin (no date) Makonnen Habtewold
3 Apr 58	*FA* Yilma Deressa
	Fin M. Woldemaskal
17 Apr 61	List published of the cabinet then in office:
	PM Akilou Habtewold
	FA Mikael Imru
	Fin Yilma Deressa
23 Mar 66	Decree giving the PM power to appoint the cabinet (previously the Emperor did it)
11 Apr 66	*FA* Ketema Yifru
18 Feb 69	*Fin* Mammo Tadesse
19 Aug 71	*FA* Minassie Haile
27 Feb 74	Government resigns
28 Feb 74	*PM* Lij Endalkatchew Makonnen
3 Mar 74	*PM/FA* Lij Endalkatchew Makonnen
	Fin none
21 Mar 74	*Fin* Negash Desta
29 May 74	*FA* Dejazmatch Zewde Gabre Selassie
12 Sep 74	Provisional military government headed by Gen. Aman Mikhail Andom takes power and deposes Emperor
15 Nov 74	Gen. Andom resigns
17 Nov 74	*Head of Executive Committee of the Military Council* Maj. Mengistu Haile Mariam
23 Nov 74	Gen. Andom executed
28 Nov 74	*Chairman of Provisional Military Administration Council* Brig.-Gen. Teferi Benti
6 Dec 74	*FA* Kifle Wodajo
3 Feb 77	Teferi Benti assassinated
11 Feb 77	Provisional Military Council to be known as the Dergue and appoint a council of ministers. Lt-Col. Mengistu Haile Mariam head of the Dergue and all its committees

11 Mar 77	FA	Feleke Gedle-Ghiorgis (Wodajo had defected)
At 30 July 80	Fin	Ato Tefera Wolde-Senayet (defected late 82)
23 Apr 83	Fin	Ato Tesfaye Dinka
	FA	Lt-Col. Goshu Wolde (defected 27 Oct 86)
4 Nov 86	FA	Lt-Col. Berhanu Bayeh
16 Mar 87	Fin	Ato Wole Chekol
19 Sep 87	PM	Capt. F. Selassie Wogderesse

GABON

Independence as an autonomous republic within the French Community

28 Nov 60	Independence	
	Pres/PM	Léon M'Ba
1963	FA	Jean François Ondo
1964	FA	Pierre Avaro
20 Mar 65	FA	Jean Engone
	Fin	Léonard Badinga
20 Apr 67	FA	Jean Rémy Ayouné
	Fin	Pierre Mebaley
28 Nov 67	Pres/PM	Albert Bernard Bongo
July 68	Fin	Augustin Boumah
8 Feb 71	FA	Georges Rawiri
Feb 72	Fin	Paul Moukambi
4 Oct 73	Pres/FA	Albert Bernard Bongo
16 Apr 75	V Pres/PM	Léon Mébiane
15 Mar 76	FA	Paul Okumba D'Okwatsegue
	Fin	Jérome Okinda
17 Oct 76	FA	Martin Bongo
28 Feb 80	Fin	Jean-Pierre Lemboumba-Lépandou

THE GAMBIA

17 Feb 65	Independence. Pierre N'Jie had been appointed Chief Minister in Mar 61. PM at Independence, Dauda Kairaba Jawara
Sep 72	Reference to
	FA Andrew Camara *Fin* S. M. Dibba
9 Apr 77	Reference to
	Pres/PM Sir Dauda Kairaba Jawara *FA* Lamine Jabang *Fin* Lamine Bora M'Boge
13 June 77	*Fin* Assane Moussa Camara (formerly Andrew Camara)
19 Aug 78	*V Pres* Assane Moussa Camara *Fin* Alhaji Mohamadu Cadi Cham
16 Jan 81	*Fin* Saikou Sabally
12 May 82	*Fin* Sherif Sisay

GHANA (formerly GOLD COAST)

5 Mar 52	*PM* Kwame Nkrumah
10 Mar 52	Nkrumah institutes cabinet government, but there are no FA or Fin Ministers
17 June 54	*Fin* Agbeli Gbedemah
5 Mar 57	Independence
18 Jan 59	*FA* Kojo Botsio
9 Apr 59	*FA* Ako Adjei
1 July 60	Republican constitution (cabinet as before)
May 61	Reshuffle between 2 May and 20 May *Fin* F. K. D. Goka
29 Aug 62	Adjei dismissed
3 Sep 62	PM Nkrumah takes on the FA portfolio; Adjei is arrested
17 Mar 63	*FA* Kojo Botsio

19 Feb 64	Goka resigns; PM Nkrumah takes on Fin portfolio
12 June 65	*FA* Alex Quaison-Sackey *Fin* Kwesi Amoako-Atta
24 Feb 66	Nkrumah deposed; National Liberation Council formed under Maj.-Gen. Joseph A. Ankrah
1 July 67	Executive Council of the National Liberation Council formed: *Chairman* Lt-Gen. Joseph A. Ankrah *FA* J. W. K. Harlley *Fin* Brig. Akwasi A. Afrifa
7 Sep 69	Civilian cabinet: *PM* Kofi Abrefa Busia *FA* Victor Owusu *Fin* J. H. Mensah
28 Jan 71	*FA* William Ofori-Atta
13 Jan 72	Coup
15 Jan 72	Office of PM abolished by proclamation, Parliament dissolved, constitution suspended
29 Jan 72	Formation of Commissioners' Council: *Head of Council and Finance Commissioner* Lt-Col. Ignatius Kutu Acheampong *Commissioner for FA* Maj.-Gen. Nathan A. Aferi
1 Jan 74	*FA* Maj. Kwame Baah
9 Oct 75	Reorganisation: National Redemption Council replaced by Supreme Military Council *FA Commissioner* Roger J. A. Felli
15 June 77	*Fin Commissioner* A. K. Appiah
1 Jan 79	*Pres of Supreme Military Council and head of state* Fred W. K. Akuffo
4 June 79	Coup. Armed Forces Revolutionary Council: *Chairman* Flight-Lt Jerry Rawlings *Fin* Joseph L. S. Abbey *FA* Gloria A. Nikoi
24 Sep 79	Civilian government:

	Pres Hilla Limann *FA* Isaac K. Chinebuah *Fin* Amon Nikoi
1 Dec 80	*Fin* George Benneh
31 Dec 81	Coup; Provisional National Defence Council installed
21 Jan 82	*Chairman* Flight-Lieut. Jerry Rawlings *FA* Obed Y Asamoah *Fin* Kwame Amoah
9 May 82	*Fin* Kwesi Botchwey

GUINEA

2 Oct 58	Independence
	Pres/PM/FA Ahmad Sekou Touré *Fin* Drame Alioune
Jan 68	*FA* Louis Lansana Beavogui *Fin* Diallo Saifoulaye
16 May 69	*FA* Diallo Saifoulaye *Fin* Ismaël Touré
26 Apr 72	*PM/FA* Louis Lansana Beavogui
11 Dec 76–	Reshuffle
Feb 77	*FA* Fily Sissoko *Fin* Fodé Mamadou Touré *Minister of the Domain of Economy and Finance* (over F. M. Touré) Ismaël Touré
11 Apr 79	Ismaël Touré dismissed
28 Apr 79	*Fin* Mamadi Keita
5 June 79	*FA* Abdoulaye Touré
22 May 81	*Fin* Boubacar Diallo
27 Mar 84	President died; interim government
3 Apr 84	Army coup
5 Apr 84	*PM* Diarra Traoré *Fin* Kémoko Keita *FA* Fanciné Touré

18 Dec 84	*PM*	post abolished; President assumes powers
	Fin	Sory Doumbouya
22 Dec 85	*FA*	Jean Troaré
	Fin	Lamine Bolivogui

GUINEA-BISSAU

10 Sep 74	Independence	
18 Mar 77	Reference to	
	PM (from 1973) Maj. Francisco Mendes	
	FA	Victor Maria Saudé
	Fin	Carlos Correia
28 Sep 78	*PM*	Maj. João Bernardo Vieira
14 Nov 80	*PM*	post abolished, replaced by head of a revolutionary council (still Vieira)
17 May 82	*PM*	Vitor Saudé Maria
	FA	S. Lamine Mane
	Fin	V. Freire Monteiro
10 Mar 84	*PM*	post abolished: Maria dismissed
16 May 84	*Chairman* (Council of State) Gen. J. Bernardo Vieira	
17 July 84	*FA*	Julio Semedo

IVORY COAST (known as CÔTE D'IVOIRE since 1986)

4 Dec 58	Independence as an autonomous republic within the French Community	
1 May 59	*PM/FA* Félix Houphouët-Boigny	
11 Aug 60	Full independence	
4 Jan 61	*Fin*	Raphaël Saller
5 Jan 70	*FA*	Arsène Assouañe Usher
	Fin	Henri Konan Bédié
1977	*FA*	Siméon Ake
	Fin	Abdoulaye Koné

KENYA

1 June 63	Ministry in preparation for independence:
	PM/FA Jomo Kenyatta *Fin* James Gichuru
12 Dec 63	Independence
10 Dec 64	First republican cabinet:
	Pres/PM Jomo Kenyatta *FA* Joseph Murumbi *Fin* James Gichuru
3 May 66	Murumbi appointed a V Pres; FA portfolio to be dealt with by a committee under Pres Kenyatta
5 Jan 67	*FA* James Myamweya (mention of his having replaced Mbiyu Koinange, who is said to have served from 3 May 66, so maybe he headed FA committee)
24 July 69	*Fin* Robert Ouko (said to have replaced Joseph Odero Jowi, but no date given for the beginning of Jowi's term)
22 Dec 69	*FA* Njoroge Mungai *Fin* Mwai Kibaki
3 Oct 74	*FA* Munyua Waiyaki
10 Oct 78	*Pres* Daniel T. Arap Moi
28 Nov 79	*FA* Robert J Ouko
25 Feb 82	*Fin* Arthur K Magugu
1 Oct 83	*Fin* George Saitoti *FA* Elijah W Mwangale
1 June 87	*FA* Zachary Onyonka

LESOTHO

11 May 65	*PM/FA* Chief Sekonyana Maseribane *Fin* Benedict Leseteli
7 July 65	*PM* and *FA* Chief Leabua Jonathan
3 Oct 66	Independence
Jan 70	Constitution suspended

27 Apr 73		Interim Assembly meets (still mention of ministers – Peete mentioned as FA Minister).
5 July 74	*FA*	J. R. Kostsokoane
12 Nov 75	*FA*	C. D. Molapo
	Fin	E. R. Sekhonyana
1977	*PM*	Chief Leabua Jonathan
	FA	Charles Molapo
	Fin	E. R. Sekhonyana
17 July 81	*FA*	Mooki Malapo
Nov 81	*Fin*	K T J Rakhetla
17 Aug 82	*FA*	Charles Molapo acting
24 Feb 83	*FA*	E R Sekhonyana, in addition to being Finance (actual title Economic Affairs) Minister
16 Aug 84	*FA*	V. Montsi Makhele
18 Sep 85	*Fin*	Peete N. Peete
20 Jan 86		Coup; Jonathan overthrown by Maj.-Gen. Lekhanya
24 Jan 86		Military Council formed:
	FA	Lengolo Monyake
	Fin	E R Sekhonyana

LIBERIA

No mention of any cabinet or ministers during the whole of Pres Tubman's reign (1944–71)

3 Jan 72	*Pres/PM*	Richard Tolbert
	FA	Rocheford Weeks
	Fin	Cyril Bright
2 July 74		Rocheford Weeks suspended
16 July 74	*FA*	Cecil Dennis
28 Apr 75	*Fin*	Edwin Williams
12 Jan 76	*Fin*	James T. Phillips
1 Aug 79	*Fin*	Ellen Johnson-Sirleaf
13 Apr 1980		Military coup

Chairman of People's Redemption Council Master-Sgt Samuel K. Doe
FA   Gabriel Baccus Matthews
Fin   Perry Zulu

24 Feb 81	*Fin*	George Dunye
29 Oct 81	Dunye dismissed	
Nov 81	*Fin*	J. Irving Jones
26 Nov 81	*FA*	H. Boima Fahnbulleh
4 July 83	*FA*	Ernest Eastman
15 Jan 86	*FA*	J. Bernard Blamo
4 Apr 86	*Fin*	Robert Tubman
24 Mar 87	*Fin*	John Bestman

LIBYA

30 Mar 51   Provisional pre-independence government formed

PM   Mahmoud Bey Muntasser
FA   Ali Bey Jerbi
Fin   Said Mansour Gadara

24 Dec 51   Independence

25 Dec 51   *PM/FA*   Mahmoud Bey Muntasser
Fin   Said Mansour Gadara

15 Feb 54   Muntasser resigns

19 Feb 54   *PM/FA*   Mohamed Saqizly
Fin (till 60)   Ali Ounaizi

8 Apr 54   Government resigns

12 Apr 54   *PM*   Mustapha Halim
FA   Abduffalan Albufeiri

25 May 57   Government resigns

26 May 57   *PM*   Abdul Majid Kobar
FA   Wahbi Bouri

17 Jan 60   General election

6 Feb 60   *PM/FA*   Abdul Majid Kobar

Fin (Minister of the Economy)   Mohamed bin-Othman al-Said

17 Oct 60	*PM*	Mohamed bin-Othman al-Said
	FA	Abdul Qadir Allam
	Fin	Salim al-Qadi
4 May 61	*FA*	Sulaiman Jerbi
	Fin	Ahmed al-Hasairi
29 Jan 62	*FA*	Wanis Gaddafi
15 Oct 62	*Fin*	Mohamed Sulaiman Bu Rabaida
20 Mar 63	*PM/FA*	Mohieddine Fekini
	Fin	Said Mansour Gadara
22 Jan 64	*PM*	Mahmoud Muntasser
	FA	Husain Maziq
	Fin	Salim Lutfi Qadi
21 Mar 65	*PM*	Husain Maziq
	FA	Wahbi Bouri
2 Oct 65	*FA*	Ahmed Bishti
1 Sep 69	Coup	
8 Sep 69	*PM/Fin*	Mahmoud Sulaiman al-Maghrabi
	FA	Salah Bousseir
16 Jan 70	*Pres/PM*	Col. Mu'ammar Mohamed al-Gaddafi
	Fin	Mohamed al-Rabeye
16 Sep 70	*FA*	Maj. Mohamed Najm
	Fin	Capt. Omar al-Meheishi
17 Oct 70	Meheishi resigns	
8 Dec 70	Najm resigns	
13 Aug 71	*Fin*	Maj. Abdul Salam Jallud
10 July 72	*PM*	Abdul Salam Jallud
16 July 72	*FA*	Mansour Rashid Kikhya
	Fin	Mohamed Zarrouk Ragab
Apr 73	Kikhya resigns	
14 Nov 74	*FA*	Maj. Abdul Moneim al-Huni
	Fin	Mohamed Zarrouk Ragab
Nov 75	Huni flees to Egypt	
23 Oct 76	*FA*	Ali Abdessalam at-Turayki

Mar 77	Cabinet renamed 'General People's Committee'; no post of Prime Minister; the Secretary of the General People's Committee is given instead.
2 Mar 79	*Sec* Jadallah at-Talhi *Econ* Abu Bakr as Sharif
at 7 Jan 81	*Econ* Abu Zeid Umar Dorda
3 Mar 82	*FA* post abolished *Econ* Musa Abu Furaywah
16 Feb 84	*Sec* Muhammad az-Zarrouk Ragab *Foreign Liaison* Ali Abdessalam at-Turayki
3 Mar 86	*Sec* Jadallah Azouz at-Talhi *Foreign Liaison* K Hasan al Mansour *Econ* Ibrahim Mohammed al Bishari

MADAGASCAR (MALAGASY REPUBLIC)

26 June 60	Independence *PM* (from 1 May 59) Philibert Tsirinana *FA* M. Sylla
22 July 67	*FA* Jacques Rabemananjara
18 May 72	*Pres/PM* Maj.-Gen. Gabriel Ramanantsoa
27 May 72	*FA* Lt-Cdr Didier Ratsikara *Fin* Albert Marie Ramoroson
26 Jan 75	Government dismissed and dissolved
5 Feb 75	Head of state hands over his powers to Col. Richard Ratsimandrava, who forms a government: *FA* Pastor Albert Zakariasy *Fin* Maj. Désiré Rakotoarijaona
11 Feb 75	Ratsimandrava assassinated. New military directorate under Gen. Gilles Andriamahazo; no change in cabinet
15 June 75	*Head of state and government* Didier Ratsiraka
16 June 75	*FA* Rémi Tiandrazana *Fin* Rakotovao Razakaboana
11 Jan 76	*PM* Lt-Col. Joël Rakotomalala *FA* Jean Bemananjara

30 July 76	PM Rakotomalala killed in a helicopter crash
12 Aug 76	*PM* Justin Rakotoniaina *FA* Bruno Rakotomavo
4 Aug 77	*PM* Lt-Col. Désiré Rakotoarijaona *FA* Richard Christian Rémi
15 Jan 82	*Fin* Pascal Rakotomavo
21 Oct 83	*FA* Jean Bemananjara
21 Feb 85	*PM* Victor Ramahatra

MALAWI (formerly NYASALAND)

1 Feb 63	Internal self-government, following break-up of Federation of Rhodesia and Nyasaland
	PM/FA Hastings Banda *Financial Secretary* (permanent official) H. E. Phillips
5 July 64	Full independence
	FA none listed *Fin* J. Z. U. Tembo
7 Sep 64	*FA* mention of W. K. Chiume, who was dismissed on this date, his portfolio being taken over by Banda on 10 Sep 64
1 Jan 69	*Fin* Aleke Banda
Apr 72	*Fin* D. T. Matenje
8 July 77	*Fin* Edward Bwanalie
11 Nov 77	*Fin* D. T. Matenje
29 Feb 80	*Fin* Lewis Chimango
7 Jan 81	*Fin* Chaziya Phiri
4 Apr 84	*Fin* Edward C I Bwanali
2 Jan 86	All portfolios transferred to President Banda
16 Jan 86	Banda retains FA portfolio *Fin* Chimwemwe Hara
1 July 86	*Fin* Dalton Katopola
3 June 87	*Fin* Louis Chimango

MALI (formerly SOUDAN)

20 June 60	Independence; the Mali Federation, consisting of Senegal and Soudan, comes into being
	PM Modibo Keita
20 Aug 60	Senegal withdraws from the Federation
22 Sep 60	The Soudan creates itself the Republic of Mali
20 Jan 61	*Pres/PM/FA* Modibo Keita
mid-61	*FA* Barema Bocoum
1965	*Pres/PM/FA* Modibo Keita
19 Nov 68	National Liberation Committee set up:
	Chairman Lt Moussa Traoré (Reference to Louis Nègre as former Fin Minister)
23 Nov 68	Provisional government
	PM Capt. Yoro Diakité *FA* Jean Marie Koné *Fin* Louis Nègre
15 Sep 69	*FA* Sori Coulibaly
19 Sep 69	*PM/head of state* Moussa Traoré
10 Sep 70	*FA* Capt. Charles Semba Sissoko *Fin* Lt Baba Diarra
2 June 74	New constitution approved by referendum
25 Sep 75	*Fin* Founeké Keita
8 Mar 78	Sissoko arrested
	FA Lt-Col. Youssouf Traoré
1978	*FA* Alioune Blondin Beye *Fin* Madi Diallo
2 Aug 80	*Fin* Ydrissa Keita
31 Dec 84	*Fin* Dianka-Kaba Diakité
6 June 86	*PM* Mamadou Dembelé *FA* Modibo Keita
19 Feb 87	*Fin* Soumana Sacko

MAURITANIA

| 28 Nov 60 | Independence |
| | *Pres/PM/FA*   Mokhtar Ould Daddah |

20 Sep 61   Resignation of Fin Minister Maurice Compagnet, but no date given for the beginning of his term

27 July 65   *FA*   Sidi Ould Sheikh Abdellahi

21 Feb 66   *FA*   Malam Ould Braham

Oct 66   *FA*   Birame Mamadou Wane (arrested July 1968)

1 Feb 68   *Fin*   Sidi Mohamed Dagane

9 Apr 70   *FA*   Sheikh Abdellahi replaces Hamdi Ould Mouknass, but no date is given for the beginning of Mouknass's term

18 Aug 71   *Fin*   Soumare Diara Mouna

23 Aug 75   Reorganisation into 'super-ministries': *Minister of State for the National Economy* (in charge of three departments) Sidi Ould Sheikh Abdellahi
Fin (one of the three)   Mouly Ould Mohamed
FA   Hamdi Ould Mouknass

31 Jan 77   Mouly Ould Mohamed sacked and his ministry joined to that of Trade. No name given for the Trade Minister, who becomes Minister of Trade and Finance

7 May 77   *Fin*   Ba Ibrahima (said to have replaced Ethmane Sidi Ahmed Yessa, but no date given for the beginning of Yessa's term)

4 Aug 77   The super-ministries are abolished

 FA/Fin   unchanged

31 May 78   *Fin*   Ahmed Ould Daddah

10 July 78   Military coup overthrows Pres Daddah. Military Committee for National Recovery (later Salvation) set up

 Pres   Mustapha Ould Mohamed Salek
 FA   Ahmedou Ould Abdalla
 Fin   Sidi Mohamed Ould Bigeira

21 Mar 79   *Fin*   Mouly Ould Mohamed

6 Apr 79   *PM*   Ahmed Ould Boussief (dies 25 May 79)

28 May 79   *PM*   Mohamed Khouna Ould Kaydalla

3 June 79	*Pres*	Mohamed Ould Ahmed Louly
	Fin	Ahmed Ould Zein
	FA	Ahmedou Ould Abdalla
4 Jan 80	*Pres/PM*	Mohamed Khouna Ould Kaydalla
	FA	Mohamed El Mokhtar Ould Zamel
15 Dec 80	*PM*	Sidi Ahmed Ould Bneijara
25 Apr 81	Military government installed under Lt-Col. M. O. S. Mohamed Taya	
	FA	Capt. D. O. Ahmed Mahmoud
	Fin	D. Boubou Farba
10 Aug 81	*FA*	Maj. Ahmed Ould Minneh
13 July 82	*Fin*	M. Sidina Ould Sidiya
Aug 82	*Fin*	S. Ould Ahmed Deya
8 Mar 84	*PM/Pres.*	Khouna Ould Haydalla
13 Dec 84	*PM*	Col. M. O. S. Mohamed Taya
	FA	C. S. A. Ould Babamine
	Fin	A. Amadou Babaly
29 Dec 84	*FA*	Ahmed Ould Minneh
29 Oct 85	*Fin*	M. S. Ould Lekhal
25 Dec 86	*FA*	M. Lemine Ould N'Diayane

MAURITIUS

12 Mar 68	Independence	
	PM	Sir Seewoosagur Ramgoolam
	FA	Gaetan Duval
2 Mar 73	*PM/FA*	Sir Seewoosagur Ramgoolam
1 June 76	*Fin*	Sir Veerasamy Ringadoo
	FA	Sir Harold Walter
15 June 82	*PM*	Aneerood Jugnauth
	Fin	P. Raymond Berenger
	FA	J. C. G. R. de l'Estrac
28 Mar 83	Fin portfolio to PM	
	FA	Anil Gayan

at 28 June 85   *Fin*   Seetanah Lutchmeenaraidoo

6 Jan 86   Gayan resigned as FA

13 Jan 86   *FA*   Madun Dulloo

8 Aug 86   *FA*   Sir Satcam Boolell

MOROCCO

7 Dec 55   Appointment of first cabinet

PM   Si M'Barek Ben Mustapha el-Bekkai
Fin   Abdelkader Bendjelloun
FA   none

2 Mar 56   Independence. Morocco incorporates the former international zone of Tangier

26 Apr 56   *FA*   Ahmed Balafrej

27 Oct 56   *Minister of Economic Affairs*   Abderrahim Bouabid (no Fin minister listed)

16 Apr 58   Government resigns

12 May 58   *PM/FA*   Ahmed Balafrej
Minister of Economic Affairs   unchanged

22 Nov 58   PM Balafrej resigns

24 Dec 58   *PM/FA*   Moulay Abdallah Ibrahim

20 May 60   Government dismissed; King Mohamed forms a cabinet as PM

FA   Driss M'Hammedi
Fin   M'Hammed Douiri

2 June 61   *PM/FA*   King Hassan II

22 Dec 61   *FA*   Ahmed Balafrej

4 Jan 63   *Fin*   Driss Slaoui

13 Nov 63   *PM*   Hadj Ahmed Bahnini
FA   Ahmed Reda Guedira

15–21 Aug 64   Reshuffle

FA   Ahmed Taïbi Benhima
Fin   Mohamed Cherkaoui

8 June 65   State of emergency; parliamentary government ended

	PM	King Hassan II
	Fin	Mamoun Tahiri
23 Feb 66	*FA*	Mohamed Cherkaoui
11 Mar 67	*FA*	Ahmed Laraki
6 July 67	End of state of emergency	
	PM	Mohamed Benhima
6 Oct 69	*PM*	Ahmed Laraki
	FA	Abdelhadi Boutaleb
25 Mar 70	*Fin*	Abdelkrim Lazarak
12 Oct 70	*FA*	Youssef Ben Abbes
23 Apr 71	*FA*	Karim Lamrani
4 Aug 71	Cabinet resigns	
6 Aug 71	*PM*	Karim Lamrani
	FA	Abdellatif Filali
	Fin	Mohamed Medeghri
12 Apr 72	*Fin*	Mustapha Faris
24 May 72	*FA*	Ahmed Taïbi Benhima
19 Nov 72	*PM*	Ahmed Osman
	Fin	Bensallem Guessous
25 Apr 74	*FA*	Ahmed Laraki
	Fin	Abdelkader Benslimane
5 Oct 77	Cabinet dismissed	
10 Oct 77	*FA*	Mohamed Boucetta
	Fin	Abdellatif Ghissassi
22 March 79	*PM*	Maati Bouabid
27 Mar 79	*Fin*	Abdel Kamal Reqhaye
5 Nov 81	*Fin*	Abdel Latif Jawahri
19 Nov 83	*PM*	Mohamed Lamrani
30 Nov 83	*FA*	Abdelwahed Belakziz
17 Feb 85	*FA*	Abdel Latif Filali
7 Apr 86	*Fin*	Mohamed Berrada
30 Sep 86	*PM*	Azzedine Laraki
	FA	Mohamed Saqqat

MOZAMBIQUE

20 Sep 74	Transitional government
	PM Joaquim Alberto Chissano
	Fin Mário Fernandes da Graça Machungo
25 June 75	Independence
1 July 75	*Pres* Samora M. Machel
	FA Joaquim Alberto Chissano
	Fin Salamão Munguambé
22 Jan 79	*Fin* Rui Baltasar dos Santos Alves
24 Apr 86	*Fin* Abdul Magid Osman
26 July 86	*PM* M. F. da Graca Machungo
19 Oct 86	President Machel killed in an air-crash
11 Jan 87	*FA* Pascual Manuel Mucumbi

NAMIBIA

22 Mar 90	Independence
	Pres Sam Nujoma
	PM Hage Geingob
	FA Theo Ben Gurirab
	Fin Otto Herrigel

NIGER

2 Aug 60	Independence
	Pres/PM Hamani Diori
1970	*FA* El-Hadj B. Courmo
15 Apr 74	Coup
17 Apr 74	*Head of the Supreme Military Council and head of state* Lt-Col. Seyni Kountché
	FA Capt. Moumouni Amadou Djermakoye
	Fin Quartermaster Tondi Moussa
1977	*Fin* Tondi Moussa
	FA Moumouni Amadou Djermakoye

10 Sep 1979	*FA*	Daouda Diallo
24 Jan 83	*PM*	Oumarou Mamane
14 Nov 83	*PM*	Hamid Algabid
	FA	Ide Oumarou
	Fin	Boukari Adji
23 Sep 85	*FA*	M. Sani Bako

NIGERIA

20 Dec 59	Pre-independence government set up

	PM	Sir Abubakar Tafawa Balewa
	Fin	Chief Festus Okotie-Eboh
	FA	none

30 Sep 60	Independence

PM/FA Sir Abubakar Tafawa Balewa

1963	Nigeria becomes a republic

PM/FA Sir Abubakar Tafawa Balewa (1 Jan 65)

17 July 65	*FA*	Jaja Wachuku
1 Dec 65	*FA*	Alhaji Nuhu Bamali

15 Jan 66	Coup; PM and Fin Minister both killed
16 Jan 66	Maj.-Gen. Johnson Aguiyi-Ironsi sets up a military government with a Federal Executive Council. Office of PM suspended
29 July 66	Coup; Aguiyi-Ironsi killed

1 Aug 66	*Head of military government* Lt-Col. Yakubu Gowon
24 Jan 75	New Federal Executive Council headed by Gowon

	FA	Okoi Arikpo
	Fin	Alhaji Shehu Shagari

29 July 75	Gowon overthrown

Head of state and government Brig. Murtala Ramal Mohamed

6 Aug 75	*FA*	Lt-Col. Joseph Namvan Garba
	Fin	A. E. Ekukinam

13 Feb 76	Gen. Mohamed assassinated

Head of state and government Lt-Gen. Olusegun Obasanjo
FA/Fin   unchanged

15 Mar 77	*Fin* Maj.-Gen. James Oluleye
1 Oct 79	Civilian government returned

Pres Alhaji Shehu Usman A. Shagari
FA   Ishaya Andu
Fin   Sunday Matthew Essang

15 Jan 81	*Fin* Victor Masi
10 Nov 83	Ishaya Andu sacked, not replaced as FA
	Fin Alhaji Adamu Ciroma
31 Dec 83	Military coup led by Maj. Gen. Mohammed Buhari
3 Jan 84	Supreme Military Council formed
18 Jan 84	Cabinet appointed:

FA   Ibrahim Gambari
Fin Onaolapo Soleye

27 Aug 85	Military coup led by Maj. Gen. Ibrahim Babangida
10 Sep 85	*FA* Bolaji Akinyemi
	Fin Kalu I. Kalu
24 Jan 86	*Fin* S. E. Okongwu
21 Dec 87	*FA* Ike Nwachukwu

RHODESIA AND NYASALAND

7 Sep 53	The PM of Southern Rhodesia, Sir Godfrey Huggins (from 1954 Lord Malvern), resigns to become PM, FA and Fin Minister of an interim federal government
15 Dec 53	*Fin* Donald McIntyre
31 Oct 56	Lord Malvern retires
1 Nov 56	*PM/FA* Sir Roland (Roy) Welensky
3 Sep 62	*Fin* J. M. Caldicott
31 Dec 63	Federation dissolved

RHODESIA (SOUTHERN RHODESIA)

2 Feb 44	*PM*	Sir Godfrey Huggins
	Fin	Max Danziger
	FA	none
23 Sep 46	*Fin*	Edgar C. F. Whitehead
15 July 48	Government defeated	
21 July 48	Parliament dissolved	
12 Nov 48	*PM/FA*	Sir Godfrey Huggins
	Fin	Edgar C. F. Whitehead
7 Sep 53	*PM*	Reginald Stephen Garfield Todd
	Fin	Donald McIntyre
17 Dec 53	*PM/Fin*	Reginald Stephen Garfield Todd
28 Jan 54	*Fin*	Cyril Hatty

11 Jan 58   Hatty resigns (with all other members of the Todd cabinet).

14 Jan 58	New Todd cabinet	
	Fin	A. E. Abrahamson
17 Feb 58	*PM*	Sir Edgar C. F. Whitehead
	Treasury	Cyril Hatty

(Whitehead didn't have a seat in the house; a member resigned so that he could win his seat in a by-election, but Whitehead lost. Parliament was dissolved 18 Apr 58 pending a general election for 5 June 58, after which all was well)

23 Sep 62	*Fin*	Geoffrey Ellman-Brown
17 Dec 62	*PM*	Winston Field
	Fin	Ian Douglas Smith
14 Apr 64	*PM/FA*	Ian Douglas Smith
	Fin	J. J. Wrathall
20 Aug 64	*FA*	Clifford Dupont

11 Nov 65   Unilateral Declaration of Independence; Dupont becomes Officer Administering the Government and leaves FA Ministry vacant

31 Dec 65	*FA*	Lord Graham (Duke of Montrose)
11 Sep 68	*FA*	John Howman

2 Aug 74	*FA* Pieter K. van der Byl
13 Jan 76	*Fin* David Smith
21 Mar 78	New Executive Council sworn in
11–12 Apr 78	Ministerial Council chosen; the Government being a coalition, portfolios are held jointly. Smith remains PM, but chairmanship of the Ministerial Council is held in rotation by its members

> *Fin*   David Smith and Ernest Bulle
> *FA*   Pieter K. van der Byl and Elliott Gabellah

RWANDA

1 July 62	Independence

Pres/PM   Grégoire Kayibanda

5 July 73	Coup led by Maj.-Gen. Juvénal Habyarimana
8 Dec 77	*Pres/PM* Juvénal Habyarimana

FA   Lt-Col. Aloys Nsekalije
Fin   Denis Ntirugirimbabazi
(The above ministers are listed as having retained posts which they held before the 8 Dec 77 government reorganisation, but there is no date for their original appointments.)

11 Jan 79	*FA* François Ngarukiyintwali
Early 1982	*Fin* J. Damascene Hategekimana
9 Apr 87	*Fin* Vincent Ruhamanya

SÃO TOMÉ AND PRÍNCIPE

12 July 75	Independence

Pres   Manuel Pinta da Costa
PM/FA   Miguel Trouvoada

11 Dec 75	*FA* Leonel Mário D'Alva
1 Oct 78	*FA* Mária do Nascimento da Graça Amorim
Apr 79	Post of PM abolished

| March 1980 | Post of PM revived for President |
| | |

23 Feb 85	*FA* President da Costa
3 Feb 86	*FA* F Bandeira de Menezes
17 Jan 87	*FA* Guilherme Posser da Costa
	Fin Prudencio Rita

SENEGAL

25 Nov 58	Independence as autonomous republic within the French Community
20 June 60	Independent as part of Mali Federation
20 Aug 60	Independent republic, having withdrawn from the Mali Federation
	PM Mamadou Dia
	FA Doudou Thiam
12 Nov 62	*FA* André Guillabert
	Fin Valdiodio Ndiaye (replaces A. Peytavin, but no date is given for the beginning of Peytavin's term)
17 Dec 62	*Pres/PM* Léopold Sédar Senghor
19 Dec 62	*FA* Doudou Thiam
	Fin André Peytavin
6 Mar 68	*FA* Alioune Badara Mbengue
22 Feb 70	Referendum on separating the posts of Pres and PM
26 Feb 70	*PM* Abdou Diouf
28 Feb 70	*FA* Amadou Karim Gaye
	Fin Jean Collin
10 Apr 71	*Fin* Babacar Bâ
19 June 72	*FA* Coumba Ndaffène Diouf
5 Apr 73	*Pres/PM* Léopold Sédar Senghor
	FA Assane Seck
21 Nov 75	Reference to the cabinet as
	PM Abdou Diouf
	FA Assane Seck
	Fin Babacar Bâ

13 Mar 78	Government resigns
15 Mar 78	*PM* Abdou Diouf *FA* Babacar Bâ *Fin* Assane Seck
1980	Senghor resigns
	Pres Abdou Diouf *FA* Mustapha Niasse
1 Jan 81	*PM* Diouf becomes President
2 Jan 81	*PM* Habib Thiam *FA* Moustapha Niasse (in office by this date) *Fin* Assane Seck
6 Nov 82	*Fin* Mamadou Toure
3 Apr 83	*PM* post taken by FA Moustapha Niasse, in preparation for its abolition, which followed
Oct 84	*FA* Ibrahima Fall

SEYCHELLES

1970	*PM* James Richard Mancham
29 June 76	Independence
	Pres/FA James Richard Mancham *PM* France Albert René *Fin* C. Chetty
5 June 77	Coup
	Pres/Fin France Albert René *FA* Guy Sinon
28 June 79	*FA* Jacques Hodoul
July 87	*FA* France Albert René

SIERRA LEONE

14 Aug 58	First cabinet and full ministerial system:
	PM M. A. S. (from 1961 Sir Milton) Margai *Fin* M. S. Mustapha *FA* none

27 Apr 61		Independence
	FA	J. Karefa-Smart
28 May 62	*Fin*	Albert Michael Margai
28 Apr 64		Death of Sir Milton Margai
29 Apr 64	*PM*	Albert Michael Margai
	FA	C. B. Rogers-Wright
	Fin	R. G. O. King
23 Nov 65	*FA*	Maigore Kallon
1967		Sierra Leone becomes a republic
23 Mar 67		Army Coup. National Reformation Council set up:
	Chairman/Fin	Lt-Col. Andrew Juxon-Smith
	FA	William Leigh
18 Apr 68		Counter-coup. National Reformation Council dissolved; National Interim Council set up
26 Apr 68		Cabinet formed by PM Siaka Probyn Stevens (membership unstated)
11 Sep 70	*Fin*	Sembu Forna (replaces Mohammed Forna, but no date given for the beginning of Forna's term)
21 Apr 71	*PM*	J. J. Koroma
	FA	Solomon A. J. Pratt
23 Mar 75		Desmond Fashole Luke resigns as FA Minister but no date given for the beginning of his term
1 Apr 75	*FA*	Francis Minah
Mid-July 75	*PM*	Christian A. Kamara-Taylor (said to be ex-Fin Minister)
	Fin	Sorie I. Koroma
9 May 77	*FA*	Abdulai Conteh
	Fin	A. B. Kamara
1980	*Fin*	Francis Minah
at Dec 80	*Fin*	Sama S Banya
May 82	*Fin*	S. Jusu Sheriff
5 Sep 84	*FA*	Sheka Kanu
	Fin	Abdulai Conteh

27 June 85   *Fin*   J. Amara-Bangali

15 July 85   *FA*   Alhaji A. Karim Koroma

28 Nov 85   President Stevens replaced by Joseph Saidu Momoh

11 June 86   *Fin*   Sheka Kanu

3 Apr 87   *Fin*   Hassan Gbassay Kanu

SOMALIA

1 July 60   Independence as union of the former British Somaliland
                Protectorate and the Italian trusteeship territory of Soma-
                lia. The British protectorate had already become indepen-
                dent on 26 June 1960. First PM and cabinet appointed

12 July 60   *PM*   Abdelrashid Ali Shermarke
                FA   Abdallah Issa
                Fin   Abdul Cadir Mohamed Aden

14 June 64   *PM*   Abdirizak Hadji Hussein
                FA   Ahmed Yussuf Dualeh
                Fin   Awil Hadji Abdellahi

6 July 67   *PM/FA*   Mohamed Ibrahim Egal
                Fin   Hadji Farrah

22 May 69   *Fin*   Sufi Omar Mohamed

15 Oct 69   Pres Shermarke assassinated

21 Oct 69   Army coup

1 Nov 69   *Chairman of the Revolutionary Council* Gen. Mohamed Siad
                  Barre
                FA   Omar Arteh Ghalib
                Fin   Abdi Avaleh

31 Mar 70   *Fin*   Ibrahim Meigag Samater

8 Apr 76   Ghalib sacked. No successor appointed

3 July 76   *Fin*   Abdurahman Nur Hersi

27 July 77   *FA*   Abdurahman Jamma Barreh

7 Feb 1980   *Fin*   Abdellahi Ahmed Adow

31 May 84   *Fin*   M Shaikh Usman

1 Feb 87   *PM*   Lt-Gen. M. Ali Samater

SOUTH AFRICA

1945	*PM/FA* Jan Christian Smuts *Fin* J. H. Hofmeyr
1948	*Fin* F. C. Sturrock
3 June 48	*PM/FA* D. F. Malan *Fin* N. C. Havenga
30 Nov 54	Malan retires
2 Dec 54	*PM/FA* Johannes Gerhardus Strijdom *Fin* Eric Louw
4 Jan 55	*FA/Fin* Eric Louw
31 July 56	*Fin* J. F. Nande
24 Aug 58	*PM* Hendrik Frensch Verwoerd
20 Oct 58	*Fin* T. E. Dönges (Verwoerd had been elected head of the Nationalist Party on the death of Strijdom (24 Aug 58), so he automatically became PM. An acting PM – C. R. Swart – had been sworn in on 21 Aug 58 when Strijdom became too ill to go on. Parliament had adjourned from 25 Aug to 3 Sep; Verwoerd took over on 3 Sep and reorganised his cabinet (as above) on 20 Oct 58)
21 Nov 63	Louw retires
9 Jan 64	*FA* Hilgard Muller
6 Sep 66	Verwoerd assassinated *Acting PM* T. E. Dönges
18 Sep 66	*PM* Balthazar Johannes Vorster
23 Jan 67	*Fin* Nicolaas D. Diederichs
31 Jan 75	*Fin* Owen P. Horwood
1 Apr 77	*FA* Roelof F. ('Pik') Botha
20 Sep 78	Vorster resigns *Pres* Nicolaas D. Diederichs
28 Sep 78	*PM* Pieter Willem Botha
4 June 79	*Pres* Marais Viljoen
28 June 84	*Fin* Barend du Plessis

| 15 Sep 84 | *PM* post combined with executive Presidency, held by Pieter W. Botha |

SUDAN

9 Jan 54	Ministry set up to manage the transition to self-government:
	PM Ismail al-Azhari
	Fin Hamad Tewfik
	FA none
10 Nov 55	Azhari cabinet resigns, but the opposition unable to form a government and Azhari voted back on 16 Nov 55
1 Jan 56	Independence
2 Feb 56	*FA* Mubarek Zarrouk
	Fin Ibrahim Ahmed
4 July 56	Cabinet resigns
5 July 56	*PM* Abdallah Khalil
	FA Mohamed Ahmed Mahgoub
	Fin Ibrahim Ahmed
17 Nov 58	Coup
18 Nov 58	*Pres/PM* Ferik Ibrahim Abboud
	FA Ahmed Kheir
	Fin Abdul Magid Ahmed
12 Nov 63	*Fin* Said Mamoun Biheiry
30 Oct 64	*PM* Serr al-Khatim Khalifa
	FA Mohamed Ahmed Mahgoub
	Fin Mubarak Zarrouk
18 Feb 65	Khalifa resigns and forms a new government on 23 Feb 65 with the above posts unchanged
2 June 65	Khalifa government resigns
10 June 65	Mohamed Ahmed Mahgoub elected PM
17 June 65	*FA* Mohamed Ibrahim Khalil
	Fin Ibrahim al-Mufti
27 July 66	*PM* Sadiq al-Mahdi
31 July 66	*FA* Ibrahim al-Mufti
	Fin Hamza Mirghani

15 May 67	Mahdi resigns
18 May 67	*PM* Mohamed Ahmed Mahgoub
29 May 67	*PM/FA* Mohamed Ahmed Mahgoub *Fin* Hussein al-Sharif al-Hindi
2 June 68	*FA* Ali Abdul Rahman al-Amin
25 May 69	Coup
	PM/FA Babikar Adwallah *Fin* Mansour Mahgoub
27 Oct 69	Adwallah resigns
28 Oct 69	*Pres/PM* Maj.-Gen. Jaafar Mohamed al-Nimeri *FA* Babikar Adwallah *Fin* Mansour Mahgoub
23 July 70	*Pres/PM/FA* Jaafar Mohamed al-Nimeri
3 Aug 71	*FA* Mansour Khaled
8 Apr 72	*Fin* Musa al-Mabarek (replaces Mohamed Abdul Halim Abdul Rahman, but no date given for the beginning of Rahman's term)
9 Oct 72	*Fin* Ibrahim Elias
8 May 73	New constitution; presidential government introduced. Cabinet dismissed 7 May 73 and a new one installed 10 May 73:
	Pres/PM Jaafar Mohamed al-Nemery *FA* Mansour Khaled *Fin* Ibrahim Moneim Mansour
25 Jan 75	*Fin* Ma'mun Bihairi *FA* Khaled sacked but not replaced
16 May 75	*FA* Gamal Mohamed Ahmed
11 Feb 76	*FA* Mahgoub Makawy
9 Aug 76	*PM* Rashid al-Tahir Bakr
9 Feb 77	*FA* Mansour Khaled *Fin* Sharif al-Khatim Mohamed
10 Sep 77	*Pres/PM/Fin* Jaafar Mohamed al-Nimeri *FA* Rashid al-Tahir Bakr *1st V Pres* Abou Kassem Mohamed Ibrahim *Fin* Osman Hashim Abdul Salam

17 Aug 80	*Fin*	Badr ad-Din Sulaiman
3 June 1980	*FA*	Rashid el Tahir Bakr dismissed
	FA	M. M. Mubarak (No date given for replacement)
24 Nov 81	*Fin*	I Munim Mansur
2 May 84	*FA*	Hashim Osman

23 May 84   Council dissolved and replaced by Presidential Council of
              Advisers

25 Dec 84   *Fin*   Abd Al-Rahman Abd al-Wahab

6 Apr 85   Coup; military government installed under Gen. Abdel-
              Rahman Swar ad-Dahab

15 May 86   Civilian cabinet government resumed:

PM   Sadiq el-Mahdi
FA   S Z al-Abidin al-Hindi
Fin   Omar al-Bashir

3 June 87   *FA*   M Tawfiq Ahmed

22 Aug 87   collapse of government; but restored (Oct)

June 89   Further military coup led by Omar Hassan Ahmad al-Bashir

SWAZILAND

6 Sep 68   Independence; government had been elected Apr 67

PM   Prince Makhosini Dlamini

12 Apr 73   King Sobhuza II announces all parties disbanded, the inde-
              pendence constitution repealed, supreme legislative and
              executive power to be vested in himself and the ministers
              to continue at his discretion as an advisory council. In this
              capacity Prince Makhosini continues in office

19 Jan 76   Prince Makhosini resigns

PM   Col. Maphevu Diamini

12 Feb 76   *Fin*   Laurence Funwake Simelane

1977   *FA*   Mhlangano Matsebula
              Fin   Robert P. Stephens

12 Feb 79   *Fin*   Laurence F. Simelane

Oct–Nov 79	*PM*	acting, Benjamin Nsibandze
Nov 79	*PM* *FA*	Prince Mbandla Dlamini Prince Mbandla Dlamini
at Apr 80	*FA*	L. M. Mncina
at Jan 82	*FA*	R. V. Dlamini
23 Mar 83	*PM*	Prince Bhekimpi Dlamini
21 Nov 83	*Fin*	Sishayi S Nxumalo
8 June 84		R. V. Dlamini and Nxumalo dismissed
Aug 84	*FA* *Fin*	Moses Mhambi Mnisi Sibusiso Barnabas Dlamini
9 July 86	*FA*	Shadrack Sibanyoni
4 Oct 86	*PM*	Sotsha Dlamini

TANGANYIKA

9 Dec 61		Independence. A PM and Ministers had been appointed after the general election of 30 Aug 60:
	PM *Fin* *FA*	Julius K. Nyerere (after independence Pres) Sir Ernest Vasey none
22 Jan 62	*PM* *Fin*	Rashidi M. Kawawa Paul Bomani
12 Mar 63	*FA*	Oscar Kambona
27 Apr 64		Union with Zanzibar to form Tanzania (q.v.)

TANZANIA

27 Apr 64		Union of Tanganyika (q.v.) and Zanzibar (q.v.) to form new state of Tanzania
	Pres/PM *FA* *Fin*	Julius K. Nyerere Oscar Kambona Paul Bomani
30 Sep 65	*Fin*	Amir H. Jamal

22 Feb 67	*FA*	Hasnu Makame
17 Feb 72	*PM*	Rashidi M. Kawawa
	FA	John Malesela
	Fin	Cleopa Msuya
9 Nov 75	*FA*	Ibrahim Kaduma
	Fin	Amir Jamal
13 Feb 77	*PM*	Edward Sokoine
	FA	Benjamin Mkapa
	Fin	Edwin Mtei
Nov 78	*Fin*	Amir H. Jamal (resigns 1 Nov 79)
5 Nov 79	*Fin*	Amir Jamal
7 Nov 80	*PM*	Cleopa David Msuya
	FA	Salim Ahmed Salim
23 Feb 83	*PM*	Edward Sokoine
	Fin	Cleopa Msuya
24 Apr 84	*PM*	Salim Ahmed Salim
	FA	Benjamin Mkapa
5 Nov 85	*PM*	Joseph Warioba

TOGO

24 Aug 56	Independence within the French Community
16 Sep 26	Cabinet government introduced

	PM	Nicolas Grunitzky
	FA	none
	Fin	unknown

27 Apr 60	Full independence
	Pres/PM Sylvanus Olympio
13 Jan 63	Pres Olympio murdered
16 Jan 63	*Pres/PM/FA* Nicolas Grunitzky
	Fin Antoine Meatchi
16 May 63	*FA* Georges Apedoamah
13 Jan 67	Army coup. Government set up under
	Pres/FA Col. Kléber Dadjo
	Fin Benoît Bedou

14 Apr 67	Government dissolved and new government set up:
	Pres Lt-Col. Étienne Eyadéma
	FA Joachim Hunlede
	Fin Boukari Djobo
4 Aug 69	*Fin* Jean Tévi
21 Aug 73	*Fin* Edouard Kodjo
Mar 75	The cabinet (having taken African forenames some time previously) appears as
	Pres/PM Gen. Gnassingbe Eyadéma
	FA Ayi Houenou Hunlede
	Fin Alien Kodjo
6 Sep 76	*FA* Edem Kodjo
	Fin Yaou Grunitzky
July 78	*FA* Anani Akakpo-Ahianyo
Nov 78	*Fin* Teti Tere Benissan
13 Sep 84	*FA* Atsu-Koffi Amega
	Fin Komlan Alipui
12 Mar 87	*FA* Yaouvi Adodo

TUNISIA

17 Aug 50	*PM* Mohamed Chenik (appointed six years ahead of full independence)
28 Mar 52	Chenik dismissed
	PM Salaheddin Baccouche
12 Apr 52	Baccouche forms a cabinet, but this does not include a minister of FA or Fin – both portfolios still handled by the French administration
18 Jan 54	Baccouche resigns
2 Mar 54	*PM* Mohamed Salah Mzali
7 Aug 54	*PM* Tahar Ben Ammar
17 Sep 55	*Fin* Hedi Nouira
20 Mar 56	Independence

10 Apr 56	*PM/FA* Habib Ben Ali Bourguiba *Fin* Hedi Nouira
25 July 57	Bourguiba also becomes head of state
30 July 57	*FA* Sadok Mokkadem
30 Dec 58	*Fin* Ahmed Mestiri
16 Aug 62	*FA* Mongi Slim
11 Nov 64	*PM* Bahi Ladgham (PM's title changes to 'President of the Republic', under Pres Bourguiba. He retains most of the functions of a PM) *FA* Habib Bourguiba Jr *Fin* Ahmed Ben Salah
8 Sep 69	*Fin* Abderrazak Rassaa
7 Nov 69	Post of PM revived
12–17 June 70	Cabinet reshuffle *FA* Mohamed Masmoudi
1 Nov 70	*Interim PM* Hedi Nouira (later confirmed in office)
6 Nov 70	*FA* Mohamed Masmoudi *Fin* Abderrazak Rassaa
26 Oct 71	Cabinet resigns
29 Oct 71	Cabinet reformed *Fin* Mohamed Fitouri
14 Jan 74	*FA* Habib Chatti
26–27 Dec 77	*Fin* Abdelaziz Mathari
Dec 77	*FA* Mohamed Fitouri
1 Mar 80	*PM* Mohamed M'Zali
24 Apr 80	*FA* Hassan Belkhodja *Fin* Mansour Moalla
15 Apr 81	*FA* Beji Caid-Essebsi
18 June 83	*Fin* Salah Ben M'barka
28 Apr 86	*Fin* Rashid Sfar
8 July 86	*PM* Rashid Sfar *Fin* Ismail Khelil

2 Oct 87	*PM* Abidine Ben Ali
7 Nov 87	*PM* Hedi Baccouche

UGANDA

1 Mar 62	Independence
	PM Benedicto Kiwanuka *Fin* Lawrence Sebalu
30 Apr 62	*PM/FA* A. Milton Obote *Fin* A. K. Sempa
24 Aug 64	*FA* Sam Odaka *Fin* L. Kalule-Settala
25 Jan 71	Army coup
2 Feb 71	Council of Ministers formed:
	Head Gen. Idi Amin *FA* Wanume Kibedi *Fin* E. B. Wakhweya
29 Apr 73	Kibedi dismissed
Early May 73	*FA* (acting) Paul Etiang
10 Oct 73	*FA* Lt-Col. Michael Ondoga
19 Feb 74	*FA* Elizabeth Bagaya
28 Nov 74	Miss Bagaya dismissed
	Pres/FA Idi Amin
18 Jan 75	Wakhweya resigns
29 Jan 75	*FA* Lt-Col. Juma Oris Abdallah
20 Feb 75	*Fin* (acting) A. C. K. Oboth-Ojumbi
6 Apr 77	M. S. Kiyingi retires as Fin Minister, but no date given for the beginning of his term
Jan 78	Reference to Brig. Moses Ali as Fin Minister
11 Apr 79	Provisional government:
	FA Otema Alimadi *Fin* Samuel Sebagereka

25 June 79   *Fin*   Jack Sentongo
                    FA   President Godfrey Binaisa (but Otema Alimadi con-
                          tinued as the working head of the department)

22 Dec 79   *FA*   Otema Alimadi

12 May 80   President Binaisa replaced by a Military Commission with
                   Paulo Muwanga as Chairman (from 13 May)

18 May 80   *Fin*   Lawrence Sebalu

Dec 80   President Milton Obote returns to power

18 Dec 80   *PM*   Otema Alimadi
                   FA   President Obote
                   Fin   President Obote

29 July 85   Obote replaced by a military government with Lt-Gen. Tito
                   Okello as Chairman

30 July 85   *PM*   Paulo Muwanga
                   FA   Olara Otunnu
                   Fin   Abraham Waligo

25 Aug 85   *PM*(and *Fin*)   Abraham Waligo

30 Jan 86   *PM*   Samson Kisekka
                   FA   Ibrahim Mukiibi

21 Nov 86   *Fin*   Ponsiano Mulema
                   Fin   Crispus Kiyonga

UPPER VOLTA see BURKINA FASO

ZAÏRE(formerly REPUBLIC OF THE CONGO)

30 June 60   Independence

24 June 60   *PM*   Patrice Lumumba
                   FA   Justin Bomboko
                   Fin   Pascal Nkayi

11 Sep 60   Joseph Ileo appointed PM by Pres Kasavubu, but Lumumba
                   refuses to give up office

14 Sep 60   Coup by Col. Joseph Désiré Mobutu

9 Feb 61   Pres Kasavubu finally succeeds in getting Ileo into office as
                   PM

12 Feb 61	Lumumba murdered	
Aug 61	*PM*	Cyril Adoula
	FA	Auguste Mavika-Kalanda
	Fin	Emmanuel Bamba
1 Dec 63	Mavika-Kalanda arrested	
	PM/FA	Cyril Adoula
2 Mar 64	Parliament suspended by Pres Kasavubu	
30 Jun 64	Adoula resigns, and is asked to head a caretaker government preparing for elections under a new constitution	
10 July 64	*PM/FA*	Moïse Tshombe
	Fin	Dominique Ndinga
12 Oct 65	Tshombe government dismissed	
	PM	Evariste Kimba
19 Oct 65	Kimba forms his cabinet:	
	FA	Cléophas Kamitatu
	Fin	Jean Litho
18 Dec 65	*FA*	Joseph Kulumba
14 Sep 66	*FA*	Justin Bomboko
26 Oct 66	*Pres/PM*	Gen. Joseph Désiré Mobutu (replaces Gen. Mulamba, but no date given for the beginning of Mulamba's term)
5 Oct 67	*Fin*	Paul Mushiete
17 Aug 68	*Fin*	Victor Nendaka
1 Aug 69	*FA*	Cyril Adoula
	Fin	Louis Namwisi
7 Dec 70	*FA*	Mario Cardoso
21 Feb 72	*FA*	Jean Nguza (Nguza Karl-I-Bond)
	Fin	M. Barute (Barute wa Ndwale)
8 Mar 73	*FA*	Umba Di Lutete
7 Jan 75	*FA*	Bula Mandungu (said to have replaced Batwanyele Losembe, but no date for beginning of his term)
	Fin	Bofossa W'amb'ea Nkoso
4 Feb 76	*FA*	Nguza Karl-I-Bond

23 Feb 77		Reorganisation: Nguza becomes also chairman of the Political, Economic and Financial Committee and thus supervises Bofassa's Fin Department
1 July 77		Executive Council deemed to have resigned; new officers appointed: *PM* (*'First Commissioner'*) Mpinga Kasenga
13 Aug 77		Nguza arrested and dismissed; temporary successor Engulu Baanganpongo Bakolele Lokanga
19 Aug 77	*FA*	Umba Di Lutete
	Fin	Kiakwama Kia Kiziki
13 Dec 77	*Fin*	Emony Mondanga
6 Mar 79	*PM*	Bo-Boliko Lokonga Monse Mihambo
	FA	Nguza Karl-I-Bond
18 Jan 80	*Fin*	Namwisi Ma Nkoy
27 Aug 80	*PM*	Nguza Karl-I-Bond
	FA	Inonga Lokonga L'Ome
18 Feb 81	*FA*	Bomboko Lukumba
17 Apr 81	*PM*	Nsinga Udjuu
9 Oct 81	*FA*	Yoka Mangodo
5 Nov 82	*PM*	Kengo Wa Dondo
	FA	Kamanda Wa Kamanda
18 Mar 83	*Fin*	Ngole Ilike
1 Nov 83	*FA*	Umba Di Lutete
	Fin	Kiakwama Kia Kiziki
1 Feb 85	*FA*	Mokolo Wa Mpombo
12 Apr 85	*Fin*	Djamboleka Okitongana
31 Oct 86	*PM*	post temporarily abolished, powers transferred to President
	FA	Kengo Wa Dondo
	Fin	Mabi Mulemba
	PM	Mabi Mulemba
22 Jan 87	*FA*	Ekila Liyonda
	Fin	Nyembo Shabani

ZAMBIA (formerly NORTHERN RHODESIA)

23 Jan 64	Pre-independence cabinet:
	PM Kenneth David Kaunda
	Fin Arthur Wina
	FA none
23 Oct 64	Independence
	Pres/PM Kenneth David Kaunda
24 Sep 64	*FA* Simon Mwanza Kapwepwe
7 Sep 67	*FA* Reuben Kamanga
	Fin Elijah Mudenda
23 Dec 68	*FA* not known
25 Aug 69	*Pres/PM* Kenneth David Kaunda
Dec 69	*FA* Elijah Mudenda
Mar 70	Reference to Moto Nkama as FA Minister
7 Oct 70	*FA* Elijah Mudenda
	Fin John Mwanakatwe
28 Aug 73	*PM* (under new constitution) Mainza Chona
10 Dec 73	*FA* Vernon Mwaanga
	Fin Alexander Chikwanda
1 Dec 75	*Fin* Luke Mwananshiku
10 May 76	*FA* Siteke Mwale
May 76	*Fin* John Mwanakatwe
24 Apr 77	*PM* Elijah Mudenda
20 May 77	*PM* Mainza Chona
2 June 80	*PM* Daniel M. Lisulo
	FA Wilson M. Chakulya
	Fin Kebby Musokotwane
7 Dec 80	*FA* Lameck Goma
18 Feb 81	*PM* Nalumino Mundia
	Fin Kebby Musokotwane
13 Jan 83	*Fin* (and *PM*) Nalumino Mundia

3 Nov 83	*Fin*	Luke Mwananshiku
24 Apr 85	*PM*	Kebby Musokotwane
4 June 86	*FA* *Fin*	Luke Mwananshiku Basil Kabwe
28 Jan 87	*Fin* (and *PM*)	Kebby Musokotwane
13 May 87	*Fin*	Gibson Chigaga
10 Mar 89	*PM*	Gen. Malimba Masheke

ZANZIBAR

24 Jun 63	Government elected to manage the run-up to independence

PM Sheikh Mohamed Shamte Hamadi
Fin Sheikh Juma Aley

9 Dec 63	Independence

FA Sheikh Ali Muhsin

12 Jan 64	The Sultan and government overthrown. New government installed:

PM Sheikh Abdallah Kassim Hanga
FA Sheikh Mohamed Abdul Rahman 'Babu'
Fin Hasnu Makame

27 Apr 64	Union with Tanganyika to form Tanzania (q.v.)

ZIMBABWE (formerly RHODESIA, q.v.)

11 Mar 80	*PM* *FA* *Fin*	Robert Mugabe Simon Mzenda Enos Nkala
10 Jan 81	*FA*	Witness Mangwende
16 Apr 82	*Fin*	Bernard Chidzero
3 Jan 84	Cabinet reorganisation; no change to Fin or FA	
30 Dec 87	Mugabe becomes first Executive President; post of PM abolished	

FA Dr Nathan Shamuyarira

4 CONSTITUTIONS AND PARLIAMENTS

ALGERIA

In 1945 Algeria was regarded as an integral part of France. The northern territories, where most of the sizable European (*colon*) minority lived, were considered metropolitan areas. Administration was by a governor-general assisted by Consultative and Superior Councils; three senators and 10 deputies represented the territory in Paris. In 1944 60 000 Muslims were granted French citizenship and thus the right to vote.

The Algerian Statute of 1947 created an Algerian Assembly. The 120 members were elected by two electoral colleges, one Muslim, the other European; representatives were also elected to the French National Assembly, the Council of the Republic, and the Assembly of the French Union.

A war against France began in 1954 and a nationalist government-in-exile was formed. In 1958 Muslims were given full voting rights and a large majority was recorded as supporting the new constitution for a French Fifth Republic. A referendum in 1961 held in both France and Algeria accepted the right of Algeria to self-determination. In 1962 Algerian–French peace talks led to the formation of an interim provisional government in Algeria. The same year the country became an independent republic. In 1963 a new constitution declared Algeria to be a Popular and Democratic Republic under an executive president and a National Assembly elected from a single party.

A military coup in 1965 suspended the National Assembly and a 26- (later 22-) member Revolutionary Council ruled the country. Under a new constitution, approved by referendum in November 1976, an executive president was to be elected for six years; legislative powers lay with a national People's Assembly elected for five years from a single party list. Elections for the 261-member Assembly occurred in 1977. An amendment to the constitution in 1979 reduced the presidential term of office to five years and obliged the president to appoint a prime minister. Under the constitution Algeria was a socialist state with Islam the national religion. The fundamental source of national policy and law was the National Charter. In 1989 a new constitution was approved recognizing the right to form opposition political associations and dropping all references to Socialism.

ANGOLA

By the Organic Charter incorporated into the Portuguese constitution of 1933, the colony of Angola was declared to be an integral part of Portugal. The colony was subject to decrees from the Colonial (later Overseas) Ministry in Lisbon and was administered directly by a governor-general.

In 1958 Angola was designated an overseas province and given a measure of local autonomy. The Governor-General was assisted by a Provincial Council and also a Government Council. A 36-member Legislative Council was established in 1953 with a majority of its members drawn from various interest groups in the territory. In 1963 advisory economic and social councils were set up consisting of seven *ex officio* members and eight elected from various corporate bodies. The Organic Law of 1972 enlarged the Legislative Council to 53 members, of whom 32 were elected by direct suffrage. Seven representatives were also elected to the National Assembly in Lisbon.

A long guerrilla war against Portuguese rule was waged by rival nationalist movements. Following the military coup in Lisbon in April 1974, which led to the end of the dictatorship in Portugal, Angola was proclaimed an independent people's republic in November 1975. The rivalry and conflict between the nationalist movements developed into a long civil war. The Marxist-Leninist MPLA–PT (People's Movement for the Liberation of Angola-–Worker's Party) formed the central government at Luanda; its rule was challenged by UNITA (Union for the Total Liberation of Angola) which controlled the southern and eastern areas of the country. UNITA received military and economic aid from South Africa and also the United States.

The independence constitution, as amended in 1976, provided for an executive president who presided over a Council of Ministers and also the Council of the Revolution, a temporary body established until a People's Assembly could be elected. The MPLA–PT was the sole legal party. A legislative People's Assembly was established in November 1980. Of the 223 members, twenty were nominated by the Central Committee of the MPLA–PT, the remaining being chosen for a 3-year period by electoral colleges drawn from representatives elected by all 'loyal' citizens. The elections scheduled for 1983 were postponed for three years.

BENIN (DAHOMEY until 1977)

In 1945 Dahomey was a colony of French West Africa administered by a governor. By the constitution of the Fourth Republic, 1946, it became an overseas territory of the French Union within the structure of French West Africa administered from Dakar. A territorial assembly of 30 members was established, elected on a double electoral-college system. A narrow franchise elected representatives to the French National Assembly and the Council of the Republic in Paris and also to the Assembly of the French Union. Representatives from Dahomey were also elected to the Grand Council at Dakar, which had certain powers over the federal budget of French West Africa.

The *loi cadre* of 1956 provided for a larger measure of self-government. An Executive Council was created responsible to an enlarged territorial assembly of 60 members. The territorial assembly had more extensive powers and was elected by universal adult suffrage. In 1958 the French Fourth Republic collapsed and under the new de Gaulle constitution of the Fifth Republic Dahomey became a self-governing member of the French Community. In 1959 a constitution similar to that of the French Fifth Republic was adopted. An independent republic was proclaimed in 1960. Under a new constitution an executive president ruled with a Council of Ministers drawn from a single-chamber National Assembly. A military coup in 1963 dissolved the National Assembly and abrogated the constitution. In 1964 a new constitution provided for a single-party state and a 42-member Assembly; the same year the army again took power and dissolved the Assembly and governed through a Committee of National Renovation. A further military coup in 1967 established a Military Revolutionary Council. A constitution was introduced in 1968 which provided for a one-party state and an executive president elected for a five-year term. The constitution was suspended by the army in 1969 and a three-man military directorate was appointed to run the country.

A fifth military coup occurred in 1972 and a 12-man National Council of Revolution ruled the country. Discussions for a new constitution began in 1977. Direct elections were held in November 1979 for a new National Revolutionary Assembly. This body, composed of 336 People's Commissioners, was designated 'the supreme authority of the state'. The National Council of Revolution was disbanded and the military regime converted itself into a civilian one. In 1980 the National Revolutionary Assembly unanimously elected the president. A newly-elected Assembly in 1984 was reduced in size to 196 People's Commissioners.

BOTSWANA (BECHUANALAND until 1966)

The territory became a British protectorate in 1885. It was governed by the eight major chiefs, with a British commissioner, under the direction of the High Commissioner for British Southern Africa, with authority to issue proclamations. Chiefly powers were slightly limited in the 1930s and their views represented through the African Advisory Council. The Resident Commissioner was also advised by a European Council and a joint body. Chiefs' powers were, for the first time under colonial rule, comprehensively defined by the African Administration Proclamation, 1954, and an attempt to democratise these powers was made by establishing African local councils in

1957. The almost autocratic powers of the chiefs were further limited with the introduction of universal adult suffrage in 1966.

A constitution was granted in 1961 which provided for a Legislative Council with an elected majority. African members were indirectly elected; European and Asian members were directly elected by communal voting. There was an Executive Council with an official majority and unofficial members drawn from the Legislative Council. An African Council was set up to replace the old advisory council of chiefs, and this elected from among its own members the African members of the Legislative Council. The protectorate became independent as a republic in 1966, with a constitution drafted in 1965 and still in force with minor amendments. Executive power is vested in the President, who is responsible to the National Assembly and an *ex officio* member of it. The National Assembly is composed of the Speaker, the Attorney-General who is without a vote, thirty-four directly-elected members and four specially-elected members chosen by the members of the Assembly. There is also a 15-member House of Chiefs to advise the government, especially on matters relating to chieftancy and any amendments to the constitution; it is composed of the chiefs of the eight principal tribes and elected representatives of the sub-chiefs.

BURKINA FASO (UPPER VOLTA until 1984)

In 1945 Upper Volta was a region of the French colony of Ivory Coast. In 1947 it was constituted a separate overseas territory under a governor and administered as part of French West Africa. In 1948 a territorial assembly of 50 members was established. The franchise was limited and based on a double electoral-college system; five representatives from the assembly went to the Grand Council in Dakar, and representatives were also elected to the French National Assembly and the Council of the Republic, and the Assembly of the French Union at Versailles.

In 1951 the franchise was extended. By the *loi cadre* of 1956 Upper Volta became a self-governing territory; the double electoral system was ended and the enlarged territorial assembly of 70 seats was elected by universal adult suffrage. In the constitutional referendum of 1958 Upper Volta voted to become an autonomous republic within the French Community. In 1960 it became an independent republic.

A constitution adopted in 1960 provided for an executive president and a unicameral national assembly. Following a bloodless coup by the military in 1966 the constitution was suspended. A military government under Gen. Lamizana ruled the country. A new constitution was approved by referendum in 1969 and introduced in the following year. This provided for an elected National Assembly under a civilian prime minister, but President Lamizana was to remain President for a further five years.

A confrontation between the Prime Minister and the National Assembly in 1974 led the army to suspend the constitution and dissolve the legislature. Legislative functions were taken over by a 65-man Consultative Council for National Renewal, which was composed of civilians and military officers. Widespread opposition to military rule forced President Lamizana in 1976 to set up a Constitutional Commission, which recommended an executive president and political activity by no more than three parties. A draft constitution was introduced in 1977 and approved by referendum; the President and National Assembly were to be elected for five years, and the 57 seats in the National Assembly were to be contested by three political parties.

In November 1982 a new military regime seized power and established a provisional 'council of the people's salvation'. Acute rivalries within the regime led to a further coup in August 1983 when power was assumed by the Conseil national de la révolution (CNR). Committees for the defence of the revolution were set up throughout the country. On the anniversary of the coup, in August 1984, the name of the country was changed to Burkina Faso.

BURUNDI (RUANDA-URUNDI until 1962)

Burundi, a former German territory, was administered as part of Ruanda-Urundi by Belgium, first as a League of Nations mandate and then, after 1946, as a United Nations trust territory. The territory was ruled by a vice-governor-general directly responsible to the Minister of Colonies in Brussels.

An Advisory Council was created in 1947 consisting of officials and three persons representing the interests of Africans. In 1960 the first elections were held for municipal councils. In 1961 an interim government was hastily formed of representatives from the municipal governments, who constituted a Legislative Assembly. The Hutu King (Mwami) Mwambutsa IV was confirmed as ruler while the Belgians retained reserve powers over foreign affairs, defence, finance, and law and order. Burundi became an independent state in 1962 with a new constitution which provided for a Legislative Assembly of 33 members and a Senate of 16 members.

In 1966 the King was deposed by the army and the constitution suspended. A republic was proclaimed and Burundi was declared a one-party state under a president, who chaired the National Council of Revolution. A Supreme Council of Revolution of 30 members was set up in 1971.

The new constitution of 1974 confirmed Burundi as a one-party state. In 1978 the office of prime minister was abolished and the President became head of the government. The President chaired the 11-member Executive Committee which was responsible to the Supreme Council. A new constitution, approved by a national referendum in November 1981, provided for a national assembly to be elected by universal adult suffrage. The first elections were held in October 1982. The national assembly meets twice a year and like the president is elected for a period of five years. The sole legal political party is the Union pour le progrès national (UPRONA).

CAMEROON

The territory was formerly German but was divided between France and Britain after the First World War, and was administered by both states first as League of Nations mandates and then, after 1946, as United Nations trust territories. The British ruled Northern and Southern Cameroons while the French administered the largest part of the territory.

Under the British, Northern Cameroons was administered as part of Northern Nigeria and was eventually represented in the Nigerian federal legislature. The Southern Cameroons was governed by a commissioner subject to the Governor (later Governor-General) of Nigeria. In 1955 Southern Cameroons was given a Legislative Council with a majority of representatives drawn from native authorities; the executive was presided over by the Commissioner and consisted of two *ex officio* members of the Legislative Council and four members of the Legislative Council selected by the Governor-General. In 1958 the executive had an unofficial majority led by a prime minister; the Governor-General of Nigeria became the High Commissioner for Southern Cameroons.

French Cameroon was an associated territory administered by a high commissioner. A Consultative Economic and Social Council of 34 members was established in 1942. In 1945 this was succeeded by a territorial assembly, which was elected by a double electoral-college system; by 1952 the Assembly had 50 members. Elections on a similar basis sent four deputies to the French National Assembly, three senators to the Council of the Republic and five members to the Assembly of the French Union. In 1956 a larger measure of self-government was granted and the enlarged territorial assembly was elected by direct universal suffrage. The Commissioner worked in consultation with the Executive Council, over which he presided.

A serious revolt broke out in French Cameroon in 1957 and lasted until 1962. In 1959 the territory was given full internal autonomy; in 1960 Cameroon became independent and a new constitution established a unitary state under a presidential system of government.

In 1961 Northern Cameroons joined Nigeria; by a referendum the people of Southern Cameroons elected to join the Cameroon Republic, which by constitutional amendment became a federal republic. The former Republic of Cameroon was then known as Eastern Cameroon and the former British territory of Southern Cameroons became known as Western Cameroon. Local legislative and administrative bodies were maintained in each state.

In 1972 a new constitution established the country as a unitary state known as the United Republic of Cameroon. An executive president was elected for a five-year period; the 150-member National Assembly was elected by universal adult suffrage. By a constitutional amendment in 1984 the original name of the country was restored – the Republic of Cameroon.

CAPE VERDE ISLANDS

In 1946 the Cape Verde Islands formed an overseas province of Portugal administered by a governor. He was assisted by a Government Council composed of officials. By the Organic Act 1963 a Legislative Council was established; its 18 members were partially elected; by 1973 it consisted of 22 members. Representatives were also elected to the National Assembly and Corporate Chamber in Lisbon.

At the end of 1974 power was transferred to a transitional government headed by a Portuguese high commissioner. The islands became an independent republic in 1975 with a president and a National People's Assembly of 56 deputies, all drawn from a single party. The aim of the government was eventual unification with Guinea-Bissau but this was revoked in early 1981. The country's constitution was approved in September 1980. It provided for a non-executive President elected by the National Assembly for a period of five years. The National Assembly is also elected for five years by universal adult suffrage. The Prime Minister is nominated by and responsible to the National Assembly. Although a one-party state the oath of allegiance to the party has been dropped. In the elections of 1985 non-members of the ruling party were elected to the National Assembly.

CENTRAL AFRICAN REPUBLIC (UBANGI-CHARI until 1958)

The territory was a colony administered by a lieutenant-governor as part of French Equatorial Africa. The lieutenant-governor was assisted by a nominated Administrative Council. By the constitution of the French Fourth Republic Ubangi-Chari became an overseas territory ruled by a governor and with a territorial assembly. This was elected on a very limited franchise by a double electoral-college system and in 1946 consisted of 25 members. Representatives elected on a similar basis were sent to the Grand Council at Brazzaville, the French National Assembly and the Council of the Republic in Paris, and also to the Assembly of the French Union at Versailles.

In 1951 the electorate was increased and the territorial assembly enlarged to consist of 40 members; by 1956 it had 45 members. In 1957, under the *loi cadre* of 1956, the territory was given internal autonomy; the territorial assembly was elected by universal adult suffrage. During the constitutional referendum of 1958 the territory elected to become a self-governing republic within the French Community with a president and a National Assembly of 50 elected members. In late 1958 Ubangi-Chari became the Central African Republic, which in 1960 became an independent state, with a constitution which provided for a president, a Council of Ministers and an elected Assembly of 50 members.

A military coup led by Col. Bokassa in 1965 abrogated the constitution and dissolved the National Assembly, establishing a military regime under a Revolutionary Council. A new constitution in 1976 proclaimed the state as the Central African Empire, with Bokassa as Emperor. In September 1979 Bokassa was overthrown and the state reverted to its former title of the Central African Republic.

The new government lasted for two years and was brought down by a bloodless coup in September 1981. The constitution which had been declared earlier that year was suspended. A Military Committee for National Recovery (CMRN) assumed all executive and legislative power. In 1985 the CMRN was dissolved and a 22-member Council of Ministers was appointed. A new constitution was prepared and approved by referendum in 1986.

CHAD

In 1945 Chad was a colony ruled by a lieutenant-governor and administered as part of French Equatorial Africa. The lieutenant-governor was assisted by an Administrative Council composed of officials.

By the constitution of the French Fourth Republic of 1946 Chad was designated an overseas territory under a governor and given a territorial assembly. The assembly of 30 members was elected on a narrow franchise by a double electoral-college system; representatives were also elected in a similar way to the Grand Council in Brazzaville, the National Assembly and Council of the Republic in Paris, and the Assembly of the French Union in Versailles. The franchise was increased in 1951 and the territorial assembly enlarged to 45 members.

Under the *loi cadre* of 1956 the double electoral-college system was abandoned and a responsible government was elected by universal adult suffrage. An Executive Council was appointed, presided over by the Governor and responsible to the territorial assembly.

In 1958 Chad accepted the de Gaulle constitution and became an autonomous republic within the French Community. In 1960 independence was achieved with a constitution which provided for an executive president and a National Assembly. An amended constitution introduced in 1964 established a single-party state, a Council of Ministers appointed by an executive president, and a National Assembly of 105 members.

A military coup in 1975 suspended the constitution, dissolved the National Assembly, and established a Supreme Military Council of nine members. In the same year a new provisional constitution was adopted by which the President was chosen by the nine members of the Supreme Military Council. The President presided over the Council of Ministers and had supreme executive and legislative powers.

Between 1979 and 1987 Chad suffered from three civil wars. There was also foreign intervention from France and military invasion by Libya. A provisional constitution was promulgated in September 1982 and a 30-member National Consultative Council established with representatives drawn from each of the 14 prefectures and appointed by the Head of State.

THE COMOROS

A group of islands in the Indian Ocean which formed a French colony. Up to 1946 the islands were administered as part of Madagascar. By the constitution of the Fourth Republic they were separated from Madagascar and received a degree of autonomy with a General Council and one representative in the French National Assembly and one in the Council of the Republic. The franchise was limited.

In the constitutional changes of 1956 and 1958 the Comoros remained an overseas territory of France under a high commissioner. Internal autonomy was granted in 1968, with a Council of Government presided over by a prime minister and a Chamber of Deputies; the French High Commissioner retained reserve powers. The franchise was based on proficiency in French and was thus limited.

In 1974 a referendum held separately on each of the four islands supported independence. However, the vote on the island of Mayotte had a majority against any break with France. The Chamber of Deputies made a unilateral declaration of independence and reformed itself as a National Assembly with a president and an Executive Council. Mayotte remained under French control, while the other three islands became an independent republic, which was recognised by France in 1976.

In 1975 a coup overthrew the President of the Republic, abolished the National Assembly and established a National Revolutionary Council with a Revolutionary Executive Council. In 1976 the Revolutionary Council was superseded by a National Institutional Council. A further coup in 1978 led to the adoption of a federal-style constitution and a Federal Assembly of 39 members.

A referendum in 1978 approved the constitution which proclaimed the Comoros a Federal Islamic Republic. The executive president, who is elected for six years, nominates the ministers who form the Council of Government. The President also nominates the governor of each island. The Federal Assembly is elected for five years while each island council is elected for four years.

The aim of the Comoros is to incorporate Mayotte within the republic. Mayotte, in a referendum in 1976, voted to remain an overseas territory of France. In 1980 it became an overseas department ruled by a prefect and an elected General Council of 17 members; it is represented by one member each in the French National Assembly and Council of the Republic.

CONGO (MIDDLE CONGO until 1958)

In 1945 Middle Congo was a colony administered by a lieutenant-governor as part of French Equatorial Africa. In 1946, under the terms of the constitution of the Fourth Republic, Middle Congo became an overseas territory ruled by a governor, and with a territorial assembly. The assembly of 30 members was elected on a double electoral-college system; representatives elected on a similar basis were sent to the Grand Council at Brazzaville, the French National Assembly and Council of the Republic in Paris, and also to the Assembly of the French Union at Versailles. The franchise was widened in 1951 and the territorial assembly increased to 37 members; by 1956 it consisted of 45 members.

By the *loi cadre* of 1956 the territory received responsible government with the assembly elected by universal adult suffrage. Between 1958 and 1959 eleven constitutional laws established the framework of government. Congo accepted the de Gaulle constitution of 1958 and became an autonomous republic within the French Community. In 1960 it became an independent state as the Republic of Congo.

In 1963 the President was forced to resign and the National Assembly was dissolved and the constitution suspended. A new constitution was adopted following a referendum and this provided for a two-man executive. In 1968 a military coup abrogated the constitution, dissolved the National Assembly and established the National Council of the Revolution with its president as head of state. A new constitution introduced in 1970 provided for a one-party state and the country was renamed the Congo People's Republic. A new constitution approved by referendum in 1973 established an Executive Council of State, and a People's National Assembly of 115 members, with the chairman of the ruling party as President. In 1977 the constitution was abolished and replaced by an Acte Fondemental with the Party Military Committee as the chief organ of government.

A new constitution, approved by referendum, was introduced in 1979 and amended in 1984. The Chairman of the Central Committee of the sole political party, the Parti congolais du travail (PCT), is President of the Republic and elected for a period of 5 years. He chairs the executive Council of Ministers whose members are appointed by the Prime Minister and who are responsible to the ruling party. Legislative powers are vested in the 153-member People's National Assembly.

CÔTE D'IVOIRE see IVORY COAST

DJIBOUTI (FRENCH SOMALILAND until 1967; FRENCH TERRITORY OF THE AFARS AND ISSAS until 1977)

In 1957 French Somaliland was given a measure of autonomy. The Representative Council was replaced by a territorial assembly of 32 members elected by direct universal suffrage. The French Governor presided over a Council of Ministers, which was responsible to the assembly. In the constitutional referendum of 1958 the population voted to continue the connection with France.

A referendum based on a restricted franchise in 1967 voted to maintain an association with France as an overseas territory; French Somaliland was renamed the French Territory of the Afars and Issas. The National Assembly was reconstituted as a Chamber of Deputies with 40 seats, and the Council of Ministers was presided over by a chairman who was head of government. The Governor was renamed High Commissioner and retained reserve powers. The territory was represented in the National Assembly and Council of the Republic by one representative each.

In 1974 the territory was given increased powers over internal security. Djibouti became an independent republic in 1977. The government is headed by a president and the Chamber of Deputies has 65 members. The Chamber of Deputies was charged with drafting a new constitution in 1977. By the constitutional laws of 1981 the President is elected by universal suffrage for a term of office of six years; deputies to the Chamber are elected for a five-year period.

EGYPT

Egypt in 1945 was an independent kingdom with a government based on the constitution of 1923. This provided for a two-chamber legislature, a Senate of 180 members, of whom two-fifths were nominated by the King and the rest elected, and a Chamber of Deputies with 319 elected members.

By the terms of the Anglo-Egyptian Treaty of 1936 Britain had the right to maintain troops in the country to garrison and defend the Suez Canal. During the Second World War British troops effectively occupied Egypt and controlled its government.

In 1952 the royal government of King Farouk was overthrown by a military coup, a nine-man Revolutionary Command Council assumed power and the constitution was abolished. In 1953 the monarchy was abolished and Egypt became a republic. Lt-Col. Nasser assumed control of the Military Council in 1954 and became President in 1956, following an election in which voting was compulsory. British troops finally evacuated the Canal Zone in June 1956. A provisional constitution was introduced in 1956 which provided for an executive president. This was approved by plebiscite and Nasser was elected President.

In 1958 Egypt joined with Syria to form the United Arab Republic. A provisional constitution superseded that of 1956 and established presidential government and a National Assembly elected from the existing Egyptian and Syrian parliaments. There was to be a central cabinet and regional councils. A military coup in Syria in 1961 led that country to leave the union, but Egypt retained the title of the United Arab Republic.

President Nasser in 1961 announced plans for a new constitution for Egypt. An elected National Congress of Popular Forces met in the same year and approved President Nasser's National Charter embodying the aims and ideas of the Egyptian Revolution, and creating the Arab Socialist Union, which was to be the sole representative of the Egyptian people. The constitution of 1964 defined Egypt as a democratic socialist state. The National Assembly was to consist of 360 members elected by universal suffrage; the President could appoint a further 10 members to the Assembly. The Assembly would nominate the President, who had to be confirmed in office by plebiscite.

In 1971 a new and permanent constitution was introduced, based substantially on the constitution of 1964. The President had to be nominated by two-thirds of the People's Assembly and to serve for six years. The legislative body, the People's Assembly, was to be elected for five years and consist of no less than 350 members; the President had power to appoint 10 additional members. Beginning in 1977, political parties were permitted to function, but they faced considerable restrictions on their activities. A constitutional amendment of April 1980 stated that the political system depended on multiple political parties and that the Arab Socialist Union was therefore abolished.

EQUATORIAL GUINEA (SPANISH GUINEA until 1968)

Equatorial Guinea consists of two territories, the mainland area of Guinea, formerly known as Rio Muni, and the island of Bioko (formerly Fernando Po) and adjacent islands. In 1945 the territory was a Spanish colony administered by a governor-general based in Fernando Po; he was assisted by a nominated council and responsible to the Colonial Ministry in Madrid.

In 1959 Equatorial Guinea was made an integral part of Spain and entitled the Equatorial Region of Spain; it consisted of two provinces. Representatives from the territory were elected to the Spanish Cortes. Reforms to government introduced in 1963 created a joint General Assembly of elected deputies and a cabinet of eight members under a president nominated by Madrid. The Governor-General became a high commissioner with reserve powers over police, defence and foreign relations.

In 1968 the two provinces became the independent republic of Equatorial Guinea. The independence constitution provided for presidential government with a National Assembly and provincial councils for the mainland and for Bioko. A new constitution of 1973 ended provincial autonomy and the government came under the arbitrary control of President Nguema. He was overthrown by a coup in 1979 and a Supreme Military Council of 10 army officers formed a government with executive and legislative powers.

A new constitution was introduced in 1982 which provided for a transitional period of seven years for the restoration of civilian rule. The executive president, elected for seven years, can appoint and dismiss ministers. A State Council of 11 members serves as an electoral college for the presidency. Members of the House of Representatives must be between 45 and 60 years of age; they are elected for a five-year term.

ETHIOPIA

Ethiopia was an empire governed by the constitution of 1931, as restored in 1942 following the defeat of the Italians in East Africa. The Emperor had a dominant role in government with power to appoint the cabinet and members of the upper house of legislature, the House of Notables. The lower house, the Chamber of Deputies, was formally a nominated body but after 1943 its members were indirectly elected by nobles and local chiefs. In 1955 the constitution was reformed and the Chamber of Deputies of 250 members was elected by adult suffrage every four years; the House of Notables then consisted of up to 125 members. In 1966 the appointed Prime Minister was allowed to choose his own cabinet.

Eritrea, a former Italian colony under British military administration from 1942 to 1952, was federated with Ethiopia under the Ethiopian crown in December 1952. Under the constitution the government of Eritrea had executive and legislative powers in domestic affairs. The Chief Executive was elected by, but not responsible to, the Constituent Assembly. The single-chamber Assembly was elected by all adult males. In 1962 Ethiopia proclaimed Eritrea part of a unitary Ethiopian state. Since 1961 Eritrean nationalist forces have fought against Ethiopia.

In 1974 an Armed Forces Co-ordinating Committee seized power, deposed the Emperor, suspended parliament, abolished the constitution, and appointed a Provisional Military Administrative Council. Ethiopia was declared a republic. It was stated in 1984 that the sole political party, the newly-organised Worker's Party of Ethiopia, would produce a new constitution. A draft was published in 1986. It declared Ethiopia a unitary state with autonomous regions to be governed through an elected national assembly.

FRENCH EQUATORIAL AFRICA

The Federation of French Equatorial Africa was established in 1910. In 1945 it consisted of the four territories of Gabon, Middle Congo, Ubangi-Chari and Chad, each administered by a lieutenant-governor advised by a council, and subject to the Governor-General in Brazzaville. By the constitution of the French Fourth Republic of 1946, each territory was designated an overseas territory under a governor. Territorial assemblies were established which exercised control over local budgets. They were elected on a double electoral-college system from a limited franchise; the first college consisted of French citizens, the second of non-citizens. Seven deputies were elected to the French National Assembly, nine senators to the Council of the Republic, and seven councillors to the Assembly of the French Union. Five members from each territorial assembly were sent to form the Grand Council in Brazzaville.

In 1951 the electorate was increased and the territorial assemblies enlarged; the Chad assembly had 45 members, Middle Congo 37, Ubangi-Chari 40, and Gabon 37.

By the *loi cadre* of 1956 the territories were granted internal self-government. The dual electoral system was ended and the enlarged territorial assemblies elected by universal adult suffrage. The Governor presided over the executive councils, which were in effect embryonic cabinets, and acted on the advice of the Prime Minister.

In the constitutional referendum of 1958 all four territories voted to become autonomous republics within the French Community. In 1960 they became independent republics and the Federation ceased to exist.

FRENCH WEST AFRICA

The territories of French West Africa were organised in a federation in 1904. In 1945 it consisted of seven colonies: Senegal, Mauritania, Soudan, Guinea, Dahomey, Niger and the Ivory Coast. Upper Volta was separated from the Ivory Coast and constituted a separate territory in 1947.

By the constitution of the Fourth Republic, 1946, the colonies were designated overseas territories. Each territory was ruled by a governor subject to the High Commissioner of the Federation in Dakar. The High Commissioner was answerable to the Minister of Overseas France and to the French parliament. He was assisted by two advisory councils, the Disputes Council, composed of five official members, and the Government Council. The governor in each territory (except Mauritania) was aided by a secretary-general and an advisory privy council.

In each territory assemblies, known as general councils, were established with powers over the local budget. Senegal retained its pre-war Colonial

Council. The assemblies were elected by limited franchise on a double electoral-college system, the first college consisting of French citizens, and the second of non-citizens. Senegal was the exception with a single-college system. Five representatives from each assembly were sent to a 40-member advisory Grand Council in Dakar. The West African territories also sent 13 (eventually 20) elected representatives to the French National Assembly (of 622 members), and a similar number of senators to the Council of the Republic. French West Africa was represented by 27 councillors in the Assembly of the French Union, which met at Versailles. Deputies to the National Assembly were elected on a single roll; senators by dual roll. In 1951 the franchise was extended and the territorial assemblies enlarged.

The *loi cadre* of 1956 granted internal autonomy to each territory. The double electoral system was ended and universal adult suffrage introduced. The territorial assemblies were enlarged (Senegal, Guinea, Ivory Coast, Niger and Dahomey to 60 members, Mauritania to 34, Soudan and Upper Volta to 70) and given a wider measure of legislative power. The executive councils, which were in effect embryo cabinets, were drawn from within and outside the assemblies; the governor presided over meetings of the executive council but was effectively guided by the vice-president or prime minister. The Grand Council in Dakar continued to exist but the reforms of 1956 had limited its powers.

Following the constitutional referendum of 1958 seven of the West African territories voted to become autonomous republics within the French Community. Guinea alone voted to become an independent sovereign republic. The autonomous republics had complete executive and legislative control over internal affairs, but matters such as defence, foreign affairs, currency and higher education were reserved to the Executive Council of the Community.

In 1959 the French government accepted that a state could become independent but remain a member of the French Community. The French West African territories all became independent in 1960.

GABON

In 1945 Gabon was a French colony governed by a lieutenant-governor and administered as part of French Equatorial Africa. By the constitution of the Fourth Republic Gabon became an overseas territory under a governor. A territorial assembly of 30 members was established, elected on the double electoral-college system. Representatives to the Grand Council at Brazzaville, the French National Assembly and the Council of the Republic, and also the Assembly of the French Union were elected on a similar basis. The franchise was widened in 1951 and the territorial assembly enlarged to 37 members.

Under the *loi cadre* of 1956 Gabon received, in the following year, a measure of internal self-government with an enlarged territorial assembly of 40 members elected by a single electorate. In the constitutional referendum of 1958 Gabon voted to become an autonomous republic within the French Community. Two years later the country became an independent state.

A provisional constitution was adopted in 1960 which provided for an executive president and an elected single-chamber National Assembly. The constitution was revised four times between 1961 and 1986. The President is elected for a period of seven years and he exercises executive power through a Council of Ministers. The President appoints the Prime Minister. The National Assembly is elected by direct universal suffrage for a period of five years (formerly seven years). There is a single legal political party.

THE GAMBIA

The Gambia in 1945 consisted of a British Crown colony and a protectorate administered by a governor under the 1888 constitution as modified in 1902. The Executive and Legislative Councils were composed of nominated official and unofficial members appointed by the Governor.

In 1946 the Executive Council was widened to include three nominated unofficial members, including the elected member from the Legislative Council. The Legislative Council had its first elected representative, from the colony, three *ex officio* members and several nominated official and unofficial members appointed by the Governor. In 1951 a second elected representative from the Colony was added to the Legislative Council.

By the constitution of 1954 the Executive Council had an unofficial majority, with two to three unofficial members in charge of government departments. The Legislative Council had a majority of elected members, although seven out of the 11 were elected by chiefs and divisional councils in the Protectorate. The franchise was given to all males aged over 25 years in the Colony, and to all male property-owners in the Protectorate.

In 1960 a new constitution was promulgated following a general election with universal adult suffrage. It provided for a House of Representatives of 27 elected members, three nominated and four official. The Executive Council consisted of four officials and six ministers appointed from among the elected and nominated members of the House. The first chief minister was appointed in 1961; the title was changed to prime minister in 1962. Internal self-government was achieved in 1963 and full independence in 1965. The House of Representatives now had 32 elected members, four nominated non-voting members and four chiefs elected by the Chiefs in Assembly.

The Gambia became a republic, following a referendum, with a new constitution in April 1970. Under the constitution executive power was vested in the President who is Head of State and Commander-in-Chief of the armed forces. A constitutional amendment of 1982 provided for the President to be elected by direct universal suffrage to serve for a five-year period. The President appoints the Vice-President and other cabinet ministers from the members of the unicameral House of Representatives. The House has 49 members; 35 are elected by universal adult suffrage, five by chiefs; there are eight non-voting nominated members and the Attorney-General.

GHANA (GOLD COAST until 1957)

In 1945 the Gold Coast consisted of three areas, the Gold Coast Colony, Ashanti and the Northern Territories. The whole territory was administered by a British governor, while chief commissioners had local executive power in Ashanti and the Northern Territories. The two chief commissioners were official members of the nominated Executive Council, which also included five African unofficial members appointed in 1942–3. The jurisdiction of the Executive Council extended to Ashanti and the Northern Territories (since 1934). The Legislative Council operated only for the Colony. It consisted of 15 official members, five unofficial Europeans, six chiefs representing the provincial councils, and three municipal representatives elected on a limited franchise. In the Colony there were three provincial councils of chiefs and a Joint Provincial Council. Ashanti had a Confederacy Council, established in 1935. A Northern Territories Provincial Council was established in 1946.

The Burns constitution of 1946 provided that a central representative government should rule over Ashanti as well as the Colony. The Legislative Council was given an elected African majority and consisted of six official members, six unofficial members nominated by the Governor (three African and three European) and 18 elected members, of whom nine were elected by the Joint Provincial Council, four by municipalities in the Colony, four by the Ashanti Confederacy Council, and one by the municipality of Kumasi in Ashanti. The Executive Council had three unofficial members and eight official, of whom one was nominated, and the Governor still had reserve powers of veto and emergency action.

In 1950 a new constitution enlarged the Legislative Assembly (as the Legislative Council was now called) and its members were mainly elected by popular vote, either direct or indirect, over the whole country. There was a Speaker, six special members elected by commercial and mining interests, three officials, 33 members elected from the Colony, 18 from Ashanti, 19 from the Northern Territories, and five municipal members. A further 37 members were elected indirectly by the territorial councils. The Executive Council had a majority of Africans drawn from the Legislative Assembly as ministers in charge of government departments. The office of prime minister was created in 1952.

The constitution of 1954 provided the basis for independence in 1957. This created a single-chamber legislature with an eight-member cabinet of wholly

African membership. The Assembly was entirely elected by adult suffrage in 104 single-member constituencies on a population basis. It was presided over by a Speaker. The Governor still had reserve powers over defence and external affairs and might ensure the passing of any bill essential to public order.

Ghana became independent in March 1957 and comprised the former Gold Coast Colony and the trusteeship territory of Togoland. Regional Assemblies were created in 1957 as a concession to federal sentiment, but were dissolved in the following year.

A republican constitution came into force in 1960, with a President as head of state. The President had extensive powers, including the right to appoint and dismiss civil servants and dismiss the Chief Justice. A referendum approved the new constitution. In 1964 a further referendum supported the introduction of a single-party state. In early 1966 there was a military coup and the constitution was suspended by the newly-formed National Liberation Council; ministers were dismissed, parliament suspended and all parties banned. A Presidential Commission was set up under a new constitution for the Second Republic in 1969; it had three members and was dissolved in 1970, its place being taken by a president. Political parties were reinstated in 1969 and a Council of State of 12 members was established, together with the reinstated Legislative Assembly.

In 1972 the armed forces took over power from the civil government and established the National Redemption Council, suspending the constitution of 1969, abolishing the office of president and dissolving the Legislative Assembly. The National Redemption Council was replaced in 1975 by a Supreme Military Council, which became the highest legislative and administrative authority, with the head of state as its chairman; all other members were *ex officio*. The National Redemption Council was then reconstituted as a subordinate body, also composed of *ex officio* members. Government departments were headed not by ministers but by administrative commissioners.

The Supreme Military Council announced that elections for a new civilian government would take place in 1979, but it was overthrown by a junior officers' coup in the middle of that year. An Armed Forces Revolutionary Council was formed, but after the elections it surrendered power to a newly formed civilian government. A new constitution prepared by a Constituent Assembly was promulgated in 1979; it provided for an executive president elected by adult suffrage, and a unicameral legislature of 140 elected members.

Following elections a civilian government took office in September 1979. Relations between the new government and the military remained tense. In December 1981 the military again seized power. The constitution was suspended and the legislature dissolved. The new ruling body was the Provisional National Defence Council, initially with four military and three civilian members.

GUINEA

In 1945 Guinea was a French colony ruled by a lieutenant-governor and administered as part of French West Africa. Under the constitution of the Fourth Republic of 1946 it became an overseas territory ruled by a governor. A territorial assembly with 40 members was established, elected on a double electoral-college system. Representatives were sent to the Grand Council in Dakar, and elected to the French National Assembly and the Council of the Republic, and also the Assembly of the French Union at Versailles. The franchise was extended in 1951 and the territorial assembly progressively enlarged so that by 1956 it numbered 60 members.

In the constitutional referendum of 1958 Guinea was the only French African territory to reject de Gaulle's proposal for a French Community. As a result Guinea became an independent republic in October of that year. The independence constitution declared the country to be a democratic, secular and socialist republic, and the Parti Democratique de Guinée to be the sole party. It provided for an executive president elected for seven years, and a single-chamber National Assembly of 150 deputies elected for five years by universal adult suffrage. The President appoints ministers by decree and is responsible to the National Assembly. The constitution was amended in 1963. The country was named the People's Revolutionary Republic of Guinea in 1979 and a new constitution was introduced in 1982. On the death of the executive president in April 1984 the military seized power. The new government of the Military Committee for National Recovery suspended the constitution in April 1984.

GUINEA-BISSAU (PORTUGUESE GUINEA until 1974)

In 1945 Guinea was a Portuguese colony administered directly by a governor responsible to the Colonial Ministry in Lisbon. The Governor was assisted by a Government Council composed of officials. The territory was designated an overseas province of Portugal in 1951. The Organic Act of 1963 established a Legislative Council which had advisory and legislative powers; it consisted of *ex officio* members and 11 elected members representing a limited franchise. The franchise was slightly extended in 1968. Representatives from the province were elected on a similar basis to the National Assembly and Corporate Chamber in Lisbon.

A nationalist revolt led by the Partido Africano da Independência da Guiné e Cabo Verde (PAIGC) broke out in 1963. By the early 1970s the guerrilla army of the PAIGC controlled a large part of Guinea. In 1973 they proclaimed the territory an independent republic. Following the military coup in Lisbon in 1974 the Portuguese government recognised the independence of Guinea-Bissau.

Under the draft constitution of 1973 the PAIGC was the only permitted party. Government was by a National People's Assembly, with executive power vested in a Council of State of 15 members elected for a period of three years by the Assembly from among its members. The President of the Council of State was head of state.

A military coup of November 1980 led to the abolition of the National Assembly and power being taken by a Revolutionary Council of nine members (six military). A new constitution of 1984 established a National People's Assembly of 150 members elected by the regional councils from among their own members. The assembly in turn elected the President who presides over the 15-member Council of State.

IVORY COAST (CÔTE D'IVOIRE)

In 1945 the Ivory Coast was a French colony ruled by a lieutenant-governor and administered as part of French West Africa. The region of Upper Volta was included with Ivory Coast but separated from it by decree in 1947. By the constitution of the Fourth Republic in 1946 Ivory Coast was designated an overseas territory and ruled by a governor. A territorial assembly was established with 45 members elected by a double electoral-college system. Representatives were sent to the Grand Council at Dakar, and elected to the French National Assembly and Council of the Republic in Paris, and also to the Assembly of the French Union at Versailles. The franchise was extended in 1951 and the territorial assembly enlarged; by 1956 it consisted of 60 members.

Under the *loi cadre* of 1956 the territory received internal self-government. The double electoral-college system was ended and the new territorial assembly was elected by universal adult suffrage. In the constitutional referendum of 1958 the Ivory Coast voted to become an autonomous republic within the French Community. A constitution adopted in 1959 provided for an executive presidential system of government and a National Assembly. This was replaced by a new constitution in 1960, subsequently modified six times between 1971 and 1986. This provided for a president elected for a period of five years with power to appoint a Council of Ministers not drawn from the Assembly and answerable only to him. The National Assembly of 175 members is elected for five years at the same time as the President. All members of the National Assembly belong to the Parti Démocratique de la Côte d'Ivoire (PDCI).

KENYA

Kenya in 1945 was a British Crown colony and a protectorate (along the coast) administered by a governor. He was assisted by an Executive Council consisting of eight *ex officio* members and four nominated unofficial members (three Europeans and one Asian). In 1947 the 'membership' system was introduced, with groups of departments being made the specific responsibility of members of the Executive Council. The Legislative Council consisted of a Speaker, 18 elected members (11 Europeans, five Asians, one Arab) and a nominated African member appointed in 1944; a second African nominated member was added in 1947.

In 1948 a Legislative Council with an unofficial majority was introduced; this included four nominated African members selected from a list submitted through local native councils. European settlers exercised considerable economic power and political influence through the Executive and Legislative Councils; their aim was to preserve white dominance in Kenya.

The Legislative Council was enlarged under the constitutional changes implemented in 1952 to 20 members and 21 elected members of whom 14 were Europeans, and six nominated African members. An African was also nominated to the Executive Council. There were separate electoral rolls for Europeans and Asians based on property and educational qualifications.

From 1952 to 1956 the 'Mau Mau' peasant rising in central Kenya brought about a declaration of a state of emergency and a ban on African political party activity. The temporary Lyttelton constitution was introduced in 1954 and provided for a 14-member Council of Ministers, of whom eight were to be *ex officio* and six appointed by the Governor. In 1957 African membership of the Legislative Council was increased to eight, elected on a qualified franchise in eight constituencies.

By the Lennox-Boyd constitution of 1958 the Legislative Council was increased substantially. It consisted of a speaker, six *ex officio* members, 37 nominated members, 36 elected members (14 Africans, 14 Europeans, six Asians, two Arabs), and 12 'specially elected members' (four Africans, four Europeans, four Asians) chosen by the Legislative Council acting as an electoral college. The Council of Ministers had 16 members, including two Africans. Africans boycotted the Council of Ministers and the Legislative Council and demanded more rapid constitutional advance.

Following the Lancaster House Conference, 1960, the Legislative Council was increased to 65 members with an effective African majority; the council consisted of 33 openly elected seats, 10 seats reserved for Europeans and 10 reserved for Asians; the 12 specially elected members were maintained. The 12-man Council of Ministers comprised four officials and four Africans, three Europeans and one Asian; in addition there were nine parliamentary secretaries.

A second constitutional conference at Lancaster House in 1962 agreed on a strong central government with federal provisions for regional governments. After elections in 1963 Kenya received responsible government under a majority-party prime minister. The constitution provided for a two-chamber legislature, a Senate, and a House of Representatives of 129 members, which included three seats reserved for Europeans. At the end of 1963 Kenya became independent and in 1964 a republic with an executive president.

In 1966 the House of Representatives and the Senate were amalgamated into a single National Assembly. By a constitutional amendment in 1969 Kenya became a single-party state. Executive power rests with the President, Vice-President and cabinet; the National Assembly consists of 158 representatives elected for five years, 12 members nominated by the President, and two *ex officio* members.

LESOTHO (BASUTOLAND until 1966)

From 1884 Basutoland was directly administered by a commissioner as a representative of the British Crown; he was under the direction of the High Commissioner for British Southern Africa, in whom legislative power was vested and by whom it could be exercised by proclamation. The supreme native authority was the Paramount Chief. A Basutoland Native Council, established in 1903, consisting largely of chiefs nominated by the Paramount, was purely an advisory body without legislative power. This system of parallel rule remained largely unchanged for fifty years. In 1946–7 a National Treasury and also native treasuries were established and chiefs were paid a regular salary. The number of chiefs was also reduced. By 1950 the Basutoland National Council had 100 members presided over *ex officio* by the Resident Commissioner. The Council consisted of the Paramount Chief, five members nominated by the Resident Commissioner, and 94 members nominated by the Paramount Chief, of whom 36 were elected by district councils and six by various associations. The Council became more representative in 1948, when the Paramount Chief agreed to consult it over new laws and taxes. The constitution of 1959 provided for a more representative Basutoland National Council of 80 members, half of them elected from among members of district councils. The district councils were in turn elected on a common-roll franchise. The other half of the National Council was composed of chiefs, members nominated by the Paramount Chief and official members. There was an Executive Council with advisory powers, half of the members being unofficial members of the National Council. The country became independent in 1966 as the Kingdom of Lesotho, with the Paramount Chief as King. Parliament consisted of a 60-member National Assembly and a Senate, the former being elected on universal adult suffrage and the latter composed of 22 chiefs and 11 members nominated by the King.

The constitution was suspended between 1970 and 1973, when parliamentary government was restored. In 1973 a 93-member interim National Assembly was established to draw up a new constitution.

An electoral law of 1984 prepared the way for a new Assembly. The National Assembly was dissolved in January 1985 in preparation for new elections but these were cancelled later in the year. After a military coup in January 1986 the electoral law and the National Assembly were suspended.

LIBERIA

Liberia is an independent republic established in 1847. The constitution promulgated in that year was modelled after that of the United States. Executive power rested with the President, who was elected by universal suffrage for an eight-year term; the President could be re-elected for a further four-year term. Legislative power was vested in two houses, the Senate of 18 members, and the House of Representatives, consisting of 71 members. The House of Representatives was elected for four years and the Senate for six years. A number of amendments were made to the constitution.

A military coup in March 1980 overthrew the government and established a People's Redemption Council. Executive power was vested in a Head of State and in a Cabinet of 17 members subject to the PRC. A new constitution was agreed by referendum in 1984. This allowed for an executive president, to be elected by universal adult suffrage and to serve for a period of six years, and a bicameral National Assembly of Senate and House of Representatives. The new constitution came into effect in January 1986.

LIBYAN ARAB REPUBLIC (LIBYA until 1969)

Libya was formerly an Italian colony. From 1943 until 1949 it was under French and British military administration, the French controlling the province of Fezzan, and the British the provinces of Cyrenaica and Tripolitania. In 1949 the British recognised the ruler of the Senussi as the Amir of Cyrenaica, and he became king of the independent state of Libya which was established in 1951.

The constitution of 1951 established a monarchy with a federal system of government. The King was supreme head of state. The federal government consisted of a Council of Ministers appointed by the King but responsible to the Chamber of Deputies, the lower elected legislative house, consisting of 55 members. The upper legislative house was the Senate, which had 24 members, eight from each province. The King had powers to nominate half the senators and to veto legislation from the Chamber of Deputies. The three provinces were each administered by a governor assisted by an executive and legislative council. In 1963 the provincial councils were dissolved and the country became a unitary state organised into 10 administrative districts.

The King was deposed by an army coup in 1969. A republic was proclaimed and the country renamed the Libyan Arab Republic. A Revolutionary Command Council was established which governed the country with the assistance of a largely civilian cabinet of ministers.

In 1977 a new constitution was introduced and the name of the country was changed to the Popular Libyan Socialist Arab Jamahiriya (*Jamahiriya* meaning 'state of the masses'). The Revolutionary Command Council and the cabinet were abolished. A General People's Congress appointed the former

President, Col. Gaddafi, head of state. Under the terms of the constitution the Congress assisted by a General Secretariat formed a Popular Legislature; executive functions are in the hands of a General People's Committee of 26 members, subsequently reduced to 21 and then, in 1982, 19 members. Under the constitution the Qur'an is the social code of the state.

MADAGASCAR (MALAGASY REPUBLIC)

In 1946 Madagascar was designated an overseas territory within the French Union. The island was ruled by a governor-general until 1946 and thereafter by a high commissioner. He was assisted by a Government Council and a territorial assembly of 60 members established by the constitution of the Fourth Republic. The territorial assembly was elected on a double electoral-college system; Madagascar also elected on a similar basis five deputies to the French National Assembly, five senators to the Council of the Republic, and six representatives to the Assembly of the French Union.

In 1947 a serious revolt broke out in the island which was suppressed with great loss of life. The franchise was extended in 1951 and the territorial assembly enlarged. By the *loi cadre* of 1956 universal adult suffrage was introduced and the island received internal autonomy in 1957. In the constitutional referendum of 1958 Madagascar voted to become an autonomous republic within the French Community. A new constitution was promulgated in 1959, and amended in 1960, which provided for a National Assembly of 107 elected members and a Senate of 52 members. Executive power was vested in the President, who appointed ministers.

The army took over full powers in 1972 and a constitutional law gave Maj.-Gen. Ramantsoa full presidential powers for a period of five years. The legislative bodies were suspended and the President was assisted by a Higher Institutional Council and a People's National Development Council. In 1975 a National Military Directorate assumed executive power. A new constitution was approved by referendum in 1975. This provided for executive power to rest with a president elected for seven years and the Supreme Revolutionary Council; legislative authority resided with a National People's Assembly elected for five years.

MALAWI (NYASALAND until 1964)

Nyasaland was a British protectorate (proclaimed 1907) administered by a governor, who was assisted by Executive and Legislative Councils, both nominated. Local legislation was by ordinance and the Governor had the right of veto. African provincial councils were established in each of the three provinces in 1944 and 1945. These councils were advisory and composed of chiefs under the presidency of the Provincial Commissioner. An African Protectorate Council established in 1946 had advisory powers.

The constitution of 1949 allowed all communities in Nyasaland to be represented in the Legislative Council. Federation with Southern Rhodesia and Northern Rhodesia was imposed in 1953 and lasted till 1963. The constitution was altered in 1956 and the Legislative Council was changed. Nominated unofficial members no longer sat in the legislature, which now consisted of 12 officials, and six European and five African unofficial members.

A constitution granted in 1960 provided for a Legislative Council of 28 elected, three official and two nominated members. There were two electoral rolls – 20 members were elected on the lower roll and eight on the upper, the electors having different qualifications. The Executive Council had five officials chosen from among the elected members of the Legislative Council.

Self-government with a ministerial system was introduced in 1963 for all internal affairs; the Legislative Council was renamed the Legislative Assembly. By the constitution of 1964 Nyasaland became the independent state of Malawi. The Legislative Assembly consisted of 53 members, of whom 50 were elected by an adult franchise and three were European members elected on a special roll. In 1966 Malawi became a republic with a president as head of state; he is also head of the government and of the one political party. In 1971 the President became President for Life. The unicameral National Assembly by 1983 had 101 elected members, but the President could also nominate additional members.

MALI (FRENCH SOUDAN until 1959; FEDERATION OF MALI 1959–60)

In 1945 the French Soudan was governed by a lieutenant-governor and administered as part of French West Africa. In 1946, in accordance with the terms of the constitution of the Fourth Republic, a territorial assembly was established. This consisted of 50 members and was elected on a double electoral-college system. Representatives were also sent to the Grand Council at Dakar, and elected to the French National Assembly and Council of the Republic, and the Assembly of the French Union. The franchise was extended in 1951 and representation in the territorial assembly enlarged to 70 members by 1956. Under the *loi cadre* of 1956 the territory was given increased internal self-government and the territorial assembly elected by universal adult suffrage.

In 1958 the Soudan voted in the constitutional referendum to become an autonomous republic within the French Community. At a conference at Bamako in 1958 representatives from four of the French West African territories proposed the creation of a federation. Dahomey and Upper Volta decided against joining the federation, which was formed in 1959 by the Soudan and Senegal and named the Mali Federation. France recognised the independence of the federation in 1960. Shortly after independence the federation broke up, with the former Soudan retaining the name of Mali.

The constitution of the former federation was adapted to Mali. This provided for presidential government with a National Assembly of 80 members. In 1968 President Keita dissolved the National Assembly by decree and assumed full legislative powers. Later that year he was overthrown by a military coup, which established a 14-man Military Committee of National Liberation. In 1974 a referendum was held on a new constitution, but despite an overwhelming vote of approval the military government announced it would continue to govern for a further five years. The constitution of 1974 proposed an elected president and a single-chamber National Assembly elected on a single-party basis. In 1979 a Constitutional Congress of 137 members (104 civilians, 27 military, and six representatives from youth and women's organisations) formed a national political party, the Union Démocratique du Peuple Malien (UDPM).

A constitution of 1974 was adopted in 1979, amended in 1981 and 1985. This provided for an executive president elected by universal adult suffrage for a period of six years, and an 82-member National Assembly elected for a three-year period.

MAURITANIA

In 1945 Mauritania was a French colony administered by a lieutenant-governor and administered as part of French West Africa. By the constitution of the Fourth Republic a territorial assembly was established, elected by a single electoral roll; representatives were sent to the Grand Council at Dakar, and elected to the French National Assembly and Council of the Republic, and the Assembly of the French Union. The franchise was extended in 1951 and the territorial assembly enlarged; in 1956 it consisted of 34 members.

In 1957 the territory received internal self-government under the terms of the *loi cadre* of the previous year. In the constitutional referendum of 1958 Mauritania voted to become an autonomous republic within the French Community. The territorial assembly became the Legislative Assembly in 1959 and adopted a new constitution.

The constitution promulgated in 1961, a modification of that of 1959, declared Mauritania to be an Islamic republic. An executive president headed the government, assisted by a council of 16 ministers appointed by him; the National Assembly had 70 members and was elected by universal adult suffrage for five years. After 1964 all members of the National Assembly were drawn from one party.

In 1976 part of the former Spanish territory of Western Sahara was added to the republic and seven representatives added to the National Assembly. A military coup in 1978 overthrew the government, suspended the constitution and established a Military Committee of National Recovery. A Military Committee for National Salvation took over executive powers in 1979. A constitutional charter was adopted which established a prime minister responsible to the Military Committee; the prime minister as head of government could not simultaneously be head of state. Mauritania relinquished control of the southern portion of Western Sahara in 1979. A provisional constitution was announced in late 1980 but it was abandoned the following year.

MAURITIUS

Under the constitution of 1885 Mauritius was a colony ruled by a governor and an Executive Council appointed by him; there was a legislature (the Council of Government) of 27 members, 10 of them elected on a limited franchise.

The constitution of 1947 provided for an Executive Council of four officials, two appointed members and four members elected by the Legislative Council. The Legislative Council consisted of three *ex officio* members, 12 nominated members and 19 members elected on the basis of 'simple literacy'. The constitution of 1958 provided for a Legislative Council of 40 members elected from single-member constituencies and 12 nominated members. Universal adult suffrage was introduced. The constitution was revised in 1964 to provide for a Council of Ministers presided over by the Governor.

Internal self-government was achieved in 1967 and under the revised constitution the Legislative Assembly was enlarged to 70 members. Responsible ministerial government was introduced and the island became an independent state within the Commonwealth in 1968. A constitutional amendment in 1969 provided for a cabinet of up to 20 ministers presided over by a prime minister, and a legislature of a speaker, 62 elected members, and eight additional members.

MOROCCO

In 1945 Morocco was a sultanate but divided into three territories: a French protectorate over most of the country, a Spanish protectorate in the north, and the international zone of Tangier. The enclaves of Ceuta and Melilla were Spanish state territories and remained so in 1990.

Under the French protectorate the Sultan was a nominal ruler; real power lay with the French representative, the Resident-General, who acted as the Sultan's foreign minister. The Sultan's authority extended to all three areas of Morocco; as reorganised in 1947 it comprised a council, or Makhzan, of 60 members, presided over by the Grand Vizier; delegates from the council were attached to the French heads of the five main government departments. A Government Council, established in 1919, represented the interests of French settlers and a small number of Moroccans, and dealt with financial and economic affairs.

The Spanish protectorate was administered by a high commissioner. From 1941 to 1945 the Spanish suppressed the international administration in Tangier but this was reinstated at the end of the Second World War and Spanish troops withdrew. The International Committee of Control consisted of representatives for Belgium, France, Italy, Netherlands, Portugal, Spain, the United Kingdom and the United States; its structure was reformed in 1953.

In an attempt to curb growing nationalist unrest in Morocco, the French sent the Sultan into exile from 1953 to 1955. In 1956 the French agreed to Moroccan independence; the Spanish protectorate and Tangier were integrated with the newly-independent kingdom of Morocco. Spanish Ifni was ceded to Morocco in 1969 and the northern half of Spanish Western Sahara in 1976.

From 1956 to 1960 Morocco was an absolute monarchy with royal government exercised through a three-member Crown Council and a National Consultative Assembly of 76 nominated members. A constitution approved by referendum and introduced in 1962 declared the country to be a democratic and social monarchy and a Muslim state. A two-chamber elected parliament was established which had limited legislative power and was subject to royal veto. The House of Representatives with 144 members was directly elected for four years. The House of Councillors was indirectly elected, two-thirds of its members coming from an electoral college composed of the recently-created provincial councils, and one-third being drawn from members of various economic and social interest groups.

A new constitution was approved by referendum in 1972. This provided for a constitutional monarchy and a single-chamber legislature of 264 deputies, 176 deputies by general election and 88 deputies by direct vote through an electoral-college representing various councils and economic interests. An amendment of 1980 extended the chamber's term from four to six years. The King as head of state has the power to appoint the prime minister and other ministers and also to dissolve the National Assembly.

MOZAMBIQUE

Mozambique was declared an integral part of Portugal by the Organic Charter incorporated into the constitution of 1933. The colony was subject to decrees from the Colonial (later Overseas) Ministry in Lisbon and administered directly by a governor-general.

In 1958 Mozambique was designated an overseas province and given a measure of local autonomy. The Governor-General was assisted by a Provincial and a Government Council. The Organic Act of 1953, modified in 1963, established a Legislative Council of 29 members; there were two *ex officio* members and the remaining members were elected on a narrow franchise by a mixture of direct suffrage and from various economic and social interest groups. Advisory economic and social councils were set up in 1963 consisting of seven *ex officio* members and eight elected members representing the interests of various corporate groups. Seven representatives from Mozambique were sent to the National Assembly in Lisbon.

From 1964 to 1974 the nationalist party Frelimo waged an armed struggle against the Portuguese in Mozambique. Following the military coup in Lisbon in 1974 a transitional government was established under a high commissioner. Mozambique became an independent republic in June 1975.

By the constitution of 1975 revised in 1978, executive powers are vested in a president who presides over the People's Assembly; a Council of Ministers is answerable to the President. Considerable powers rest with the Central Committee of Frelimo, the only permitted political party, and also a 15-member Permanent Commission of the Assembly. The legislative function lies with the People's Assembly, which consists of up to 210 elected members.

NAMIBIA (formerly SOUTH WEST AFRICA)

South West Africa was a former German colony administered by South Africa as a League of Nations mandate. In 1946 South Africa refused to submit the territory to United Nations trusteeship. The status of South West Africa was contested and in 1966 the United Nations terminated the mandate; in 1971 the International Court of Justice ruled that South Africa's presence in the territory was illegal. The United Nations referred to the territory as Namibia.

In 1945 the Administrator of the territory was assisted by an Advisory Council and a Legislative Assembly of 12 elected and six nominated members. The South West Africa Amendment Act, 1949, abolished the Advisory Council and introduced a wholly elected Legislative Assembly of 18 members. The Executive Council had four members chosen from the legislature. South West Africa was represented in the South African House of Assembly by six members and in the Senate by four members, two of whom were elected and two nominated by the Governor-General of South Africa. The franchise was restricted to registered voters, who were all white. After 1950 apartheid policies were introduced into the country; in 1966 the apartheid and security laws of South Africa were applied to the territory retroactively to 1950. African nationalists of the South West African People's Organisation (SWAPO) began a guerrilla war against the South African presence in 1966 and this intensified throughout the 1970s.

Following the Odendaal Report of 1964 South Africa began to divide Namibia into 'homelands'; the first was created in 1968 in Ovamboland, which received executive and legislative councils. In 1969 South Africa transferred most of the administrative functions of the Legislative Assembly to the appropriate government departments in South Africa and Namibia became virtually a fifth province of the Republic.

In 1973 the South African government established an Advisory Council to discuss a constitution for Namibia; it rejected United Nations attempts to alter the status of Namibia. The withdrawal of Portugal from Angola in 1975 put pressure on South Africa to seek an internal solution. A constitutional conference, the Turnhalle Conference of 1975–7, attempted to establish a transitional government leading to an independent Namibia which would remain sympathetic to South Africa. A draft constitution of 1977 appointed an administrator-general to organise elections for a Constituent Assembly in preparation for independence. South Africa rejected a proposal for United Nations supervised elections. The elections of 1978, based on adult suffrage, were boycotted by SWAPO. Following the elections the 50-member Constituent Assembly constituted itself as the National Assembly with legislative powers over Namibian affairs. Executive power was retained by the Administrator-General assisted by an Executive Council of 12 drawn from the National Assembly. SWAPO forces continued to fight against the new government and South African forces occupying the country.

In mid-1980 a Ministerial Council of 12 members was formed; the following year it was increased to 15 members and given wider executive powers. In 1983 the Ministerial Council was dissolved and executive and legislative powers resided with the Administrator-General.

In June 1985 a 'transitional government of national unity' took office. It consisted of a cabinet of eight ministers, assisted by deputies, drawn from the National Assembly of 62 members. The members of the National Assembly were not elected but represented certain political parties. A 17-member Constitutional Council, similarly composed, was appointed to draft a constitution for an independent Namibia.

On Independence (21 Mar 1990), Namibia adopted a liberal, democratic constitution. The constitution stipulated a multi-party, democratic republic with an independent judiciary, a Bill of fundamental human rights and an Executive President who may serve two five-year terms. The death penalty was abolished.

NIGER

In 1945 Niger was a colony ruled by a lieutenant-governor and administered as part of French West Africa. By the constitution of the Fourth Republic of 1946 Niger was designated an overseas territory and placed under a governor. A territorial assembly was created and representatives were elected by a double electoral-college system to the Assembly, and also to the Grand Council at Dakar, the French National Assembly and Council of the Republic, and the Assembly of the French Union. The franchise was increased in 1951 and the territorial assembly enlarged from 30 members to 50 members.

In 1957 the double electoral-college system of voting was replaced by universal adult suffrage and Niger was given internal self-government. In the constitutional referendum of 1958 the territory voted to become an autonomous republic within the French Community. The first constitution was framed in 1959 and replaced with another when Niger became independent in 1960. This provided for an executive president elected for five years by universal adult suffrage. The President was assisted by a Council of Ministers, who were responsible to him. A single-chamber National Assembly of 60 members, all from a single party, was elected for five years.

In 1974 the constitution was suspended following a military coup. Executive and legislative powers were taken over by a group of army officers who constituted themselves as a Supreme Military Council. A predominantly civilian cabinet was established in 1976. There was no formal constitution but a National Charter provided for consultative non-elective institutions at both national and local level. A draft 'national charter' was introduced in 1986 and put to a referendum the following year.

NIGERIA

In 1945 Nigeria was administered by the constitution of 1922. This provided for an Executive Council of official members, to which two unofficial African members were added in 1943, and a Legislative Council consisting of 26 official members, 15 nominated unofficial members, and three members elected from Lagos and one from Calabar.

The Richards constitution of 1946 extended the authority of the Legislative Council to the whole of Nigeria, and established under it a house of chiefs and a house of assembly for the Northern province; these together were called the Northern Regional Council. The Western and Eastern provinces were created and given houses of assembly, which formed links between the native rulers and the Legislative Council; they were advisory bodies with a majority of unofficial members chosen by the native authorities.

Under the McPherson constitution of 1951 the Legislative Council was replaced by a House of Representatives which had a majority of members elected indirectly. The regional houses of assembly were given powers in local legislation, and the Western province gained its own house of chiefs. Elections were through electoral colleges; electors in the primary election needed residence and tax qualifications to elect members of a divisional college which in turn elected to provincial colleges. The provincial colleges elected members to each regional house of assembly, which then elected from among its own members those who would represent it in the House of Representatives. The Central Executive Council became a council of ministers drawn from the regions on the advice of regional legislatures. Officials remained in charge of defence, justice and finance. Ministers of the regions were nominated by regional lieutenant-governors with the approval of the houses of assembly.

By the 1954 Lyttelton constitution Nigeria became a federation. The Governor was replaced by a Governor-General and the regional lieutenant-governors by governors. There was a federal House of Representatives with a speaker, 184 elected members, three officials and six special members. The federal Council of Ministers had authority over all matters on which the House of Representatives might legislate. The House of Representatives had exclusive power in external affairs, migration, citizenship, defence, external trade, customs and excise, currency, banks, loans, mining and communications. There was then a concurrent list, on which federal law prevailed in case of conflict. Elections to the House of Representatives varied with the regions. In the North there were indirect elections, with franchise confined to adult male taxpayers. In the West there were direct elections, as also in the East and in Lagos, based on adult suffrage. The Southern Cameroons were at this time a region of the federation with a house of assembly of mainly elected members and an executive council with an unofficial majority. In 1961 the region joined the Republic of Cameroon.

In 1960 there were further constitutional changes as preparation for independence. The federal House of Representatives was elected in single-member constituencies, and a Senate was established with revisionary powers; its members were nominated by regional governments with the approval of the majority in each regional parliament, and there were four members for Lagos and four appointed by the Governor-General. The regional parliaments consisted of a house of chiefs, an elected house of assembly (five appointed members serving in the Northern regional house) and an executive council of prime minister and other ministers. Full independence followed in October 1960, and Nigeria became a republic in 1963.

In 1966 the government was overthrown by a military coup, which was in turn suppressed by the head of the army, Gen. Aguiyi-Ironsi, who then suspended the constitution and set up a Supreme Military Council. He abolished all political parties and tribal associations and dissolved the federal system of government. He was in turn overthrown in July 1966 and the federal system was restored in September as the Federal Military Government. A constitutional decree of 1967 placed all executive and legislative powers with the Supreme Military Council, which was composed of regional military governors and the heads of the armed forces. A federal Executive Council was also formed from military and civilian commissioners.

In 1967 the republic was divided into 12 states; six in the former Northern Region, three in the former Eastern Region, one in the West, a Mid-West state and a state of Lagos. Following this, the military governor of the Eastern Region states seceded from the federation and renamed the region the Republic of Biafra; this led to civil war, which ended with federal victory in 1970.

In 1976 the number of states was increased from 12 to 19. A draft constitution of 1976 provided for a return to civilian government within three years; there was to be an elected National Assembly and an executive president. In 1977 a 230-member Constituent Assembly was inaugurated to discuss the draft constitution. Up to 1979 central government remained a military government; local government was by native authorities of local-government bodies controlled by state legislation. In 1979 elections took place and a civilian government headed by a president took over from the military government.

The constitution of 1979 provided for an executive president, a 96-member senate, and a 450-member house of representatives. In late December 1983 the military again seized power and a new Supreme Military Council assumed executive and legislative authority. All political parties were dissolved. An 18-member Federal Executive Council was established, which included more civilian than military members who were drawn from most states of the federal republic. A further military coup took place in August 1985. The Supreme Military Council and the Federal Executive Council were dissolved. Executive power now resided in a 28-member Armed Forces Ruling Council which contained only military members. The new government created a National Council of Ministers and a National Council of State, both subject to the Armed Forces Ruling Council.

FEDERATION OF RHODESIA and NYASALAND

The federation was created in 1953 from the British territories of Southern Rhodesia, Northern Rhodesia and Nyasaland, and lasted until 1963. Britain retained ultimate responsibility for external affairs. Defence, immigration, European education, European agriculture and health became the responsibility of the new federal legislature, which sat in the Southern Rhodesian capital of Salisbury.

The federation had a governor-general and a unicameral assembly elected on two common rolls with qualified franchise. In 1960 there were 44 seats for elected members of any race, eight for Africans, four for specially elected

Africans and three for Europeans responsible for African interests. The constitution provided for an African Affairs Board as a standing committee of the Assembly. It consisted of the three Europeans representing African interests and one specially elected African member from each territory. It had power to make representations to the Federal Assembly, assist a territorial government when asked to, and require any measure which it thought discriminatory to be reserved to the crown. The Federal Assembly had a majority, returned by roll voters in constituencies, and a minority returned by roll voters in electoral districts. Both franchises were qualified by property and educational standards.

RWANDA (RUANDA-URUNDI until 1962)

Ruanda, a former German territory, was administered as part of Ruanda-Urundi by Belgium, first as a League of Nations mandate and then, after 1946, as a United Nations trust territory. The territory was ruled by a vice-governor-general directly responsible to the Minister of Colonies in Brussels. An Advisory Council was set up in 1947 consisting of officials and three persons representing the interests of Africans.

The first elections held in the country were in 1960 for municipal councils. In 1959 the Belgians announced that Rwanda was to become independent, and representatives of the municipal councils were hastily convened into the Rwanda Council of 48 members, which constituted a national government in October 1960. A state of civil war existed throughout the country between the Hutu majority and the Tutsi feudal minority, who opposed the prospect of a government in the hands of the Hutu.

In 1961 the Tutsi king was deposed and a republic established. Internal self-government was achieved in early 1962 and the country was proclaimed an independent state in July the same year. The constitution of 1962 provided for an executive presidential government elected for four years, assisted by a council of 12 ministers. The National Assembly was to consist of 47 members elected by universal suffrage every four years.

A military coup in 1973 led to a change in the executive functions of the constitution: under the Second Republic supreme authority was in the hands of the Committee of Peace and National Unity. In 1975 Rwanda was declared to be a one-party state led by the Mouvement Révolutionnaire National pour le Développement (MRND).

A new constitution was introduced in 1978. This provided for an executive president, elected for a five-year period, who presides over the Council of Ministers. Legislative powers are jointly exercised by the President and also the National Development Council which is elected for five years by universal direct suffrage.

ST HELENA, ASCENSION ISLAND AND TRISTAN DA CUNHA

St Helena and its dependencies Tristan and Ascension form a Crown colony administered by Britain. In 1945 St Helena was administered by a governor assisted by an Executive Council of five members and an Advisory Council of six unofficial members chosen to represent all sections of the community.

A government representative was responsible for Ascension, while Tristan had a chief with three administrative officers; the chief was chairman of the island council. An administrator was appointed in 1948 and he chairs the island council of six nominated and 15 elected members.

In 1967 St Helena received a Legislative Council consisting of the Governor, two official members and 12 elected members; government departments were run by committees of the Council, whose chairmen, together with the two official members, form the Governor's Executive Council.

SÃO TOMÉ and PRÍNCIPE

The islands of São Tomé and Príncipe, together with the fort of São João Baptista de Ajuda on the coast of Dahomey, formed in 1945 an overseas province of Portugal. They were administered by a governor directly responsible to Lisbon, who was assisted by a Government Council composed of officials. The fort of São João Baptista was taken over by Dahomey in 1960.

By the Organic Act of 1963 a Legislative Assembly was established composed of 10 elected and three *ex officio* members; the province was also represented in the National Assembly and the Corporative Chamber in Lisbon.

The military coup in Lisbon in 1974 led to negotiations between nationalists from the islands and the new Portuguese government. A transitional government was formed in São Tomé under a high commissioner and in 1975 the islands became an independent republic. By the constitution of 1975 executive power lies with the President and his ministers, who are responsible to the People's Assembly. The People's Assembly is elected for four years and draws its 22 members from the sole party, the Movement for Liberation of São Tomé and Príncipe.

A new constitution was approved in 1982. A 40-member National People's Assembly, elected for five years, in turn elects the executive president of the republic.

SENEGAL

Senegal was a colony administered as part of French West Africa. In 1946 the constitution of the Fourth Republic transformed the pre-war Colonial Council into a territorial assembly of 50 members. The franchise was limited and based on a single electoral roll. Representatives were also sent to the Grand Council in Dakar, and elected to the French National Assembly and the Council of the Republic, and the Assembly of the French Union.

The franchise was extended in 1951. By the *loi cadre* of 1956 Senegal received internal self-government; the assembly was enlarged to 60 members and elected by universal adult suffrage. An Executive Council, presided over by the Governor, functioned as an embryo cabinet. In 1958 the territory voted to become an autonomous republic within the French Community. Senegal joined with the Soudan to form the Mali Federation in 1959 but separated to become an independent republic in the following year.

The constitution of 1959 provided for a National Assembly of 80 members. A revised constitution of 1960 introduced a government with executive power divided between a President and a Prime Minister. The President was elected for seven years and he appointed the Prime Minister, who held executive power subject to the National Assembly.

In 1963 a referendum approved a new constitution, subsequently amended at various times. This provided for an executive president elected for four years, later increased to five years, by universal adult suffrage. The National Assembly of 100 members is also elected at the same time.

SEYCHELLES

The islands were ruled by a governor assisted by an Executive Council and a Legislative Council with a majority of official members. In 1948 four elected members were added to the Legislative Council of six official and two nominated unofficial members; the franchise was based on property, income and educational qualifications. In 1960 the Legislative Council was reconstituted with a presiding governor, four *ex officio* members, five elected members and three nominated members, one of whom was unofficial. The Executive Council had a similar structure.

In 1970 a new constitution provided for a Legislative Assembly of 15 elected members, three *ex officio* members and a ,speaker. Internal self-government was achieved in 1975 and independence in 1976. The 1976 constitution provided for executive power to be held by the President and a prime minister responsible to an elected National Assembly of 25 members.

In 1977 a coup ousted the President and the National Assembly was suspended. The constitution was reintroduced but modified to give full executive powers to the President.

In 1979 a new constitution was proclaimed. This provides for the election of both an executive president and a 23-member National Assembly. The President appoints the advisory Council of Ministers and also two appointees to the National Assembly to represent the inner and outer islands. Candidates for election must be members of the sole party.

SIERRA LEONE

Sierra Leone consisted of two territories, the Colony, which extended along the littoral, and the Protectorate in the hinterland. Both Colony and Protectorate were administered by a governor assisted by a single executive and legislature.

In 1945 the Legislative Council had 11 official members and 10 unofficial members, of whom three were elected for a five-year term on a limited (male) franchise from the Colony; there was no franchise in the Protectorate. The Executive Council was increased in 1943 to include two African unofficial members (one a chief), who were drawn from the Legislative Council; another member was added in 1948. In 1946 district councils and a Protectorate Assembly were established in the Protectorate; the Assembly was composed of 26 paramount chiefs, 11 official members and three nominated members (one Creole and two Protectorate Africans).

Under the constitution of 1951 the Executive Council had an unofficial majority and the Legislative Council a large elected majority, members being elected by the Protectorate for the first time. Seven members were elected from the Colony and 12 by the district councils of the Protectorate; two were elected by the Protectorate Assembly; two were nominated by the Governor; and seven were *ex officio* members. The Governor had an Executive Council of four official members and six unofficial members appointed from among the unofficial members of the Legislative Council. The Protectorate was administered by a chief commissioner responsible to the Governor, and, although it was represented in the Legislative Council, it retained the Protectorate Assembly. This now consisted of representatives from each district council and six members nominated by the Governor to represent other interests; it met in an advisory capacity.

In 1952 departments of government were assigned as the special responsibility of certain members of the executive. In 1953 a full ministerial system was introduced, the ministers all being elected members of the Legislative Council. A chief minister was appointed in 1954.

A new constitution in 1956 replaced the Legislative Council with a House of Representatives which had a speaker, four official members, 14 directly elected from the Colony and 25 directly elected from the Protectorate, 12 paramount chiefs elected by district councils in the Protectorate, and two nominated members with no voting rights.

In 1958 the executive was made collectively responsible to the legislature. The government consisted of at least seven elected ministers appointed on the advice of the Chief Minister. The Governor retained his responsibility for 'peace and good government', external affairs, defence, internal security, police and public service. In 1960 he ceased to preside over the executive and was replaced by the Chief Minister; he also transferred to the ministers his powers on police and internal security. The territory became fully independent in 1961.

Under the constitution of the independent state the Queen was represented by a governor-general appointed on the advice of the Prime Minister. There was a House of Representatives of not less than 60 members elected from constituencies established by an electoral commission.

In March 1967 there were two successive military coups, the first of which overthrew the newly elected government and the second of which proclaimed the National Reformation Council; the Council consisted of eight members. In April 1968 it was in turn overthrown by non-commissioned officers of the army and police force, who formed the Anti-Corruption Revolutionary Movement. This movement appointed an interim council, and constitutional government was restored on 26 April.

In 1971 the state became a republic under the President as head of state; he was also head of the cabinet. A new constitution, approved by referendum in 1978, declared Sierra Leone to be a single-party state. The executive president was elected for seven years by members of the National Delegates Conference of the All-People's Congress (APC), the sole party. The House of Representatives consisted of 60 elected members, whose nominations were endorsed by the Central Committee of the APC.

SOMALIA

In 1945 Somalia was divided into two territories. British Somaliland in the north was a protectorate but under wartime military administration, which lasted to 1948. Civil government was then resumed under a governor who had sole legislative and executive authority. A Legislative Council was established in 1957, with an official majority and six appointed members. In 1959 it was enlarged to include 12 elected members and 17 appointed members. The next year it became the Legislative Assembly, with 33 elected members.

Italian Somalia in the south was occupied by British forces in 1941 and placed under military administration until 1949. The territory then passed under British Foreign Office administration until 1950, when Italy resumed control as trustee for the United Nations. The trusteeship was governed by a UN Advisory Council with representatives from Egypt, Colombia and the Philippines; advisory or departmental bodies were mainly under Somalis. A territorial council of 35 members appointed by the trusteeship administration had to be consulted by the Italians on all important matters relating to the territory. Following elections in 1956 the territorial council was replaced by a Legislative Assembly of 70 elected members; this was enlarged to 90 members in 1959. A constitution for the territory was drafted by the Assembly between 1957 and 1960.

In 1960 British Somaliland became an independent republic. Six days later it merged with Italian Somalia, when that territory also became independent, to form the Somali Republic. The president of the southern legislature was proclaimed provisional head of state and the two legislatures were united at Mogadishu to form a single-chamber National Assembly of 123 members, 33 from the north and 90 from the populous south.

The constitution of the former trust territory was adopted by referendum in 1961 as the constitution for the unified republic. This provided for a president elected by the National Assembly and a prime minister as head of government; the National Assembly was elected for five years.

A military coup in 1969 suspended the constitution and dismissed the National Assembly. The new government which assumed power consisted of a 73-member Supreme Revolutionary Council. In 1976 the Council was replaced by a civilian government. Somalia is a single-party state with the Central Committee of the Somali Socialist Revolutionary Party having considerable executive powers.

A new constitution was approved in 1979 and amended in 1984. This stated that party and state were indivisible. The executive president, elected by direct universal suffrage for seven years, had powers to appoint and dismiss ministers. The People's Assembly of 171 deputies was elected by secret ballot for a period of five years.

SOUTH AFRICA

South Africa was established as a Union in 1910 from the four self-governing territories of Cape Colony, Natal, Orange Free State and the Transvaal. In 1945 it was a sovereign state within the Commonwealth governed by a governor-general appointed by the Crown and exercising executive power in conjunction with a cabinet drawn from the legislature. Legislative power was vested in a House of Assembly of 153 elected members, and a Senate of 48 members. The Senate consisted of members elected by the members of the provincial councils and those nominated by the Governor-General.

Money bills had to originate in the lower house; the Senate's powers to block them were restricted, as they could still be passed on recommendation from the Governor-General. Each province after Union was administered by a provincial council elected for three years, each council having an executive committee presided over by an administrator appointed by the Governor-General. The term was later extended to five years.

Members of the Union parliament had to be white, but this did not apply to members of the provincial council. The franchise was restricted to whites except in Cape Province, where a small number of Africans and Coloureds had the vote. The Coloureds voted on the common roll until 1956, when they were placed on a separate roll and could elect four white representatives to the Assembly and one to the Senate. Africans in the Cape were placed on a separate roll by the Representation of Natives Act 1936; by this they could elect three white representatives to the Assembly. Africans in the rest of the Union elected three white senators through electoral colleges. An African Representative Council was set up in 1936. Under the policies of apartheid all African representation in the Assembly was abolished in 1959 and replaced by a system of regional and territorial Bantu authorities. Coloured representation in the Assembly was ended in 1969.

A referendum was held in 1960 to decide whether the Union should become a republic; it was restricted to white voters. A republic was proclaimed in 1961 and South Africa also left the Commonwealth. The constitution of the republic provided for a president as head of state, elected by an electoral college for seven years. The executive consisted of the State President and the cabinet. The Senate had some elected members and another eight who were nominated by the State President to represent the four provinces. The House of Assembly had 159 members elected for a period of five years. From 1949 to 1977 representatives from South West Africa (Namibia) were elected to both the Senate and the House of Assembly.

In the late 1970s various schemes were proposed for a tricameral legislative system with separate parliaments for the white, 'Coloured', and Indian populations, although sovereignty would remain with the white legislature. The Senate was replaced by an advisory President's Council consisting of nominated white, 'Coloured' and Indian members. A referendum of November 1983, in which only white voters participated, approved constitutional changes. In August 1984 elections took place for an Indian House of Delegates and a 'Coloured' House of Representatives.

South Africa introduced a new constitution in September 1984. This provides for an executive State President elected by an electoral college consisting of up to 88 members of Parliament with the white House of Assembly having a dominant voice. Ministers are appointed by the State President from the three racially separate Houses of Parliament.

Legislative power is vested in the State President and the Parliament. Parliament consists of three Houses: the House of Assembly (white) with 166 directly elected members, four nominated and eight by indirect election; the House of Representatives ('Coloured') with 80 elected members, two appointed by the State President, and three more elected by members; the House of Delegates (Indian) with 40 directly elected members, two appointed by the State President, and three more elected by members.

Africans are not permitted to vote and have no representation in the South African Parliament.

A 60-member President's Council, consisting of up to 20 members from the House of Assembly, 10 from the House of Representatives, and five from the House of Delegates, plus 25 appointed by the State President, may advise the president on any matter.

The Promotion of Bantu Self-Government Act, 1959, provided for the establishment of self-governing ethnic states for all Africans. Under this and further legislation implementing apartheid, all Africans within the Republic were to be deprived of their South African citizenship and to become citizens of ten independent black homelands. The first of these to be created was Transkei in 1976; Bophuthatswana followed in 1977, Venda in 1979, and Ciskei in 1981. None of these 'independent' states has gained any international recognition. Since 1988, as a result of the political changes in South Africa, the governments of Ciskei, Venda and Transkei have announced that they wish to be reintegrated into South Africa.

BOPHUTHATSWANA

The constitution of 1977 provides for an executive president directly elected by universal suffrage. The single chamber Legislative Assembly has 108 members, 72 elected, 24 nominated by regional authorities, and 12 appointed by the President.

CISKEI

The constitution of 1981 created an executive President who appoints the members of the executive council. The National Assembly is composed of 50 elected members and 37 hereditary chiefs. Following a military coup in 1990 a four man Military Committee and an eight member Council of State rule the territory.

TRANSKEI

The constitution of 1976 created an executive President who is elected by the National Assembly for a seven-year period. An Executive Council of not more than 15 members is appointed by the president. The National Assembly has 150 members, 75 elected and 75 chiefs and paramount chiefs. Military rule was established after a coup in 1987.

VENDA

The 'independence' constitution of 1979 provided for an executive president who presides over a cabinet of ministers all drawn from the National Assembly. The single chamber National Assembly has up to 92 members of whom 45 are directly elected, the others being chiefs, appointees of the President, and representatives of the regional councils.

SPANISH SAHARA

The Spanish occupation of the Western Sahara began in 1860 and the interior was finally conquered and annexed in 1934. The enclave of Ifni was effectively occupied by Spanish forces in 1932–3.

Until 1958 both territories were regarded as colonies and administered jointly by a military regime. In 1958 the two territories were formed into separate provinces and a new system of administration established under the 'Fundamental Laws of Spain'. Each province was under a governor-general, who in practice was always a military man. Local elected councils met under a president. In Spanish Sahara in 1963 the council consisted of seven Spaniards and seven Saharan representatives; the council was responsible for 12 government departments. Three representatives were elected to the Cortes in Madrid. A General Tribal Assembly to represent all Saharans was set up in 1967. It had 82 members and was to be elected every four years. In 1973 the Assembly was increased to 102 members.

Morocco and Mauritania both claimed large parts of the territory and from 1956 onwards a Moroccan-backed guerrilla movement fought against the Spanish authorities. A northern strip of Spanish Sahara was ceded to Morocco in 1958 and Ifni was returned in 1969. In 1976 the Spanish withdrew from the territory, which by agreement was divided between Morocco and Mauritania. A Saharan independence movement, Polisario, began a guerrilla war against both the occupying Moroccan and Mauritanian forces and proclaimed a Saharan Arab Democratic Republic. In 1979 Mauritania withdrew from the southern part of the territory, which was then occupied by the army of Morocco.

SUDAN (ANGLO-EGYPTIAN SUDAN until 1955)

The Sudan was an Anglo-Egyptian condominium established in 1899. The Anglo-Egyptian Treaty of 1936 confirmed a joint administration under a British governor-general. Britain effectively controlled the territory.

In 1944 an Advisory Council was established for northern Sudan. It was composed of 18 Sudanese elected or nominated from the provincial councils that already existed in the six northern provinces, eight other Sudanese nominated by the Governor-General, and two members elected by the Chamber of Commerce.

Executive and Legislative Councils were set up in 1944. The Governor-General's Council ceased to exist and was superseded by the Executive Council of 12–18 members, of whom half had to be Sudanese. A Sudanese chief minister was appointed; the Governor-General retained the power of veto. The Legislative Assembly represented the whole of the Sudan, with 52 members elected directly and indirectly to represent the north and 13 members elected by the southern provincial councils. The franchise was limited.

In 1952 the Self-Government Statute was passed. This established a Council of Ministers composed entirely of Sudanese and responsible to a two-chamber legislature; the legislative body consisted of a House of Representatives with 97 seats, of which 68 were elected directly, and the Senate, with 30 elected members and 20 members nominated by the Governor-General. The Governor-General acted on the advice of the Prime Minister and had reserve powers over defence and foreign affairs.

The new constitution was intended as transitional, leading to independence. A major problem was Egypt's claim to the Sudan and its refusal to accept constitutional advancement for the territory. Political changes in Egypt in 1952 led to the Anglo-Egyptian Agreement of 1953, which guaranteed Sudan's right to self-determination. Another problem for the Sudan was the provinces of the south, which under British administration had for years been treated separately from the northern provinces; many southerners demanded a federal government. In 1955 a revolt broke out in the southern provinces and this has continued virtually ever since.

In 1956 the Sudan became an independent republic. A transitional constitution was introduced which continued the parliamentary system but transferred the Governor-General's powers to a Supreme Commission of five Sudanese, including one southerner. A military coup took over power and suspended the constitution in 1958. A 12-man Supreme Council of the Armed Forces became the supreme constitutional authority, with Gen. Abboud as President; a seven-member Council of Ministers headed government departments. Gen. Abboud resigned as President in 1964 and his place was taken by a five-member Council of Sovereignty; the Supreme Council was replaced by a civilian cabinet. In 1965 parliamentary government was reintroduced, with a president elected by the Constituent Assembly.

A second army coup in 1969 suspended the constitution and placed government in the hands of a 10-man Revolutionary Council and a cabinet of 21 members. In 1973 a new constitution with an executive president was introduced; a 304-member National People's Assembly was to be elected every four years, with up to 10 per cent of its members appointed by the President. A regional constitution for the southern Sudan provided for a regional executive headed by a president and a 60-member Regional People's Assembly responsible for a wide range of local affairs.

A military coup occurred in April 1985 and the constitution was suspended. Power was transferred in a civilian régime in May 1986 following multi-party elections to a 301-member constituent assembly which was changed with preparing a new constitution. A 5-member Supreme Council headed the state. Constitutional development was held up by conflicting views on the Southern question and the place of Islamic law.

SWAZILAND

Swaziland was a British protectorate administered by a high commissioner who had power to make laws by proclamation. The High Commissioner was represented in the territory by a resident commissioner. Native administration was in the hands of chiefs and their councils; ultimate authority in native affairs lay with the National Council, or Libandla, and an inner or privy council, the Liqoqo. The Resident Commissioner was advised by the Council through the paramount chief, the Ngwenyama, and by a special standing committee in his dealings with Swazi affairs.

In 1950 the traditional system was reformed with the creation of a Swazi National Treasury and also a High Court and lower African courts. A European Advisory Council (created 1921) consisted of elected representatives of the small European community to advise on European affairs.

In 1963 a new constitution established an Executive Council of three *ex officio* members and five elected members presided over by the British-appointed Commissioner; a 24-member Legislative Council was also created, composed of 16 elected members, five of whom had to be white, and eight nominated members. The Legislative Council had powers of legislation over minerals, and mineral ownership was formally vested in the Ngwenyama on behalf of the Swazi nation.

In 1967 the country achieved internal self-government as a protected state with the Ngwenyama as King and head of state. The legislature was a House of Assembly of 24 elected and six nominated members, and a Senate composed of 12 members, six elected by the House of Assembly and six appointed by the King. The House of Assembly was elected by universal adult suffrage. Swaziland became an independent kingdom in 1968.

In 1973 the King assumed supreme power and repealed the constitution. In 1977 he announced the abolition of the system of parliamentary government and its replacement by traditional tribal institutions known as Tinkhundla.

A new constitution of 1978, based on traditional authorities, endorsed the power of the king. The two-chamber parliament (Libandla) comprises a House of Assembly with 50 members, and a 20-member Senate. Members of both chambers are elected from each traditional authority while the king appoints 10 members to each house. The function of parliament is to advise the king.

TANGANYIKA/TANZANIA

Tanganyika came under effective British control in 1919 and was administered as a League of Nations mandate. A governor headed the administration, assisted by an Executive Council of nominated members. In 1945 the Legislative Council (established 1926) was enlarged to seven official, eight *ex officio* and up to 14 unofficial members (seven Europeans, four Africans, three Asians). The League of Nations agreement was replaced by the United Nations trusteeship in 1946.

In 1948 the member system was introduced into the Executive Council – that is to say, each department of government was the responsibility of one member of the council. A speaker was appointed to the Legislative Council in 1953.

The constitution of 1953 provided for 31 official members and 30 unofficial in the Legislative Council, the latter being 10 Africans, 10 Asians and 10 Europeans, all nominated after consultation with the bodies they represented. The members of the Executive Council with responsibility for departments became ministers in 1957. The first elections to the Legislative Council were held in 1955–9; each constituency elected one African, one Asian and one European member. Voters were all over 21 with an educational or property qualification. Unofficial members were appointed as ministers from 1959. The tripartite system of voting ended in 1959 and in the elections of the following year for the 71-member Legislative Council 50 seats were open to members of any race, 11 were reserved for Asians, and 10 for Europeans.

The constitution of 1960 provided for an elected majority in the Legislative Council and ministers responsible to parliament. In 1961 internal self-government was introduced, with the withdrawal of official members from the Council of Ministers and restriction of the powers of the Governor. The National Assembly had 71 members elected on a common roll and some nominated members. Full independence was attained in December 1961, when the trusteeship agreement with the UN came to an end. A republican constitution with the President as head of state was adopted in 1962. In 1964 Zanzibar joined Tanganyika to form the united republic of Tanzania.

An interim constitution for Tanzania was adopted in 1965. It provided for a National Assembly of 107 elected members from Tanganyika, 10 appointed members, 15 members elected by the Assembly after nomination by various national interests, 20 regional commissioners, up to 32 members of the Zanzibar Revolutionary Council, and up to 20 other Zanzibari members appointed by the President after consultation with the President of Zanzibar. The number of members elected from Tanganyika was later reduced to 96. There is only one political party. In 1977 a permanent constitution was adopted; it is an amended version of the 1965 draft constitution.

The Revolutionary Council of Zanzibar adopted a separate constitution in 1979. By amendment to the Tanzanian constitution in 1984 the powers of the 231-member National Assembly were increased.

TOGO

Togo was a former German colony administered by France as a League of Nations mandate and then, after 1946, as a trust territory of the United Nations. By the constitution of the Fourth Republic Togo was designated an associated territory ruled by a commissioner and separate from the Federation of French West Africa. A territorial assembly was established with powers over the budget; in 1952 it consisted of 30 members elected by a single electoral roll. Togo was represented in the French National Assembly by one deputy, in the Council of the Republic by two senators, and in the Assembly of the French Union by one member.

By statute in 1955 Togo became an autonomous republic within the French Union. The Legislative Assembly was elected by universal adult suffrage and had considerable power over internal affairs; there was an elected executive presided over by a prime minister responsible to the legislature. These changes were promulgated in a constitution approved by referendum in 1956.

In 1960 the trusteeship was ended and Togo became an independent republic with a provisional constitution. A new constitution of 1961 established an executive president, elected for seven years, and a weak National Assembly. A military coup in 1963 suspended the constitution. The same year another constitution was promulgated, which provided for an executive president elected for five years and a weak National Assembly.

A second army coup in 1967 suspended the constitution. A committee of National Reconciliation was established and Colonel Eyadéma became a plebiscitary president with executive and legislative powers heading a government composed of army officers and civilians.

The 1979 constitution, approved by referendum, provides for an executive president elected by adult universal suffrage for seven years. The President appoints the Council of Ministers. The National Assembly has 77 members (increased from 67 in 1985) who are elected for a period of five years.

TUNISIA

Tunisia became a French protectorate in 1881. Although there were indigenous institutions under the Bey of Tunis, effective executive power was by the decrees of 1943–4 exercised through the French Resident-General.

In 1945 a Legislative Assembly in which European settlers and Tunisians were equally represented was established; the government of the protectorate comprised six Tunisian ministers and six French directors. The powerful settler lobby wanted the system of co-sovereignty under French control to continue, while the Tunisian nationalists demanded internal autonomy and the restoration of sovereignty.

In 1951 the French established a Tunisian cabinet headed by a prime minister. Settler opposition to this led to French repression of the Tunisian government and an insurrection among the nationalists from 1952 to 1955. In 1954 the French promised internal autonomy, which was granted in 1955. The country was administered by a high commissioner through an elected Constituent Assembly of 98 members. In 1956 Tunisia became an independent state; the Constituent Assembly deposed the Bey and a republic was proclaimed in 1957, with Habib Bourguiba as executive president.

Under the constitution promulgated in 1959 the country is ruled by an executive president and a National Assembly, elected simultaneously for five years. The President is assisted by a Council of State and also by an Economic and Social Council; the National Assembly has 90 members and meets for two sessions of not more than three months each year.

UGANDA

The territory was a British protectorate administered by a governor. Native rulers with rights regulated by treaty had some powers over their subjects; the province of Buganda was recognised as a native kingdom under its Kabaka, who was assisted by a council of ministers and an assembly, the Lukiiko.

In 1946 the Executive Council consisted of the Governor plus seven official members and one nominated unofficial member; the Legislative Council consisted of nine official and nine nominated unofficial members, including three Africans. The Legislative Council was enlarged at various times from 1949 to 1954 and by that date included 14 Africans elected from the newly formed district councils and the Lukiiko. A constitution introduced in 1955 provided for ministers in the Executive Council.

In 1958 the Legislative Council was given a majority elected on an extended franchise, and the Executive Council became a Council of Ministers with a non-official majority. In 1961 internal self-government was introduced with federal status for Buganda. There was a National Assembly entirely elected on universal adult suffrage, and full responsible government. The Governor retained responsibility for external affairs, defence and security pending full independence, which followed in 1962. In 1963 the constitution was amended to provide Buganda with its own head of state; at the same time the Governor-General was replaced by a president elected by the National Assembly for a five-year term.

In early 1966 Prime Minister Milton Obote suspended the constitution and assumed all executive powers; a few weeks later he abrogated the constitution. In 1967 Uganda became a republic with executive authority vested in the President assisted by a cabinet of ministers. The power and status of all the kingdoms were reduced and the country was organised into four regions, one of which was Buganda.

In 1971 President Obote was overthrown by Gen. Amin, who set up a military government. In 1978 President Amin announced the formation of an advisory United National Forum; it was to consist of about 1000 members and only to meet occasionally. In 1979 President Amin was overthrown following a Tanzanian-backed invasion of Uganda. The victorious Uganda National Liberation Front established a provisional government under President Lule. He was dismissed after a few weeks and President Binaisa assumed power, with executive functions in the hands of a National Consultative Council.

Following elections President Milton Obote came into office in 1980.

A military coup occurred in July 1985 and the constitution was suspended and the 126-member National Assembly dissolved. A Military Council assumed executive authority.

ZAÏRE (BELGIAN CONGO until 1960; then REPUBLIC OF THE CONGO until 1971)

The administration of the Belgian Congo was based upon the Charte Coloniale of 1908, which centralised executive and legislative control in the hands of the Governor-General subject to the Minister of Colonies. The Council of Government was reorganised in 1947 with a non-official majority, but its functions remained purely advisory. By 1951 the Council included eight African members representing African interests. By 1955 the Council consisted of the Governor-General, the Vice- Governor-General, the six provincial governors, the commander of the *Force publique*, up to six unofficial notables nominated by the Governor-General, 16 members representing various commercial and settler associations, and the eight Africans representing African interests. A standing committee of the Council held quarterly meetings. Each of the six provinces was administered by a governor assisted by an advisory provincial council.

Until 1958 the only elections held in the country were those on a limited franchise for municipal governments. Following serious riots in the Congo in 1959 the Belgians announced constitutional reforms. An interim constitution of 1960 proposed a federal parliamentary government with a two-chamber legislature, the House of Representatives based upon direct and proportional representation, and a Senate with equal representation from each of the six provinces. The President was to be elected by a congress of parliament; the Prime Minister was to be appointed by the President and his cabinet had to include at least one minister from each province. Provincial assemblies were also proposed.

The Belgian Congo became independent in June 1960. Shortly after independence serious disturbances broke out in various parts of the country and the *Force publique* mutinied. In September 1960 the Army announced that it was 'neutralising' all politicians; it installed a College of Commissioners to govern the country. The province of Katanga attempted to secede and the Congo went into a constitutional crisis with rival claimants to central government authority. The constitution of 1962 provided for a constitutional president, a prime minister, and a federal structure of 21 provinces with local and restricted powers. President Kasavubu dissolved parliament and suspended the constitution in 1963 and granted the Prime Minister full legislative powers.

A new constitution was introduced in 1964 which reduced the powers of the legislature but increased those of the head of state. A military coup led by

Gen. Mobutu in 1965 briefly suspended the National Assembly and then governed through it by presidential decree. A national referendum in 1967 approved a new constitution, the third since independence, which was further revised in 1971, 1974, and 1977, and promulgated in 1978. This provided for an executive president elected for seven years, and a single-chamber National Legislative Council of 268 deputies. The President was to be leader of the sole political party, the Mouvement Populaire de la Révolution (MPR), and would be assisted by a National Executive Council consisting of state commissioners, who would also be heads of government departments.

ZAMBIA (NORTHERN RHODESIA until 1964)

In 1945 the British protectorate of Northern Rhodesia was administered by a governor assisted by an Executive Council of five official and three nominated unofficial members. The Legislative Council consisted of nine official members, eight elected members, three unofficial members appointed to represent African interests, and two nominated unofficial members. By 1948 the number of unofficial members on the Executive Council had been increased to four or five and the Governor was obliged to regard the unanimous advice of the unofficial members as the advice of the Executive, even if the officials disagreed. He had either to accept it or to refer his rejection to the Secretary of State. In 1949 two unofficial members held ministerial portfolios.

In 1953 Northern Rhodesia became part of the Federation of Rhodesia and Nyasaland despite widespread African protests. Britain retained ultimate responsibility for external affairs, while defence, immigration, European education, European agriculture and health were transferred to a new federal legislature. Northern Rhodesia continued as a protectorate, and its government retained control over African affairs, local government, housing, police, internal security, industrial relations, lands, mining and irrigation.

By 1955 the Legislative Council had been enlarged to 26 members. It consisted of eight official and 12 elected members, plus two nominated by the Governor to represent African interests, and four Africans elected by the African Representative Council (established 1945–6). The constitution of 1960 was an attempt by the British Secretary of State to balance power between the African majority and the small white minority. It provided for a Legislative Council with an elected majority – 12 members elected by European constituencies, six by special African constituencies, two to seats reserved for Africans and two to seats reserved for Europeans. There was a franchise on a common roll with qualifications. Ministers were to be appointed to the Executive Council on the advice of the lower house.

The federation come to an end in 1963. Northern Rhodesia became the independent republic of Zambia in 1964, after ten months of internal self-government. The constitution provided for a president, to be elected for the first term by the Legislative Assembly but thereafter by the electorate at each general election. There is a single-chamber parliament, the National Assembly of 110 members; the government is led in the Assembly by the Vice-President, appointed by the President. Since 1972 Zambia has been a one-party state.

A new constitution was introduced in 1973. This provided for an executive president elected by popular vote; the President would appoint a prime minister. The Central Committee of the ruling United National Independence Party (UNIP) has greater powers than the cabinet; of its 28 members 25 are elected at the UNIP General Conference, and three are nominated by the President. The cabinet is appointed by the President. The National Assembly consists of 125 elected members, all drawn from UNIP, and 10 appointed by the President. There is also a House of Chiefs, with 27 members representing each province of the country.

ZANZIBAR

Zanzibar was a sultanate and a British protectorate administered by a British Resident. Executive and Legislative Councils were established in 1926. The Executive Council, of which the British Resident was chairman, continued as an entirely official body until 1956; the Legislative Council in 1945 consisted of three ex officio and five official members, with six unofficial members appointed to represent the various communities. Arabs received the largest representation in the Legislative Council, although they did not constitute the majority of the island population. In 1956 the membership of the Executive Council was altered to allow more Zanzibari representatives; the Legislative Council was expanded and six of its 12 unofficial members were to be elected.

A new constitution of 1960 opened the franchise to women on the same qualifications of property and education as applied to men. The Legislative Council now had 22 elected members, three ex officio and up to five nominated members, and was presided over by a speaker. The Executive Council had three ex officio members and five unofficial members, including a chief minister. In 1962 the Executive Council was replaced by a Council of Ministers, the franchise was widened by the removal of property and educational qualifications, and the official members were removed from both the Executive and the Legislative Councils. Full ministerial government was introduced, as a preliminary to independent status, achieved in December 1963, when the Legislative Council was replaced by a National Assembly.

In 1964 the sultanate was abolished by a revolution and the People's Republic of Zanzibar established. Zanzibar joined with Tanganyika to form a united republic which was named Tanzania; it retained its own executive and legislature. The First Vice-President of the united republic is the head of the executive in Zanzibar under the title of President of Zanzibar.

ZIMBABWE (SOUTHERN RHODESIA until 1965; RHODESIA until 1978; ZIMBABWE–RHODESIA, 1978–80)

By the constitution of 1923 Southern Rhodesia became a self-governing colony with internal autonomy except in legislation affecting the African population and mining royalties. A governor appointed by the Crown administered the country through an Executive Council drawn from and responsible to the single-chamber Legislative Assembly, which in 1946 had 30 members, all white and elected on a restricted franchise.

The Federation of Rhodesia and Nyasaland was formed in 1953. Britain retained ultimate responsibility for external affairs; defence, immigration, European education, European agriculture and health were transferred to the new federal legislature. Salisbury, the capital of Southern Rhodesia, became the federal capital. Southern Rhodesia continued to have the status of a self-governing colony. It retained control over African affairs, local government, housing, police, internal security, industrial relations, lands, mining and irrigation.

The constitution of 1961 transferred to Southern Rhodesia some powers still vested in the British government and included the Declaration of Rights. It created the Governor's Council, consisting of the Prime Minister and up to 11 ministers, to replace the Executive Council. The constitution stated that certain of its basic provisions might not be altered without majority approval by each of the four main races voting separately in referendum, *or* the approval of the British government, which could refuse to give a decision if it was thought a referendum desirable. The only reserved powers remaining related to the Sovereign and the Governor, international obligations and loans under Colonial Stock Acts. The Legislative Assembly was enlarged to 65 members – 50 seats reserved to Europeans voting on the upper roll, and 15 to Africans on the lower roll.

In 1963 the Federation came to an end. Southern Rhodesia reverted to the status of a self-governing colony but took additional powers over matters previously transferred to the federal government in 1953.

In 1965 the Prime Minister of Rhodesia declared a state of emergency, overriding normal constitutional safeguards, and issued a unilateral declaration of independence. His government was dismissed by the Governor, but continued to carry on effective internal administration. The British government reasserted its formal responsibility for Rhodesia and passed an enabling bill which gave it power to deal with the situation by orders-in-council. In 1969 a new constitution was passed in Rhodesia which declared the country to be a republic. The constitution further provided for a president elected for five years and a bicameral legislature consisting of a House of Assembly and a Senate. The House of Assembly had 66 members, 50 elected by a white roll and 16 by an African roll; the Senate had 23 members. The British government declared the constitution illegal. Attempts to reach an agreement (which would allow legal independence under agreed conditions) were made in 1966, 1968, 1970–72, 1974, 1975 and 1976.

African nationalist forces began a guerrilla war in north-east Rhodesia in 1972. From 1973 onwards the white government under Ian Smith discussed a possible internal settlement with other African nationalist leaders. Negotiations failed and the war escalated. In 1977 both the Smith government and the guerrilla leaders rejected an Anglo-American proposal for a constitutional settlement. In the following year a transitional government was formed by the white ruling party and African nationalists not involved in the guerrilla war. This provided for executive power to be shared between the white Prime Minister and three African ministers, who would take turns to chair the Executive Council. The Council of Ministers was equally divided between European and African ministers, who were similarly to share the role of chairman. The state was renamed Zimbabwe–Rhodesia and the transitional government set about drafting a constitution on the basis of majority rule and adult suffrage.

The constitution of 1979 provided for a 100-seat House of Assembly; 28 seats were reserved for whites, 20 being elected and eight chosen by the 92 elected members of the House from among white members of the former House of Assembly. The Senate consisted of 30 members, 10 white and 10 black senators elected by the House of Assembly, and 10 senators elected by chiefs. In May 1979 Bishop Muzorewa became Prime Minister of Zimbabwe–Rhodesia. His government failed to receive international recognition or to bring about the lifting of economic sanctions, and the guerrilla war in the country intensified. These events forced the transitional government to agree to constitutional talks in London with the British government; the nationalist groups in the guerrilla war also agreed to participate in the talks.

At the Lancaster House talks in London it was finally agreed by all parties that Britain would resume responsibility for Rhodesia and supervise elections to produce a government which would then rapidly lead the country to legal independence. A British governor was installed in Salisbury late in 1979. Under the constitution agreed in London the new state of Zimbabwe was to be a republic with a president as constitutional head of state. Executive power was to rest with the Prime Minister and Executive Council, responsible to the House of Assembly of 100 members. 20 of the seats in the House were to be reserved for white electors, the rest having no racial restrictions. There was to be a Senate of 40 members chosen by various electoral colleges.

Elections were held in early 1980 and the nationalist groups which had been involved in the guerrilla war won an overwhelming majority. In April, Robert Mugabe became Prime Minister at the head of a coalition government and Zimbabwe was declared an independent republic within the Commonwealth. In 1987, the Presidency became an Executive Presidency (with Robert Mugabe as first Executive President). The office of Prime Minister was abolished.

5 POLITICAL PARTIES

ALGERIA

Front de Libération Nationale (FLN)
Founded in November 1954, it led the movement for independence from France. Dedicated to socialism, non-alignment and pan-Arabism, it is the only party with legal status. Since independence the party has been split many times over economic and ideological policies. The party congress nominates candidates to be president of the republic, and the FLN organises mass movements for women and young people.

Unofficial and illegal opposition comes from:

Front des Forces Socialistes (FFS)
This organisation led the Kabylia revolt against President Ben Bella in 1963–4.

Organisation Clandestine de la Révolution Algérienne (OCRA)
Founded in 1966, the OCRA supported the imprisoned Ben Bella as lawful president.

Mouvement Démocratique du Renouveau Algérien (MDRA)
Founded in 1967, the MDRA supported Krim Belkacem, who was implicated in an anti-government conspiracy of that year.

Parti de l'Avant Garde Socialiste (PAGS)
Founded in 1965, the PAGS consisted of communist and Marxist critics of the FLN. Formerly called the Organisation de la Résistance Populaire, it was allied with the French Communist Party. All its leaders were imprisoned.

Parti Communiste Algérien (PCA)
Banned in 1963, the PCA works underground and through Algerians overseas.

Mouvement pour la démocratie en Algerie (MDA)
Formed by a group of exiles in France in 1984. It aims to establish a pluralist democracy.

Islamic Salvation Front, in national and local elections in mid-1990, gained majorities in 32 out of 48 provinces.

WESTERN SAHARA

Frente Popular para La Liberacion de Sakiet el Hamra y Rio de Oro (Polisario)
Founded in 1973, the Polisario has fought for the independence of the
Western Sahara, first from Spain and later from Morocco and Mauritania.
Based in Algeria, it forms the government of the self-proclaimed Saharan
Arab Democratic Republic.

ANGOLA

Political institutions inside Angola were those of metropolitan Portugal until
independence.

Movimento Popular de Libertação de Angola (MPLA)
Formed in 1975 by the merger of several militant nationalist groups, the
MPLA was based in Zambia and led by Agostinho Neto. In the civil war
which followed independence from Portugal in 1974 the MPLA was victorious and it now forms the government. A new name, the Marxist–Leninist
Angola Workers' Party was proposed in 1977. All other parties have been
banned.

Frente Nacional de Libertação de Angola (FNLA)
Formed in 1962 by the merger of two earlier groups, the FNLA established a
government-in-exile under Roberto Holden in Kinshasa, Zaïre. Active in
northern Angola, it was strongly anti-communist. Inactive since 1984.

União Nacional para a Independencia Total de Angola (UNITA)
Formed in 1966, UNITA was based in south-eastern Angola. Since the
MPLA's victory in 1976, UNITA has continued a guerrilla war against the
Angolan government and has received support from South Africa, and from
the USA.

Frente de Libertação de Enclave de Cabinda (FLEC)
Formed in 1963, the FLEC fights a guerrilla war in Cabinda from bases in
Zaïre, but it has been plagued by repeated splits in its leadership.

Movimento para a Libertação de Cabinda (Molica)
An offshoot of the FLEC.

BENIN (formerly DAHOMEY)

Parti de la Révolution Populaire du Benin (PRPB)
Formed in 1975, the PRPB is the country's only legal party and has a
Marxist–Leninist programme.

Before 1975, political parties did not take firm root in the country, owing to government policies in successive periods of military rule. All political parties were banned in 1965, and the constitution of 1968 envisaged the establishment of a one-party political system.

Union pour le Renouveau du Dahomey (URD)
Formed in 1968, it organised support for the military-backed government of Émile Derlin Zinsou.

Front pour la Libération du Dahomey
The illegal opposition party, implicated in an abortive coup of 1977.

BOTSWANA

Botswana Democratic Party (BDP)
The ruling party of Sir Seretse Khama, it is the strongest party in Botswana, favouring close relations with South Africa and Western-style democracy.

Botswana Peoples' Party (BPP)
Until 1969 the principal minority party, advocating pan-Africanist policies and social democracy

Botswana National Front (BNF)
A left-wing pro-communist party formed after the 1965 elections, it polled the second largest number of votes in the 1969 and 1974 elections.

Botswana Independence Party (BIP)
Formed in 1965, the BIP is a small opposition party with similar policies to the BPP. Other small parties include the *Botswana Liberal Party* (formed 1983), and the *Botswana Progressive Union* (formed 1982).

BURKINA FASO (formerly UPPER VOLTA)

Union Démocratique Voltaique
Affiliated to the RDA (see Ivory Coast), the UDV was the dominant party until 1966, and from 1969 to 1974. Its support was strongest in the eastern and central regions. Revived in 1977, it was banned in 1983.

Groupement d'Action Populaire (GAP)
Active after 1977, the GAP organised support for President Lamizana.

Other parties active between 1977 and 1983 included the *Mouvement des Indépendants du Parti du Regroupement Africain* (MI–PRA), the *Union Nationale des Independants* (UNI) and the *Union Nationale pour la Défense de la Démocratie*.

The *Mouvement de Libération Nationale*, active between 1974 and 1977, later divided, part of it joining dissidents from other parties to form the *Union Progressiste Voltaique (UPV)*, the largest party, banned in 1983 after if had formed an alliance with a faction of the UDV.

The *Conseil national de la révolution (CNR)*, established in August 1983, contains three left-wing groups:

> *Ligue patriotique pour le développement (LIPAD)*, a pro-Soviet Marxist party formed in 1973,
> and
> the *Regroupement des officiers communistes (ROC)*, founded in 1983,
> and
> the *Union de la Lutte Communiste (ULC)*, formed in 1978.

BURUNDI

Parti de l'Unité et du Progrès National du Burundi (Uprona)
Formed before indepéndence, Uprona won the elections of 1961 and 1965 and became Burundi's only legal political party. Dominated by the Tutsi ruling tribe and by ex-President Micombero, the party stressed national unity with social and economic progress.

24 parties contested the pre-independence elections of 1961, but all are now banned. Unofficial opposition centres on:

Parti du Peuple (PP)
The party of the numerically dominant Hutu tribe, it was implicated in the abortive coup of 1965.

Parti Démocratique Chrétien (PDC)
A Tutsi party, it was discredited for its complicity in the assassination of Prime Minister Prince Louis Rwagasore in 1961.

CAMEROON

Union Nationale Camerounaise (UNC)
The one-party system of Western Cameroon was extended to Eastern Cameroon in 1966, when all parties merged to form the UNC. The party sponsors organisations of women, young people and trade unionists. Its policy is pan-Africanist and combines the encouragement of private initiative with a positive leading role for the state. In 1985 the UNC changed its name to the *Rassemblement démocratique du peuple camerounais* (RDPC).

Before 1966, the major parties were:

Union Camerounaise
Based in Eastern Cameroon.

Kamerun National Democratic Party
Founded in 1951 by Vice-President Foncha, it was based in the west of the country.

Kamerun United National Congress
Based in the west.

Kamerun People's Party
Based in the west.

After 1966, illegal opposition centred on

Union des Populations Camerounaises (UPC)
A pro-Chinese Communist group, banned in 1966 but active among Cameroon émigrés. The UPC operates from exile in Paris.

CAPE VERDE ISLANDS

Partido Africano da Independência da Guiné e Cabo Verde (PAIGC)
Founded in 1956 and based in Conakry, Guinea, the PAIGC was the liberation movement in Guinea-Bissau and the Cape Verde Islands until independence. The PAIGC seeks the reunion of Guinea-Bissau and the Cape Verde Islands and the Comisão National de Cabo Verde da PAIGC is the republic's only legal political party.

Following the 1980 coup in Guinea Bissau, which the government of Cape Verde opposed, the PAIGC changed its name to the *Partido Africano da Independência de Cabo Verde* (PAICV).

Independent Democratic Union of Cape Verde (UCID).
A group of emigrants based in Portugal and opposed to the PAICV regime.

CENTRAL AFRICAN REPUBLIC

Mouvement d'Évolution Social en Afrique Noire (MESAN)
Founded before independence by Barthélemy Boganda, the MESAN became the Central African Republic's single political party under the regime of President David Dacko. All other parties were banned in 1962. The new military government of 1966 under Col. J. B. Bokassa took over the MESAN as an instrument of political control and to rally support for Bokassa, who was crowned Emperor in 1977.

Rassemblement démocratique centrafricain (RDC)
Established in 1986 as the country's only legal party. An opposition alliance, the *Front Uni*, was subsequently formed, comprising the *Mouvement pour la libération du peuple centrafricain* (MLPC) and the *Front patriotique ouban-guien – Parti du Travail (FPO–PT)*, which aims to establish a democratic system.

CHAD

All political parties were banned in 1975.

Mouvement National pour la Révolution Culturelle et Sociale, formerly the *Parti Progressiste Tchadien (PPT)*
Founded in the late 1950s as the local division of the Ivory-Coast-based Rassemblement Démocratique Africain, the PPT was based among the Sara community in southern Chad. In 1962 the PPT became Chad's only legal political party, and the party adopted its new name in 1973.

Clandestine opposition parties of the Muslim north include *Parti National Africain; Union Nationale Tchadienne; Mouvement Socialiste Africain*. The *Mouvement Populaire pour la Libération du Tchad (Troisième Armée)* and the *Union Socialiste Tchadienne* (UST) were both formed in 1986.

Front de la Libération Nationale Tchadien (Frolinat)
Formed in 1966, Frolinat was the PPT government's major adversary in the civil war. In 1982 it won control of the country's government. In 1984 a faction of Frolinat formed the *Union Nationale pour l'Indépendence et la Révolution* (UNIR), under Hissène Habré.

Gouvernement d'Union Nationale de Transition (GUNT)
A coalition of opposition groups which controlled the national government from 1979 to 1982.

Front de la Libération Tchadienne (FLT)
Formerly part of the guerrilla opposition, the FLT supported the 1975 government.

Mouvement Démocratique pour la Renouvellement de Tchad (MDRT)
Formerly an opposition party based in Paris, the MDRT welcomed the 1975 government.

COMORO ISLANDS

Front National Uni (FNU)
Formed by the major opposition parties after independence, the FNU provided the government from 1975 until the coup of May 1978.

Union comorienne pour le progrès (Udzima)
Since 1982, the country's only legal party.

Mouvement de Libération Nationale des Comores (Helinocom)
Active against the French in the 1960s, it was led by Abdou Bakari Boina. Most opposition comes from groups operating in France including the FNUK–UNIKOM, a coalition of the *FNU des Komores* and the *Union des Komores*, the *Comité national de salut public*, and the *Union pour une République Démocratique des Comores* (URDC).
On Mayotte, which remains under French rule, the *Mouvement Populaire Mahorais* is the major party. It wants departmental status for the island.

CONGO

Parti Congolais du Travail (PCT), formerly the *Mouvement National Révolutionaire (MNR)*
Established by the then President Massemba-Débat, the MNR became the country's only legal party in 1963, devoted to a programme of 'scientific socialism'. A new name was adopted in 1969, after the army took power.

Opposition parties were banned in 1963, but until then the main parties were the *Union pour la Défense des Intérêts Africains* (UDIA, the party of ex-President Youlou) and the *Mouvement Socialist Africain (MSA)*.

CÔTE D'IVOIRE see IVORY COAST

DJIBOUTI

Rassemblement Populaire L'Indépendance (RPI)
The coalition which won the 1977 election, it comprises the *Front de la Libération de la Côte des Somalies (FCLS)*, which was founded in 1963 and from its base in Mogadishu, Somalia, fought for independence from France; and the *Ligue Populaire Africaine pour l'Indépendance (LPAI)*, which provides the major component of the government.

The LPAI was succeeded in 1979 by the *Rassemblement populaire pour le progrès* (RPP), which became the only legal party in 1981.

Mouvement pour la Libération de Djibouti (MLD)
Founded in 1964, the MLD is an illegal Afar party based in Ethiopia.

Union Nationale pour l'Indépendance (UNI)
Founded in 1975, the UNI is the major party of the Afar opposition. A breakaway group joined the RPI for the 1977 elections.

Mouvement Populaire de Libération (MPL)
Another Afar party, the MPL has a Marxist–Leninist policy.

In 1979 the MPL and UNI, both Afar-supported, formed the *Front démocratique pour la libération de Djibouti* (FDLD), based in Ethiopia.

Mouvement national djiboutien pour l'instauration de la démocratie (MNDID).
An opposition group operating from Ethiopia, formed in 1986, aiming to restore a multi-party democracy.

EGYPT

Arab Socialist Union (ASU)
Established in 1962 by President Nasser as the country's only legal political party, the ASU was charged with the safeguarding and development of Egypt's programme of Arab socialism. The party underwent reorganisation in 1968, and ASU membership rose to 5 million. The ASU lost its monopoly and its dominant position in 1976, and was dissolved in 1980.

The ASU was the successor to two other parties sponsored by Nasser, the National Liberation Rally and the National Union. All Egypt's old political parties were banned when the monarchy was destroyed in 1953.

Arab Socialist Party (ASP)
Founded in 1976, this centrist party supported President Sadat. It won 280 seats in the 1976 parliamentary elections.
The 1977 constitutional changes recognised four main parties: *National Democratic Party*;
Socialist Workers, founded in 1978, which forms the official opposition;
Liberal Socialists, founded in 1976, supporting private enterprise and liberalisation;
Union Progressive, founded in 1976.

In 1987 the *Socialist Workers* and the *Liberal Socialists* formed an electoral alliance with the previously-banned *Muslim Brotherhood*, founded in 1928 and active in anti-British protests in the 1940s.

New Wafd Party
A revival of the *Wafd Party* (*Wafd* = 'delegation') which led the nationalist

movement against Britain from 1919 to 1952, dominating Egyptian politics. It stood for independence from Britain and a constitutional monarchy, but pursued a pragmatic policy of compromise. Revived, and given legal recognition in 1984, this right-wing party draws support from a broad base.

EQUATORIAL GUINEA

Since the coup of 1979, no political parties have been recognised.

Partido Unico Nacional de los Trabajadores (PUNT)
Established in 1970 through the merger of all existing parties, the PUNT was the governing party.

Alianza Nacional de Restoracion Democratica (ANRD)
Founded in 1974 and based in Geneva, the ANRD forms the opposition to the present regime and publishes *La Voz del Pueblo*.

The political parties which proliferated before and just after independence were:

Movimento de Union Nacional de Guinea Ecuatorial (MUNGE)
Founded in 1964, the MUNGE represented the traditionalist right wing of the mainland people, and was in government between 1964 and 1968.

Movimento Nacional de Liberacion de la Guinea Ecuatorial (Monalige)
Formerly part of the nationalist guerrilla movement, based on the mainland, Monalige helped form the first independent government but soon fell foul of President Francisco Macias Nguema.

Idea Popular de la Guinea Ecuatorial (IPCE)
A third mainland party, the IPCE stood on the left wing.

Union Democratica Fernandina (UDF)
Based in Fernando Po, the UDF wanted loose federation with Rio Muni.

Union Bubi
The second party of Fernando Po, it helped form the first independent government.

Exiled groups seeking the restoration of democracy include:

Convergencia Social Democrática (CSD), formed in 1984 and based in France;

Co-ordinating Board of Opposition Forces, formed in 1983 representing five exiled groups, and based in Spain.

ETHIOPIA and ERITREA

No political parties were allowed to exist before 1974 under the Haile Selassie government.

Mesan (Me'ei Sone = All-Ethiopia Socialist Movement)
This party received strong trade union support, and support from the military government (*Dergue*) until it was dissolved in 1978.

Ethiopian People's Revolutionary Party (EPRP)
Formed in 1972. A Marxist group calling for a return to civilian rule, supported by the *Dergue* until 1978. Its Ethiopian People's Revolutionary Army organised urban guerrillas in opposition to the government.

Ethiopian Democratic Union (EDU)
Founded in 1975, the EDU is a conservative, anti-Marxist party which has engaged in guerrilla resistance to the *Dergue*.

Abyot Seded ('Revolutionary Flame')
The main government-supported party between 1978 and 1984. The party drew much of its support from junior officers, and was strongly pro-Soviet.

Workers' Party of Ethiopia (WPE)
Created in 1984 by the government's Commission for Organising the Party of the Working People of Ethiopia (COPWE), which was formed in 1979. Led by Lt-Col. Mengistu Haile Mariam, this Marxist–Leninist movement is the only legal party.

A number of separatist organisations have been in conflict with the government since 1974:

Afar Liberation Front (ALF)
A guerrilla group operating in the Hararge and Wollo regions.

Eritrean People's Liberation Front (EPLF)
Formed in 1970, this Marxist–Leninist group is a breakaway from the *Eritrean Liberation Front*, founded in 1958. Led by Ramadan Mohammed Nur, the EPLF draws both Christian and Muslim support, and organises the *Eritrean People's Liberation Army* of over 25 000 men.

Eritrean Unified National Council (EUNC)
Formed in 1985 by the fusion of the *Eritrean Liberation Front*, which maintains the (Muslim) *Eritrean Liberation Army*, the *People's Liberation Forces – Unified Organisation* and the *People's Liberation Forces – Revolutionary Committee*.

Oromo Liberation Front (OLF)
Active among the Oromo people of Shoa region, with Somali military aid.

Somali Abo Liberation Front
Operates in Bale region with Somali military help.

Western Somali Liberation Front (WSLF)
Formed in 1975, the Mogadishu-based WSLF seeks to unite the Ogaden region with Somalia. It maintains up to 3000 guerrillas who receive help from the Somali military.

Tigre People's Liberation Front (TPLF)
A Marxist separatist group, founded in 1975, which operates in the Tigre region.

Eritrean Liberation Parties
A united front launched in 1977 to embrace the *Eritrean Liberation Front (ELF)*, which was founded in 1958, maintains the (Muslim) Eritrean Liberation Army, and is based in Beirut, Lebanon; the *Eritrean People's Liberation Front (EPLF)*, which was founded in 1970 as a Marxist party with Muslim and Christian support, and maintains the Eritrean People's Liberation Army; and the *Eritrean Liberation Front – Popular Liberation Forces (ELF–PLF)*, a breakaway from the EPLF.

Somali Abo Liberation Front
Another separatist group.

Somali Fatherland Liberation Front (SFLF)
Founded in 1975 as the Western Somali Liberation Front, the SFLF is based in Mogadishu, Somalia. It failed in its attempt in 1977–8 to unite the Ogaden region with Somalia.

Tigre People's Liberation Front (TPLF)
A separatist movement in one province.

GABON

Parti Démocratique Gabonais (PDG)
Founded in 1968 by President Bongo as Gabon's only legal political party, the PDG was the successor to the ruling Bloc Démocratique Gabonais (BDG). This itself was part of the Rassemblement Démocratique Africain, based in the Ivory Coast. The BDG and PDG have been consistently pro-French and stand for no protest or dissent in the country.

Clandestine opposition centred on:

Union Démocratique et Sociale Gabonaise (UDSG)

An affiliate of the Senegal-based Parti du Regroupment Africain, the UDSG was banned in 1964 and its leader imprisoned.

Mouvement de la Révolution Gabonaise (MRG)
This party opposed the PDG in the 1967 elections.

Mouvement de redressement national (MORENA)
Founded in 1981, MORENA is based in France and seeks to create a multi-party democracy. In 1985, it formed a government-in-exile. Although it was allowed to put forward a presidential candidate in the 1986 election, it was not allowed to campaign on his behalf.

THE GAMBIA

People's Progressive Party (PPP)
Founded in 1958, it merged with the Gambia Congress Party in 1968. From 1965 it was the governing party and advocated closer economic and cultural links with Senegal.

National Convention Party (NCP)
Formed in 1975, and advocating a fairer society with a more equal distribution of wealth.

People's Democratic Organisation for Independence and Socialism (PDOIS)
Founded in 1986, this Marxist-inclined party advocates economic and political independence for the country.

Gambia People's Party (GPP)
Formed in 1986 by former PPP members, the GPP is socialist in outlook.

Other parties include

Gambia Socialist Revolutionary Party (GSRP)
Movement for Justice in Africa – The Gambia (MOJA–G)
(both Marxist and formed in 1980; since banned)
United Party, founded in 1952,
Progressive People's Alliance, founded in 1968 and
National Liberation Party, founded in 1975.

GHANA

In the years 1966–9, 1972–9 and since the coup of 1981, political parties have been banned.

United Gold Coast Convention (UGCC)
Formed in 1947 by the intelligentsia, notably the lawyer Dr J. B. Danquah. The first political organisation to talk in practical terms of self-government 'in the shortest possible time'. Kwame N. Nkrumah was briefly the general secretary. Defeated in the general election of 1951 and dissolved in the next year.

Convention People's Party (CPP)
Formed in 1949 by Kwame N. Nkrumah, Prime Minister and later President of Ghana, the CPP became the country's only legal political party in 1964. Its policies were a mixture of 'socialism', nationalism and pan-Africanism.

National Liberation Movement (NLM)
An Ashanti-based party formed in 1954 which demanded a 'federation' for Ghana.

Northern People's Party (NPP)
Formed in 1954 to represent the interests of the northern part of the country.

United Party (UP)
Established in 1956 by a merger of various opposition parties, principally the Northern People's Party and the NLM. It opposed Nkrumah's government but was effectively banned when Ghana became a one-party state.

Progress Party (PP)
Founded in 1969 and led by Dr Busia, it won the 1969 elections and formed the government until 1972.

National Alliance of Liberals (NAL)
The main opposition party in the 1969 elections.

(Three other parties contested the 1969 elections.)

Justice Party
Founded in 1970 by the merger of the NAL with the United Nationalist Party and the All People's Republican Party.

The following parties contested the 1979 elections:

Action Congress Party (ACP)
Popular Front Party (PFP)
Social Democratic Front (SDF)
People's National Party (PNP)
Won the election with 71 out of 140 seats, forming the government under Dr Limann.

United National Convention (UNC)
Formed a coalition with the PNP until 1980.

All People's Party (APP)
Formed in 1981 as a coalition of parties opposed to the PNP.

Ghana Democratic Movement (GDM)
Formed in 1983, this group is based in London and advocates a return to democratic party politics. Its leader, Joseph H. Mensah, was arrested in the USA in 1985 on charges of attempting to buy arms for the opponents of the military government.

GUINEA

Parti Démocratique de Guinée (PDG)
Founded in 1947 as an affiliate of the Rassemblement Démocratique Africain, the PDG was first based on Guinea's well organised, pro-communist trade-union movement. It was the country's only legal political party. Led by President Sekou Touré, it was organised on democratic centralist principles with an array of affiliated mass organisations. The PDG was dissolved following the military coup in 1984.

Front de Libération Nationale de Guinée
Formed by Guinean exiles in 1966, it was based in France, Senegal and the Ivory Coast.

Among the exiled opposition groups are:

Mouvement pour la renouveau en Guinée, formerly the *Union de peuple guinéen* (UPG), and the
Organisation unifiée pour la libération de la Guinée (OULG), which operates from the Ivory Coast.

GUINEA-BISSAU

Partido Africano da Independencia da Guiné e Cabo Verde (PAIGC)
Formed in 1956 and based in Conakry, Guinea, the PAIGC undertook political campaigning and guerrilla struggle for the liberation of Guinea-Bissau and the Cape Verde Islands from Portuguese rule. It is the country's only legal party and stands for eventual reunion with the Cape Verde Islands.

Front de Lutte pour l'Indépendance de la Guinée (Fling)
A rival to the PAIGC, it was based in Dakar, Senegal, during the war of independence.

Guinea-Bissau Bofata Resistance Movement
Formed in 1986, this Lisbon-based opposition group seeks a pluralist democracy.

IVORY COAST (CÔTE D'IVOIRE)

Parti Démocratique de la Côte d'Ivoire (PDCI)
Formed in 1946 as the main affiliate of the Rassemblement Démocratique Africain, the PDCI has been the country's only political party since independence. Led by President Houphouët-Boigny, the party was reorganised after an abortive coup in 1963 and takes a pro-French political stance.

Rassemblement Démocratique Africain (RDA)
Established in 1944, the RDA was an international political party with branches in most of France's former colonies in West Africa. Based in the Ivory Coast, its leading light was Félix Houphouët-Boigny.

KENYA

Kenya African Union (KAU)
Formed in 1944, this was the first African nationalist party, supported chiefly by the educated population on a pan-tribal basis. Its economic aims were radical, and it was banned in 1953 during the Mau Mau emergency.

Kenya African National Union (KANU)
Formed in 1960 and based on Kikuyu support, KANU later absorbed the non-Kikuyu Kenya African Democratic Union (KADU) and the African People's Party (APP). Its leaders, the late Jomo Kenyatta and Tom Mboya, stressed 'African socialism', racial harmony and centralised government. In 1982 KANU became Kenya's only legal political party.

Kenya People's Union (KPU)
The main opposition party, banned in 1969, was led by Oginga Odinga. Formed in 1966 by former members of KANU, the KPU was socialist, anti-Western and based on support from the Luo tribe.

LESOTHO

Basutoland National Party (BNP)
Formed in 1959 and led by Chief Leabua Jonathan, the conservative BNP formed Lesotho's government, which favours free enterprise and cooperation with South Africa. It claims 80 500 members.

Basutoland Congress Party (BCP)
Founded in 1952, the BCP is the main opposition party. It favours non-alignment, is strongly anti-apartheid and pan-Africanist. It claims 75 000 members. The party's militant wing is led from outside Lesotho by Ntsu Mokhehle.

Marematiou Freedom Party (MFP)
This royalist party was formed in 1962 and claims 50 000 members.

United Democratic Party
A breakaway from the BNP, it was formed in 1967.

National Independence Party
This party, founded in 1984, advocates ending Lesotho's ties with South Africa.

LIBERIA

True Whig Party (TWP)
Prior to the 1980 coup the only legal political party. The TWP had held power continuously since 1878. The party stresses national development and cultural integration of the Americo-Liberian community and the indigenous population.

Between 1980 and 1984, political parties were banned.

National Democratic Party of Liberia (NDPL)
Formed in 1984 by Samuel Doe.

Liberal Grand Coalition
A coalition of opposition groups formed in 1986 which was not granted legal recognition.

Liberian People's Party (LPP)
Founded by ex-members of the pan-Africanist *Movement for Justice in Africa* (MOJA), this party was banned in 1985.

National Patriotic Front of Liberia
Led by Charles Taylor; raised rebellion in Nimba Country in 1989 and advanced on the capital while controlling most of the country.

LIBYA

Arab Socialist Union (ASU)
Formed in 1971 as the country's sole political party. In 1975 the General National Congress of the ASU became the country's General People's Congress, which produced a new national constitution.

All political parties were banned in 1952 and before the 1969 revolution there were no legally constituted political parties, but several clandestine organisations existed; e.g. the *Baath Party*, the *Arab Nationalist Party*, and the *Muslim Brotherhood*.

MADAGASCAR (MALAGASY REPUBLIC)

Front National pour la Défense de la Révolution Socialiste Malgache
Founded in 1977 to rally pro-government political parties. All opposition
parties had been banned in 1975. The Front incorporates:

Avant-garde de la Révolution Malgache (Arema)
Formed in 1976 as the mainstay of the revolution, the Arema forms the
nucleus of the Front National.

Élan Populaire pour l'Unité Nationale (VONJY)
A nationalist party formed in 1973.

Parti du Congress de l'Indépendance de Madagascar (AKFM)
The pro-Soviet party, established in 1958.

UDECMA–KMTP
A Christian Democrat party formed in 1977.

Other independent parties include:

Mouvement National pour l'Indépendance de Madagascar (Monima)
An anti-French radical socialist party, it withdrew from the Front National in
1977.

MFM
Extreme left-wing party which supports the government.

Parti Social Démocratique (PSD)
Founded by Philibert Tsirinang in 1956, the PSD was the ruling party from
1959 to 1972. Non-Marxist but committed to Christian Socialist principles, the
PSD drew its strength from the coastal tribes and its policy was pro-French.

Mouvement pour la Rénouvation Nationale (Morena)
A small left-wing and Catholic opposition party.

Voudrona Sosialista Monima (VSM)
A Marxist breakaway from Monima, founded in 1977.

MALAWI

Malawi Congress Party (MCP)
Malawi's only authorised political party, the MCP was founded in 1959 to
succeed the Nyasaland African National Congress. Life President Dr Hastings Banda's policy is strongly pro-Western, multi-racial and with emphasis
on internal development.

Three small opposition groups are in exile:
the *Congress for the Second Republic* and the *Malawi Freedom Movement (MAFREMO)* which are based in Tanzania, and the *Socialist League of Malawi (LESOMA)*, based in Zimbabwe and believed to receive Soviet and Cuban aid. LESOMA maintains the *People's Liberation Army of Malawi*, founded in 1980.

MALI

Union Démocratique du Peuple Malien (UDPM)
Founded in 1976 as the country's sole political party, the UDPM is a democratic centralist structure.

Between 1968 and 1974 all political parties were banned by the military government. These parties included:

Union Soudanaise (US)
Founded after the Second World War as an affiliate of the Rassemblement Démocratique Africain (see Ivory Coast), this party supported the Keita government of 1960–68 and controlled the press, trade unions and other social institutions.

Unofficial opposition parties include the Paris-based *Comité de défense des libertés démocratiques au Mali*, the *Front démocratique des patriotes maliens* (FDPM) and the *Parti malien de la révolution et de la démocratie*.

MAURITANIA

Parti du Peuple Mauritanien (PPM)
Founded in 1961, through the merger of the Parti du Regroupement Mauritanien, the Union Nationale Mauritanienne, Nahda and the Union des Socialistes Musulmans Mauritaniens, the PPM became the country's only legal political party in 1964. Its policy combined moderate socialism and a non-aligned foreign policy.

The PPM was dissolved after the coup of 1978. Exiled supporters of the party in France formed the *Alliance pour une Mauritanie démocratique (AMD)*.

Organisation des nationalistes mauritaniens
An opposition group based in Senegal, formed in 1984.

MAURITIUS

Mauritius Labour Party (MLP)
The governing party, led by Sir Seewoosagur Ramgoolam, enjoys strong urban trade-union support, plus rural Hindu agricultural votes. It led the drive for independence.

Muslim Committee of Action (MCA)
Led by those Muslims who believe they can gain most by communal action, it is part of the governing coalition.

Parti Mauritien Social-Démocratique (PMSD)
The leading Francophile opposition party gains support from the Creole middle class and Franco-Mauritian landowners and was originally opposed to independence. Part of the government coalition after 1976.

Mauritian Militant Movement (MMM)
The leading Marxist party, and the largest single party in the legislative assembly since 1976.

Mauritian Militant Movement – Social Progress (MMM–SP)
An opposition party formed from the MMM.

Independent Forward Bloc (IFB)
Founded in 1958, this is a small party based on Hindu farm-labourer support.

Independence Party (IP)
A short-lived coalition of the MLP, IFB and the MCA, in 1967–9.

Mauritius People's Progressive Party (MPPP)
The Mauritian affiliate of the Afro-Asian People's Solidarity Organisation since 1963.

Republican Centre Party
Founded in 1972.

Mauritian Democratic Union (MDU)
An offshoot of the PMSD.

Mouvement Socialiste Mauritien (MSM)
Formed in 1983.

MOROCCO ·

Istiqlal
Founded in 1943, the Istiqlal led the struggle for independence but split in 1959 and lost power in 1963. It stands for equal rights, better living standards and

the absorption of the Western Sahara and Mauritania. Istiqlal was represented in the 1977 government of national unity.

Mouvement Populaire (MP)
Formed in 1957, it is the pro-royalist Berber party, shared in the government
of 1963–5 and dominates the constitutional government formed in 1977.

Mouvement Populaire Constitutionnel et Démocratique (MPCD)
Breakaway from the Mouvement Populaire.

Parti de l'Action
Formed in 1974, it calls for democracy and progress.

Parti Démocratique Constitutionnel (PDC)

Parti Démocrate de l'Indépendance (PDI)
A left-wing offshoot from the Istiqlal, now defunct.

Parti du Progrès et du Socialisme (PPS)
Formed in 1974 to succeed the Parti Marocain de la Libération et du
Socialisme (PMLS). A pro-Soviet communist party, the PPS replaces the
banned Parti Communiste Marocain, and PMLS leaders were arrested in
1969. It won one seat in the 1977 general elections.

Parti Libéral Progressiste (PLP)
Formed in 1974, it stands for free enterprise and individual rights.

Parti Socialiste Démocratique (PSD)
A small party which shared in government 1963–5.

Union Nationale des Forces Populaires, Casablanca (UNFP)
Formed in 1959 as a left-wing offshoot of Istiqlal, the UNFP campaigned for
the restoration of constitutional rule and a programme of social and economic
change. Its leader, Ben Barka, disappeared in France in 1965. It has suffered
government harassment and internal disagreements. The Rabat UNFP was
banned in 1973 and many party leaders were arrested. It remains in opposition.

Union Socialiste des Forces Populaires (USFP)
A breakaway from the UNFP, formed in 1974 from the banned Rabat section.

Organisation de l'Action Démocratique et Populaire
Founded in 1983.

Rassemblement National des Independants (RNI)
Formed in 1978 by the majority of independents in the Chamber of Representatives who supported the government.

Parti National Démocrate (PND)
Founded in 1981 as a breakaway of the RNI, the PND supports democratic
government and greater social and economic equality.

MOZAMBIQUE

Frente de Libertação de Moçambique (Frelimo)
Formed in 1962 by the merger of various small nationalist parties: the Unido Democratica Nacional de Moçambique (Udenamo), the Mozambique African Nationalist Union (MANU) and the União Africana de Moçambique Independente (Unami). Frelimo was first led by Eduardo Mondlane from Dar es Salaam in Tanzania, until Mondlane's assassination in 1969. The Frelimo styles itself as Marxist–Leninist and is Mozambique's only legal party.

Comite Revolutionario de Moçambique (Coremo)
A small nationalist group based in Zambia in the 1960s.

Resistência Nacional Moçambicana (Renamo)
An opposition group which has conducted a guerrilla war against Frelimo since 1976. It receives assistance from South Africa.

NAMIBIA

Democratic Turnhalle Alliance
Formed in 1977, it represented whites and some African delegations to the Turnhalle Conference. It was sponsored by South Africa to lead a multi-racial independent Namibia.

Namibia National Front
An umbrella body for ten African groups, including the SWANU.

National Democratic Unity Organisation (NDUO)
The party of the Herero people.

National Democratic Party
An Ovambo grouping.

Christian Democratic Action for Social Justice (CDA)
Formed in 1982 and supported mainly by Ovambos and former supporters of the NDP.

Labour Party
Supported by the 'Coloured' population.

Namibia Christian Democratic Party
Founded in 1978, this party advocates a 'Social Christian' form of free enterprise and multi-racialism. It receives mainly African support.

South West Africa Coloured People's Organisation
Founded in 1959.

South West Africa National Union (SWANU)
Founded in 1959, the SWANU was supported by South Africa's African National Congress.

South West Africa National United Front (SWANUF)
A guerrilla force formed in 1964.

South West Africa People's Organisation (SWAPO)
Founded in 1958 as the Ovambo People's Organisation and strongest among the Ovambo tribe, the SWAPO is the main nationalist movement and has organised a guerrilla war for independence. Based in Tanzania and later in Zambia, SWAPO is backed by the Organisation of African Unity (OAU) and receives aid and arms from the Eastern-bloc communist countries. Led by Sam Nujoma, it gained over 53% of the vote and 41 seats at the 1989 elections.
Under South African government, the major parties for white voters were:

National Party (NP)
A branch of South Africa's ruling party which dominated the territory's representation in the South African parliament.

Federal Party of South West Africa, formerly the *United National South West Africa Party*
Formed in 1927 as an all-white opposition party, independent from parties in South Africa.

White Republican Party
Founded in 1977 as a breakaway from the National Party, the party supports the Democratic Turnhalle Alliance.

NIGER

Parti Progressiste Nigérien (PPN)
Formed in 1946 as an affiliate of the Rassemblement Démocratique Africain (see Ivory Coast), the PPN became Niger's only legal party in 1959. Its policy was generally pro-French and conservative.

Sawaba (Freedom) Party
Founded as the Union Démocratique Nigérienne (UDN), the Sawaba was Niger's principal left-wing opposition party until its banning in 1959. It continued illegal subversive activities from abroad.

All political parties were banned in 1974 by the military government.

NIGERIA

In May 1966, the new military rulers banned all existing political parties. These parties were regional and based on particular tribal and sectional loyalties:

Northern People's Congress (NPC)
The predominant party in the Federal Parliament.

National Council of Nigerian Citizens (NCNC)
The main party of the Eastern province, the NCNC collaborated with the NPC.

Nigerian National Democratic Party (NNDP)
An opposition party of the Western Region.

Action Group
An opposition party of the Yoruba people, Western Region.

In October 1975 it was announced that party politics would be resumed in 1978. In 1979 elections were held and the country returned to civilian rule. Only parties with a nationwide organisation were able to register, i.e. regionally-based parties were excluded.

Greater Nigeria People's Party (GNPP)
Essentially a conservative party which stressed national unity; led by a Northerner.

National Party of Nigeria (NPN)
Formed by representatives of all the pre-1966 political parties drawn from all areas of the country. Polled 33 per cent of the votes in the elections of July–August 1979 with Alhaji Shehu Shagari becoming President of Nigeria.

Nigerian People's Party (NPP)
Established in 1978 but then split into various factions after disputes over personalities, leadership and finance. Led by the veteran nationalist leader Dr Nnamdi Azikiwe. Polled just over 16 per cent of votes in 1979 elections.

People's Redemption Party (PRP)
Slightly left-of-centre party with policy of 'democratic humanism' and a 'socialist democracy'.

Unity Party of Nigeria (UPN)
Founded by Chief Obafami Owolowo. Proclaimed itself a democratic socialist party which was in fact just left-of-centre. Gained 29 per cent of the votes in the 1979 elections.

In 1982 the GNPP, NPP, PRP and UPN formed the *Progressive People's Alliance*.
All political parties were banned in 1984.

RWANDA

Mouvement Révolutionnaire National pour le Développement (MRND)
Formed in 1975 as the sole political party, it seeks to remove inter-tribal conflict and promote national unity and development.

Mouvement Démocratique Républicain, formerly the *Parti de l'Emancipation Hutu (Parmehutu)*
Founded in 1959 to succeed the Mouvement Social Hutu, the Parmehutu was the only legal political party representing the country's dominant tribe. It was replaced by the MRND.

Union Nationale Ruandaise (UNR)
The party of the minority Tutsi tribe was virtually eliminated in the 1960s.

ST HELENA, ASCENSION ISLAND and TRISTAN DA CUNHA

St Helena Progressive Party
The dominant party, formed in 1973.

St Helena Labour Party
It advocates free enterprise and opposes British development plans. Its leader was banned from the island in 1975.

SÃO TOMÉ and PRÍNCIPE

Movimento de Liberação de São Tomé e Príncipe
Formed in 1972, this is the country's only legal party. Its policy stresses non-alignment and agrarian and social reform.

Comissão de Liberação de São Tomé e Príncipe
Led by Tomas Medeiros, this was the main underground nationalist party seeking independence from Portugal.

Coalizão Democrática de Oposição
A coalition of opposition groups formed in 1986, and based in Portugal.

SENEGAL

Parti Socialiste Sénégalais (PSS), formerly the *Union Progressiste Sénégalaise (UPS)*
Founded in 1949 by Léopold Sédar Senghor, the UPS was an offshoot of the French Socialist Party. With a moderate, Francophile policy, it has formed

the government since 1960. Between 1966 and 1974 Senegal was in effect a one-party state.

Parti de Regroupement Africain-Sénégal (PRA)
A left-wing opposition party, the PRA was absorbed by the UPS in 1966.

Parti Communiste Sénégalais (PCS)
An illegal party, formed in 1965 as an offshoot of the PAI.

Parti Démocratique Sénégalais (PDS)
Founded in 1974, the PDS forms the liberal democratic opposition.

Parti Africain de l'Indépendance (PAI)
Founded originally in 1957 and reorganised in 1976, the PAI forms the Marxist opposition.

Mouvement Républicain Sénégalais (MRS)
Founded in 1977, it forms the right-wing conservative opposition.

Rassemblement National Démocratique (RND)
An illegal progressive party, formed in 1976.

Ligue communiste des travailleurs (LCT)
A Trotskyist party formed in 1982.

Ligue démocratique – Mouvement pour le parti du travail (LD–MPT)
Registered in 1981.

Mouvement démocratique populaire (MDP)
Founded in 1981. Socialist.

Mouvement révolutionnaire pour la démocratie nouvelle – And Jëf (MRDN–AJ)
A Maoist party registered in 1981.

Organisation socialiste des travailleurs (OST)
An independent Marxist–Leninist party formed in 1982.

Parti Africain pour l'indépendance du peuple (PAIP)
A Marxist–Leninist party founded in 1982.

Parti de l'indépendance et du travail (PIT)
A pro-Soviet Marxist–Leninist party formed in 1981.

Parti populaire sénégalais (PPS)
A populist party registered in 1981.

SEYCHELLES

Seychelles Democratic Party (SDP)
The conservative party, formed in 1963 and led by ex-President James

Mancham. In 1978, the SDP was said by the government to have 'disappeared'.

Seychelles People's United Party (SPUP)
The left-wing party, led by Albert René, who became President of the Seychelles in the 1977 coup. In 1978, the party was renamed the *Seychelles People's Progressive Front (SPPF)*, and became the only legal party.

Among the exiled opposition parties are the *Seychelles National Movement*, based in Belgium, the *Mouvement pour la Résistance* and the *Seychelles Popular Anti-Marxist Front*.

SIERRA LEONE

All-People's Congress (APC)
Formed in 1960 by Siaka Stevens, the APC drew its strength from the Temme people and minor tribes. With a leftist republican programme, it took power in 1968. All its candidates were returned unopposed in the 1973 elections. The APC is the country's only officially recognised party.

Sierra Leone People's Party (SLPP)
Formed in 1951, it was the country's first political party. Dominant until 1967, the SLPP was based on support from the Mende tribe. Led by Milton and Albert Margai, the party was temporarily split from 1958 to 1961.

Democratic National Party (DNP)
Opposition party.

United National Alliance
Coalition of the SLPP and the DNP in the 1977 elections.

People's National Party
Shortlived breakaway party from SLPP formed by Milton Margai and Siaka Stevens. It was badly defeated in the District Council elections of 1959.

Exiled opposition groups include the *Sierra Leone Alliance Movement (SLAM)* and the *Sierra Leone Democratic Party (SLDP)*, which both operate from London, and the *National Alliance Party (NAP)*, based in the USA.

SOMALIA

Somali Socialist Revolutionary Party (SSRP)
Formed in 1976 as the country's sole political party. The Central Committee of the SSRP forms the government.

Somali Democratic Action Front (Sodaf)
The illegal opposition party, which advocates democratic elections and peace with Ethiopia.

Political parties which were banned in 1969 by the new military government included:

Somali Youth League (SYL)
The government party since independence in 1960, the SYL was strongly nationalist and irredentist towards Somali minorities in Ethiopia, Kenya and Djibouti. It relied heavily on Eastern-bloc communist aid.

Other parties remained legal under the SYL, and a total of 63 minority parties and groups fought in the 1969 elections (before the military takeover). Most supported the SYL government. These included *Somali National Congress (SNC)*, an offshoot from the SYL and other parties in 1963, which took a radical line in foreign policy; *Somali African National Union (SANU)*; *Liberal Somali Youth Party (PLGS)*; *Independent Constitutional Somali Party (DHMS)*; *Somali Democratic Union*, strongly left-wing; *Democratic Action People's Party (MPAD)*, strongly critical of the SYL in 1969.

Democratic Front for the Salvation of Somalia (DFSS)
A coalition of anti-government forces established in 1981, operating from Ethiopia. It receives support from Ethiopia, the People's Democratic Republic of Yemen and Libya.

Somali National Movement (SNM)
Formed in London in 1981, this group maintains an anti-government guerrilla force with support from Ethiopia.

Somalia First
Formed in London in 1983, its aim is to bring together the opposition forces against the government.

SOUTH AFRICA

African National Congress (ANC)
Formed in 1912, the ANC stands for a non-racial society and co-operation with left-wing and liberal organisations of other races. Led by Nelson Mandela, it was banned in 1960 and its activities were directed from Zambia. In 1990 Mandela was released and the ban on the ANC was lifted.

Black People's Convention (BPC)
Founded in 1972, as an all-African and non-tribal organisation, it was banned in 1976.

Black Unity Front (BUF)
Founded in 1976 and led by the Zulu Chief, Buthelezi. In 1978, Chief
Buthelezi founded the *South African Black Alliance (SABA)*, including the
Indian Reform Party, the *Inkatha Movement* and the *Linkoanketla Party*.

Coloured Labour Party (CLP)
The main party for people of mixed race.

Congress of Democrats
A communist front, banned since 1962.

Herstigte Nasionale Party (HNP)
Founded in 1969 by National Party dissidents of the right wing, the HNP calls
for strict application of apartheid, Afrikaans as the national language and a
society based on God's laws as defined by Calvin.

Indian National Congress of South Africa (INC)
Formed in 1896, the INC collaborates with the ANC.

Indian Reform Party

Liberal Party (LP)
Founded in 1953, the party broke up in 1968 when new legislation banned
political association among members of different racial groups.

National Party (NP)
Formed originally in 1912, the party has held power since 1948; it absorbed
many other parties, including the Afrikaner Party. An all-white party, the
National Party represents most Afrikaners and a growing number of English-
speaking South Africans, and it stands for apartheid and rigorous anti-
communism. Its policies are designed to safeguard the white nation in its
South African homeland and to lead the black inhabitants to self-government
in their homelands or 'bantustans'. Recently, its stand has changed.

New Republic Party (NRP)
Formed in 1977 by United Party members, it stands for a power-sharing
federal government.

Pan-Africanist Congress of Azania (PACA)
Formed in 1959 as a left-wing offshoot of the ANC, it rejects the multi-racial
approach. Banned in 1960, it operates from Zambia. The ban was lifted 1990.

Progressive Federal Party (PFP)
Established in 1977 from the Progressive Reform Party and part of the old
United Party, the PFP is a white organisation which advocates a federal
constitution with self-governing states based on territorial rather than racial
divisions, power-sharing between the races and an end to discriminatory
legislation. The PFP was the principal opposition party between 1977 and
1987.

Progressive Party (PP)
Formed in 1959 by United Party dissidents, the party favoured enfranchisement for all qualified persons irrespective of race. It gave way to PFP in 1977. The legislation of 1968 forced the party to become all-white.

South African Communist Party (SACP)
Formed in 1921, banned in 1950, but operated in exile. The ban was lifted 1990.

South African Party (SAP)
Formed in 1977 by the Independent United Party, the SAP rejects power-sharing and seeks federal government under white leadership.

United Party (UP)
Founded in 1937, the United Party represented most English-speaking white South Africans, and was the main opposition party from 1948 to 1977, when it was dissolved and gave way to the PFP, SAP and NRP.

Afrikaanse Weerstandsbeweging (AWB)
(Afrikaner Resistance Movement) An extreme right-wing paramilitary group founded in 1973, and led by Eugene Terre' Blanche.

Azanian People's Organisation (AZAPO)
Formed in 1978, this party aims to establish a democratic, socialist and unitary state in South Africa. White members are excluded.

Blanke Bevrydingsbeweging (BBB)
(White Protection Movement) An extreme right-wing group.

Conservative Party of South Africa (CPSA)
Founded in 1982 by right-wing Members of Parliament expelled from the National Party. Since 1987, the CPSA has been the chief opposition party.

People's Congress Party
Formed in 1983, this party draws support mainly from the 'Coloured' population.

Democratic Workers' Party
A breakaway from the *People's Congress Party*, founded in 1984.

Federal Independent Democratic Alliance (FIDA)
A moderate black African party formed in 1987. It seeks a negotiated ending of apartheid.

Labour Party of South Africa
A mainly 'Coloured' party which has a democratic and multi-racialist platform.

New Freedom Party of Southern Africa
Previously called the *Federal Party*, this party draws support from the Coloured population.

Other parties depending mainly on Indian and Coloured support include the *National People's Party*, the *Progressive Independent Party*, the *Reformed Freedom Party*, the *Solidarity Party*, the *Freedom Party* and the *Transvaal Indian Congress* (founded in 1902, and revived in 1983).

United Democratic Front (UDF)
A multi-racial coalition of anti-apartheid groups formed in 1983 in order to campaign against Indian and 'Coloured' participation in new constitutional arrangements.

SUDAN

Sudanese Socialist Union (SSU)
Formed in 1972 as the country's only legal party, the SSU provided the government's power-base in the country.

Sudanese National Front (SNF)
An umbrella for various opposition groups, including the Umma Party, the Muslim Brotherhood and the right-wing Union of Sharaf al-Hindi. It was banned in 1969, but tolerated after 1977.

Political parties were banned between 1969 and 1985.

Democratic Unionist Party (DUP)
The major government party, formed in 1967 from the former National Unionist Party and the Muslim People's Democratic Party. Legalised in 1985.

Islamic Charter Front (Mithaq)
Formed in 1964, the Mithaq organised strict Muslims.

Southern Front
Founded in 1964, it wanted self-determination for the three southern provinces and co-operated with the DUP to achieve that end.

Sudan African National Union (SANU)
A radical party of the southern provinces, it split in 1967.

Sudan Communist Party (SCP)
The party enjoyed strong trade-union and student support, but was banned intermittently in the 1960s. In the 1970s the government was strongly anti-communist. Legalised in 1985.

Sudan Socialist Party (SSP)
Formed in 1967 after the SCP was banned, the SSP acted as a communist front.

Umma Party
Legalised in 1985. A conservative party, based on the Ansar religious

brotherhood and the Mahdi family, the Umma was split for two years from 1967 to 1969.

Other parties made legal in 1985 were:

Baath Party

Muslim Brotherhood

National Alliance for Salvation (NAS)
A grouping of parties, trade unions and professional associations.

National Congress Party
This party has a platform of national unity, decentralised government and non-alignment.

Sudanese National Party

Southern Sudanese Political Association (SSPA)
The largest party in the south of the country, its aim is the unity of the region.

Opposition separatist groups include the *Sudan People's Liberation Movement (SPLM)*, which has a military branch, the *Sudan People's Liberation Army*, and the *Liberation Front for Southern Sudan*.

SWAZILAND

All political parties were dissolved and prohibited by King Sobhuza II. Prior to that, the five main parties were:

Imbokadvo National Movement (INM)
Founded in 1964, it was moderate, sympathetic to white settlers, and dominated the Swazi elections. Since 1978, the INM has been the only legal party.

Ngwane National Liberatory Congress (NNLC)
Founded in 1962, it opposed the Imbokadvo Movement and was strongly nationalistic and pan-Africanist. In 1971 it split into two factions.

Swaziland Progressive Party (SPP)
Founded in 1929, as the Swazi Progressive Association.

Swaziland United Front (SUF)
Founded in 1962, as an offshoot of the SPP.

United Swaziland Association (USA)
Representing Swaziland's white community, it supported the INM.

TANZANIA (formerly TANGANYIKA and ZANZIBAR)

Chama Cha Mapinduzi (Revolutionary Party of Tanzania) (CCM)
Formed in 1977, the CCM results from a merger of TANU and the ASP, which operated as the only legal parties on the mainland and Zanzibar respectively. The party aims for a socialist democratic state, advocates self-help methods and sponsors mass organisations for women, young people, trade unionists and co-operatives.

Tanganyika African National Union (TANU)
Founded in 1954, TANU led the movement for independence from Britain.

Afro-Shirazi Party (ASP)
Formed in 1956–7, the ASP mobilised Zanzibar's African people and came to power after the coup of 1964. It pursued a socialist programme.

TOGO

Rassemblement du Peuple Togolais (RPT)
Founded in 1969 as the only legal political party, the RPT organises support for the government.

All other political parties were banned after the coup of 1967. The major parties were:

Unité Togolaise (UT)
Led by Togo's first president, Sylvanus Olympio, the party stemmed from the Comité de l'Unité Togolaise. In power from 1960 to 1963, the Unité Togolaise enjoyed strong support from the Ewe tribe and from trade unionists.

Juvento
Originally the youth movement of the Unité Togolaise, Juvento became independent in 1959.

Mouvement Populaire Togolais (MPT)
Formed in 1954 by UDPT dissidents.

Union Démocratique des Populations Togolaises (UDPT)
Led by Togo's second president, Nicolas Grunitzky, the UDPT was formed in 1959 by the merger of the Parti Togolais Du Progrès and the Union des Chefs des Populations du Nord. These formed the main opposition to the Unité Togolaise, and were based on tribal support in the central and northern regions.

An illegal opposition group, the *Mouvement Togolais pour la Démocratie (MTD)* exists in exile.

TUNISIA

Parti Socialiste Destourien (PSD)
Formed in 1934 by Habib Bourguiba as the Neo-Destour Party, the PSD has been Tunisia's ruling party since independence. It is strongly organised among trade unionists, peasants, women, young people, etc, and stands for a programme of moderate socialism. In 1988 the PSD was renamed the *Democratic Constitutional Rally*.

In the 1974 and 1986 elections, there were no candidates from other parties.

Mouvement de l'Unité Populaire (MUP)
Advocates radical reform.

Mouvement des Démocrates Socialistes (MDS)
This party seeks a pluralist democratic system. It took part in the 1981 election and was given official recognition in 1983.

Parti de l'Unité Populaire (PUP)
An off-shoot of the MUP.

Rassemblement Socialiste Progressiste
Founded in 1983.

The *Mouvement de la Tendance Islamique* and the *Rassemblement National Arabe* were banned 1981–87.

UGANDA

Political parties were suspended in 1971 and again following the coming to power of the *National Resistance Movement* in 1986.

Uganda People's Congress (UPC)
Formed in 1960, the UPC shared in government from 1962 to 1966, ruling with full powers until 1971. During this time, under the leadership of Dr Milton Obote, the UPC was the only legal party. It was again in power between 1980 and 1985. The party's philosophy is basically socialist.

Democratic Party (DP)
Based on Roman Catholic and Bugandan support, the DP advocates a mixed economy, multi-party politics and national government.

National Liberal Party
A breakaway from the DP formed in 1984.

Front for National Salvation (Fronasa)
A guerrilla group, formed in 1973, which opposed President Amin.

Kababa Yekka (KY)
A Buganda-based movement which organised support for the Kabaka until his overthrow in 1966.

Uganda National Union (UNU)
Formed in 1969.

Conservative Party (CP)
Founded in 1979.

National Resistance Movement (NRM)
Created to oppose the UPC government of 1980–85, and the military regime in power 1985–6. The NRM's military wing, the *National Resistance Army*, under Yoweri Museveni, took power in 1986.

Uganda Freedom Movement (UFM)
Based mainly on support in Buganda, the UFM left the NRM governing coalition in 1987.

Ugandan People's Democratic Movement
A group in armed conflict with the government. It includes members of the former government armed forces. Led by John Okello, it seeks democratic reforms. The Movement draws support from the north and east of the country.

UPPER VOLTA see under BURKINA FASO

ZAÏRE

Mouvement Populaire de la Révolution (MPR)
Formed by President Mobutu in 1967, the MPR became Zaïre's only legal political party, with a policy of national unity, Zaïrean militancy and nationalism. It is generally anti-communist and anti-clerical.

Illegal parties and former parties, banned in 1965, included:

Alliance des Bakongos (Abako)
Led by ex-President Kasavubu.

Mouvement National Congolais (MNC)
The left-wing party led by Congo's first prime minister, Patrice Lumumba.

Confédération des Associations Tribales du Katanga (Conakat)
Led by Moïse Tshombe.

Parti pour la Conscience Nationale (Pacona)
Formed in 1977, the Pacona aims to depose President Mobutu, to restore a

two-chamber parliament and the traditional authority of tribal chiefs, and to rehabilitate the Roman Catholic Church.

Parti Révolutionnaire du Peuple (PRP)
Based in eastern Zaïre, the party organises guerrilla resistance to President Mobutu and has a Marxist–Leninist programme.

Other illegal groups in exile include the *Conseil pour la libération du Congo*, formed in 1980, the *Front congolais pour la restauration de la démocratie* (FCD), founded in 1982 and based in Belgium, the Marxist–Leninist *Parti ouvrier et paysan du Congo* (POP), formed in 1986, and the *Union pour la démocratie et le progrès social* (UDPS), founded in 1982 and based in Belgium.

ZAMBIA

United National Independence Party (UNIP)
Formed in 1959 and led by Kenneth Kaunda, the UNIP became Zambia's only legal party in 1972. Originally the party's strength came from the Bemba-speaking population.

Parties banned since 1972:

African National Congress (ANC)
Founded in 1944 by Harry Nkumbula as a militant nationalist organisation, the ANC fought against the Rhodesian Federation and racial discrimination. It was strongest among the Borotse people. The ANC favoured co-operation with the white-ruled governments of Southern Africa.

United Progress Party (UPP)

United Party
Active among Lozi tribesmen between 1967 and 1968, when it was banned.

National Progress Party (NPP)
The party of Zambia's white minority, the NPP held 10 seats in parliament until 1966.

ZIMBABWE

African National Council (ANC)
Formed in 1971, the ANC organised opposition to the Anglo-Rhodesian settlement proposals. Its leader was Bishop Abel Muzorewa.

African National Council – Sithole (ANC–Sithole)
Formed in 1977 by former militants of the ANC and the ZANU, the party
was led by the Revd Ndabaningi Sithole and supported the 'internal settlement' of Zimbabwe's independence.

African National Council – Zimbabwe (ANC–Zimbabwe)
As the internal wing of the ZANU, the party opposed the internal settlement.

African Progressive Party (APP)
Formed in 1974, it wanted a settlement on the basis of the 1971 proposals.

Centre Party (CP)
Formed in 1968, the CP was multi-racial and critical of the Rhodesia Front's
discriminatory legislation.

Conservative Alliance of the Republic of Rhodesia
Formed in 1969 by right-wing dissidents of the Rhodesia Front, the party
called for separation of the races.

Front for the Liberation of Zimbabwe (Frolizi)
Led by James Chikerema, the Frolizi merged into the Patriotic Front.

National Association of Coloured People

National Democratic Union
A conservative faction, created in 1979 with minority Zezuru support.

National People's Union (NPU)
A mainly black party formed in 1969, the NPU combined the former United
People's Party and the Democratic Party, and it covered those Africans who
sat in the Rhodesian parliament.

National Settlement Convention (NSC)
Formed in 1974 from the former African Settlement Convention and the
Rhodesian Settlement Forum, the NSC wanted a settlement based on the
1971 proposals.

National Unifying Force (NUF)
Formed in 1977 from the Rhodesia Party, the Centre Party and the National
Pledge Association, the NUF supported a multi-racial Zimbabwe and the
Anglo-American proposals for a settlement.

Patriotic Front (PF)
The main nationalist umbrella organisation formed in 1976 by the leaders of
the ZANU and ZAPU, the Patriotic Front opposed the internal settlement,
promoted guerrilla warfare for the liberation of Zimbabwe, and enjoyed the
support of the presidents of Angola, Botswana, Mozambique, Tanzania and
Zambia. It was based in Mozambique.

People's Movement (PM)
Formed in 1976 and led by Robert Mugabe, it maintained an internal wing in Zimbabwe.

Rhodesian Action Party (RAP)
Formed in 1977 by former members of the Rhodesia Front.

Rhodesia Front (RF)
The white party led by Ian Smith which held power from 1962 with a policy of racial segregation, white supremacy and independence from Britain. In 1977 the Front accepted the principle of universal adult suffrage and began to devise an 'internal settlement'. In 1981, the *Rhodesia Front* changed its name to the *Republican Front*, and later to the *Conservative Alliance of Zimbabwe* (CAZ).

Independent Zimbabwe Group
A faction of the former *Republican Front*, formed in 1983.

Rhodesia Party
Formed in 1972, it was an opposition white party critical of the Rhodesia Front's racially discriminatory laws and supported a qualified franchise and responsible government.

Rhodesia White People's Party
Formed in 1976, it was anti-liberal and anti-Zionist.

Southern Africa Solidarity Conference (Sascon)
A group for those opposed to majority rule and in support of closer links with South Africa.

United African National Council (UANC)
Formed originally in 1971 as the ANC, the UANC was the party of Bishop Abel Muzorewa which emerged from the nationalists' split in 1975. It supported the 'internal settlement'.

United Conservative Party (UCP)
Formed in 1975, the white right-wing opposition party which wanted separate parliaments for whites and blacks.

United Front against Surrender
Formed in 1972, the party stood for continued white supremacy.

United National Federal Party (UNFP)
Formed in 1978, the UNFP is a conservative party which advocates the federation of Matabeleland and Mashonaland.

Zimbabwe African National Union (ZANU)
Formed in 1963 after a split in ZAPU, the party is led by Robert Mugabe and until the 1980 settlement was based in Mozambique, from where it organised

guerrilla warfare. It formed part of the Patriotic Front and advanced a Marxist-Leninist programme. In the 1980 elections, it won a landslide victory.

Zimbabwe African People's Union (ZAPU)
Formed in 1961, ZAPU was banned in 1964. Led from Zambia by Joshua Nkomo, it promoted guerrilla warfare and formed part of the Patriotic Front.

Zimbabwe Democratic Party
A breakaway from the UANC, formed in 1979. A traditionalist party led by James Chikerema.

Zimbabwe Reformed African National Council
Formed in 1976.

Zimbabwe United People's Organisation (ZUPO)
Formed in 1976, the ZUPO was led by Chief Chirau, and supported the 'internal settlement'.

6 CONFLICTS, ARMED FORCES AND COUPS

MAJOR CONFLICTS

REVOLT IN MADAGASCAR 1947–8

A revolt against French rule, centring on the east coast, was suppressed after much bloodshed.

EGYPT'S WARS WITH ISRAEL 1948–73

War of Independence 1948. As soon as Israel had been established as an independent Jewish state in May 1948, it was invaded by Egypt, Iraq, Lebanon, Jordan and Syria. After initial Arab gains, the Israelis counter-attacked successfully. An armistice was agreed between Israel and Egypt on 23 Feb 1949.

Sinai Campaign 1956. After secret negotiations with France and Britain, Israel attacked Egypt on 29 Oct 1956. Israeli forces overran most of Sinai and advanced to within 30 miles of the Suez Canal when they halted in response to an ultimatum by France and Britain (see SUEZ CRISIS). Israeli troops withdrew and were replaced by a UN peace-keeping force.

Six-Day War 1967. In May 1967 Egypt demanded the withdrawal of the UN peace-keeping force and signed a defence pact with Jordan. The Israelis decided on a pre-emptive strike and launched a devastating air attack on the Egyptian air-force on 5 June 1967. Israeli forces invaded Sinai and reached the Suez Canal. A ceasefire was agreed on 10 June.

Yom Kippur War 1973. Egyptian forces crossed the Suez Canal in a well-planned surprise attack on 6 Oct 1973, Israel's Day of Atonement. Israel's Bar Lev defence line was overwhelmed as men and equipment were rushed across the canal under cover of Soviet-supplied surface-to-air missiles, but the Egyptians proved unable to extend their bridgehead. In a daring counter-stroke, Israeli forces crossed to the west bank of the canal on 15 Oct 1973 through the gap between the Egyptian Second and Third Armies, and encircled the Third Army. A ceasefire became effective on 24 Oct.

MAU MAU REVOLT 1952–60

Violence by Mau Mau, an African secret society which aimed at driving white settlers out of Kenya, led the British government of Kenya to declare a state of emergency on 20 Oct 1952. Leading Kikuyu nationalists were arrested, and Jomo Kenyatta was given a seven-year prison sentence in Oct 1953. Assassinations and terrorist attacks on the farms of white settlers and on Africans who did not support Mau Mau were countered by a British military campaign in which the insurgents were driven into the remote mountain areas of western Kenya. Some 600 British and African troops died in the operations against Mau Mau. The state of emergency ended on 12 Jan 1960.

MOROCCAN REVOLT 1953–6

Morocco had been divided into French and Spanish spheres of influence as a result of a protectorate treaty between France and the Sultan signed at Fez on 30 Mar 1912 and a convention between France and Spain signed at Madrid on 27 Nov 1912. Anti-French nationalist activity developed in the 1950s and after a period of rioting and terrorism France recognised Morocco as an independent sovereign state on 2 Mar 1956. Spain followed suit on 7 Apr 1956.

WAR OF ALGERIAN INDEPENDENCE 1954–62

In 1954 the nationalist movement in Algeria, the Front de Libération Nationale (FLN), 'declared war' on France. Despite the employment of 400 000 troops with modern equipment and the use of torture, the French were unable to crush the rebellion, which gained in popular support. On 13 May 1958 criticism of army methods led the military in Algeria to refuse to recognise the government of France. General de Gaulle came to power in June 1958, and after further fighting the French voted in a referendum on 8 Jan 1961 to support his plan for self-determination for Algeria. A mutiny by the French army in Algeria led by Generals Challe and Salan on 22 Apr 1961 was suppressed. Despite terrorism by the French settlers belonging to the Organisation Armée Secrète (OAS) in Algeria, peace-talks were conducted between the Algerian nationalists and the French at Evian-les-Bains, and Algeria was granted its independence on 3 July 1962.

SUEZ CRISIS 1956

Following the decision by the United States and Britain to withdraw aid from Egypt's Aswan Dam project, Egypt announced the nationalisation of the Suez Canal on 26 July 1956. After secret talks with Britain and France, Israel invaded Sinai on 29 Oct 1956. When Egypt rejected a cease-fire ultimatum by France and Britain, their air-forces began to attack Egyptian air-bases on 31 Oct. On 5–6 Nov French and British troops moved into the Canal Zone by sea and air, but as a result of pressure from the United Nations and world opinion, they ended hostilities at midnight on 6–7 Nov. A UN emergency force took the place of the Franco-British forces.

FRANCO-TUNISIAN CONFLICT 1958–61

Tunisian support for anti-French operations by Algerian nationalists resulted in border incidents in 1958. French bombing of the border town of Sakhiet on 25 Feb 1958 led to evacuation of all French bases in Tunisia except Bizerta by June 1959. In fighting at Bizerta on 19–22 July 1961 800 Tunisians were killed. The base was returned to the Tunisians on 30 June 1962.

INDEPENDENCE STRUGGLES IN PORTUGAL'S AFRICAN COLONIES: MOZAMBIQUE, GUINEA AND ANGOLA 1960–76

Guerrilla activity in Portugal's African colonies grew during the 1960s. This became an increasing drain on Portugal's resources. Over half Portugal's annual budget went on defence, and its army in Africa numbering 135 000 in 1974 could only be maintained by unpopular conscription at home. Following the military coup which overthrew the Caetano regime in Portugal on 25 Apr 1974, the new government opened negotiations with the African nationalists. These led to the independence of Portuguese Guinea on 10 Sep 1974 and of Mozambique on 25 June 1975.

The situation in Angola was complicated by the presence of three rival liberation movements (MPLA, FNLA and UNITA). The Marxist MPLA took control of the capital Luanda in July 1975, and received tanks and artillery from the Soviet Union; from Oct 1975 over 15 000 Cuban soldiers began to arrive to support the MPLA. The FNLA and UNITA formed a joint military command, and when independence was formally proclaimed, on 11 Nov 1975, they established a rival government in Huambo. The UNITA–FNLA forces received aid from China and also from the United States until Congress stopped further appropriations. As full-scale civil war developed, the MPLA occupied northern Angola, driving the FNLA into Zaïre. UNITA forces were then attacked and Huambo fell in Feb 1976. South African troops had advanced into Angola but now began to withdraw, remaining to protect the Cunene hydro-electric scheme and refugee camps until March. The MPLA under Agostinho Neto was recognised as the government of Angola and became a member of the United Nations in Nov 1976, but the FNLA and UNITA continued to wage a sporadic guerrilla campaign.

CONFLICT IN THE CONGO 1960–67

The Congo (now Zaïre) was granted its independence by the Belgians on 30 June 1960, but it proved to be ill prepared for this step. There was widespread disorder, the army mutinied and on 11 July 1960 Moïse Tshombe proclaimed the rich mining province of Katanga an independent state and requested

Belgian aid. Fearing for his country's independence, the Prime Minister of the Congo, Patrice Lumumba, appealed to the United Nations for assistance. A peacekeeping force, which eventually grew to some 20 000 men, was established on 14 July 1960. After he had sought and received Soviet aid, Lumumba was dismissed by the President, Joseph Kasavubu, on 5 Sep 1960, but refused to resign. On 14 Sep the army leader, Col. Mobutu, took power. Lumumba was captured by Mobutu's troops on 1 Dec 1960, handed over to the Katangese and murdered in Feb 1961. For the next two years periods of armed conflict and negotiation between the central government, the Katangese secessionists and the United Nations failed to resolve the Congo's problems. Katanga's secession was not finally ended until Dec 1962 when a UN offensive against the province forced Moïse Tshombe into exile on 15 Jan 1963.

The last UN forces left the Congo on 30 June 1964. In an attempt to find a stable government Tshombe was recalled as Premier on 10 July 1964, but there was continued fighting. Rebels established a rival government in Stanleyville and held 2000 white hostages, but Belgian paratroops intervened on 24 Nov 1964 to free them. Following Kasavubu's dismissal of Tshombe in Oct 1965, Gen. Mobutu again took power in Nov. Violence continued until July 1967, when a revolt by mercenaries in the eastern provinces was suppressed.

EGYPT'S INVOLVEMENT IN THE YEMEN 1962–7

Following the death of the Imam of the Yemen in 1962, Egypt supported an armed uprising which resulted in a new regime. A civil war then developed in the Yemen in which some 70 000 Egyptian troops and republican forces fought against royalists supported with arms by Saudi Arabia. An agreement for a ceasefire was signed in Aug 1965 and Egypt withdrew her forces in 1967.

ERITREAN SECESSION FROM ETHIOPIA 1962–90

Eritrea, formerly an Italian colony, was made a federated state of the Ethiopian Empire in 1952 and fully integrated 10 years later. A secession movement grew up in the province and by 1976 there were some 15 000 guerrillas in arms. While the Ethiopian government was also engaged in fighting in the Ogaden, the guerrillas were able to take control of almost the whole of Eritrea, with the exception of Asmara and the Red Sea ports of Massawa and Assab. However, once the Somali-backed forces in the Ogaden had been defeated, Ethiopian troops, with Soviet and Cuban assistance, launched a major counter-offensive against the Eritrean guerrillas in May 1978. The guerrillas were forced to lift the siege of Asmara, and in Nov 1978 Ethiopian troops regained control of the 72-mile road linking Massawa and Asmara. The last big town in rebel hands, Keren, fell to government forces at the end of Nov 1978. Guerrilla warfare continued, though the division of the separatist movement in Eritrea into warring factions greatly reduced its effectiveness. There was an upsurge in fighting in 1988 as Eritrean guerrillas resumed co-operation with the Tigrean separatists which had been broken off in 1985.

BORDER CONFLICT BETWEEN ALGERIA AND MOROCCO 1963

Serious border fighting took place between Algeria and Morocco in Oct 1963 in the Atlas Mountains area.

KENYA–SOMALI BORDER WAR 1963–7

The 1960 independence constitution of the Somali Democratic Republic contained a commitment to recover its 'lost territories', one of which was the Northern Frontier district of Kenya. Serious border clashes between the Kenyans and Somalis began in Mar 1963 and diplomatic relations were broken off in Dec. The conflict continued until the two countries agreed to end the fighting by the Declaration of Arusha on 28 Oct 1967.

CIVIL WAR IN THE SUDAN SINCE 1963

The Anyanya rebels demanding secession for southern Sudan began a campaign of guerrilla warfare in 1963. They were supported by the Israelis, who provided training and captured Soviet and Chinese weapons. The Sudanese government received help from Arab states, such as the United Arab Republic and Libya, and the Soviet Union. Peace talks between the government and the rebels began in Addis Ababa in Feb 1972. An agreement for a ceasefire and regional self-government for the southern provinces was reached on 28 Feb, and this was ratified on 27 Mar.

There was renewed fighting in the Sudan in the 1980s when a mutiny amongst southern troops and opposition to President Nimeri's imposition of Islamic law in 1983 led to a new guerrilla campaign. This was conducted by the Sudan People's Liberation Army led by Colonel John Garang.

SOMALI–ETHIOPIAN CONFLICT 1964–78

The Somali Democratic Republic claims the Ogaden desert region in the south of Ethiopia, as well as parts of Kenya and the tiny state of Djibouti. Clashes between Ethiopia and the Somali Republic resulted in an inconclusive border war in 1964. The turmoil in Ethiopia after the downfall of Emperor Haile Selassie in 1974 led Somalia to foster a guerrilla movement in the Ogaden, the Western Somali Liberation Front. A Somali-backed offensive during 1977 gave the guerrillas control of the southern desert area. A new situation developed, however, when the Russians switched their support from Somalia to Ethiopia. In Nov 1977 President Barre of Somalia expelled the 6000 Russian military and civilian advisers from his country, withdrew all naval and military facilities and renounced his 1974 treaty of friendship with the Soviet Union. Massive quantities of Russian military equipment were transported to Ethiopia in preparation for a counter-offensive in the Ogaden. This offensive in 1978 restored Ethiopian control of the Ogaden region.

INSURGENCY IN SOUTHERN AFRICA SINCE 1965

In Rhodesia black nationalist guerrilla activity grew after Ian Smith's Unilateral Declaration of Independence on 11 Nov 1965. By the end of 1978 it was estimated that there were some 9000–15 000 guerrillas operating inside Rhodesia and martial law had been extended to three-quarters of the country. In Mar 1978 Ian Smith reached agreement with three leaders of African organisations inside Rhodesia, Bishop Muzorewa, the Revd Ndabaningi Sithole and Chief Chirau, but the 'internal settlement' did not bring the fighting to an end. The guerrilla campaign continued, conducted by the Zimbabwe People's Revolutionary Army (ZIPRA), the military wing of Joshua Nkomo's Zimbabwe African People's Union (ZAPU), and the Zimbabwe African National Liberation Army (ZANLA), the military wing of Robert Mugabe's Zimbabwe African National Union (ZANU). Rhodesian government forces carried out raids on guerrilla camps in Mozambique and Zambia. A settlement for an end to the conflict based on a new constitution was reached at a conference at Lancaster House in London in 1979. Zimbabwe became an independent republic in 1980.

Guerrilla warfare was also being conducted in Namibia (South West Africa). Namibia was mandated by the League of Nations to South Africa in 1920. South Africa was prepared to move towards independence for Namibia, but refused to recognise the South West Africa People's Organisation (SWAPO), which was designated as the 'sole authentic representative of the Namibian people' by the United Nations in 1973. Guerrilla warfare was stepped up by SWAPO in 1978 from bases in Angola and Zambia as South Africa organised pre-independence elections in Namibia. SWAPO activity continued despite the signature of a non-aggression pact by Angola and South Africa in 1984. There were major clashes in 1988 inside Angolan territory near the Namibian border between the forces of South Africa and Angola (supported by Cuban troops). The conflict was finally ended in 1989, as Namibian independence was agreed for March 1990.

CONFLICT IN CHAD 1965–88

After 1965 there were sporadic outbreaks of fighting inspired by the Chad National Liberation Front (Frolinat). Guerrillas backed by Libya opposed the government of Chad, which was supported by France. A ceasefire agreement was signed in 1978 after talks between the government and the rebels at Sebha in Libya.

There was renewed fighting in 1979 as conflict developed between two factions in Frolinat: FAN under Hissène Habré, and the more militant FAP, backed by Libya, under Goukouri Oueddei. Habré's army defeated the FAP and captured the capital, Ndjamena, in 1982.

Fighting resumed in 1983. As FAP and Libyan forces advanced, Hissène Habré appealed for foreign help and troops were sent by France and Zaïre. The Libyan advance was halted but the north of Chad remained under Libyan control. In 1986 the situation changed when Goukouri Oueddei was wounded and taken prisoner after a dispute with his Libyan allies. His men then joined forces with government troops, and together they crossed the demarcation line into Libyan-controlled territory. In 1987 the Libyans were forced to evacuate their last important base in northern Chad at Faya-Largeau.

NIGERIAN CIVIL WAR 1967–70

Tribal rivalry in Nigeria led to a prolonged civil war when the Ibos of the Eastern Region attempted to form a breakaway state. On 30 May 1967 the military governor of Eastern Nigeria, Col. Ojukwu, declared the region an independent sovereign country under the name of the Republic of Biafra. Troops of the Nigerian federal army attacked across the northern border of Biafra on 7 July 1967. On 20 May 1968 they captured Port Harcourt, but the Ibos continued to resist tenaciously. European nations became involved in the war as suppliers of arms, equipment and advisers, and in 1969 Count Carl-Gustav von Rosen, a Swedish pilot, formed a small but effective Biafran air-force, which carried out attacks on federal territory. Exhaustion and shortage of supplies finally led to the collapse of Biafran resistance after a four-pronged federal attack in Dec 1969. Col. Ojukwu flew into exile and the Biafran army surrendered on 15 Jan 1970.

TRIBAL WARFARE IN BURUNDI AND RWANDA 1972–3

In Apr 1972 guerrillas from the majority Hutu tribe in Burundi attacked the ruling Tutsi minority, killing between 5000 and 15 000. The Burundi armed forces, which were under Tutsi command, retaliated with help from troops from Zaïre and by the end of May the death toll had risen to between 50 000 and 100 000. There was renewed fighting between the Hutu and Tutsi in Rwanda in Feb 1973. In May 1973 Hutu rebels from Rwanda and Tanzania invaded Burundi. In response Burundi troops crossed the Tanzanian border and killed 10 Tanzanians.

CONFLICT BETWEEN UGANDA AND TANZANIA 1972–9

On 17 Sep 1972 a 'People's Army' of some 1000 men supporting the ex-President of Uganda, Milton Obote, invaded Uganda from Tanzania and advanced on Kampala. However, they were repulsed by President Amin's forces and Ugandan aircraft bombed the Tanzanian towns of Bukoba and Mwanza. On 21 Sep the Somali Foreign Minister negotiated a ceasefire and a peace agreement was signed at Mogadishu on 5 Oct 1972. Spasmodic guerrilla warfare continued in the area west of Lake Victoria. More serious fighting flared up in Oct 1978 when Ugandan forces invaded Tanzania. Ugandan troops occupied some 700 square miles of Tanzanian territory but withdrew in Nov. Fighting continued on the border in 1979. In January Tanzanian forces, with armed Ugandan exiles, advanced into Uganda. Kampala fell in April 1979 and President Amin fled the country.

CONFLICT IN SPANISH SAHARA SINCE 1975

Spanish Sahara was claimed by Morocco and Mauritania. After the International Court of Justice at the Hague had ruled in favour of a plebiscite to settle the future of the territory in Oct 1975, King Hassan of Morocco called on 350 000 of his subjects to march unarmed into Spanish Sahara. They crossed the border on 6 Nov, but were recalled three days later. On 14 Nov Spain agreed to hand over Spanish Sahara to Morocco and Mauritania, and Spanish troops were evacuated in Jan 1976.

Morocco and Mauritania formed a joint administration of the territory. But the Algerian-backed liberation movement, the Polisario, proclaimed the Saharan Arab Democratic Republic and began an armed struggle. Morocco and Mauritania formed a joint military command in May 1977, and Mauritania received support from the French air force. Then in August 1979 Mauritania came to terms with the Polisario, but Morocco moved to occupy the whole of Western Sahara. In 1984 Morocco built a 1600-mile defensive wall from the Moroccan town of Zag to Dakhla on the Atlantic coast, protecting the economically important north of the territory and creating an effective stalemate.

EGYPT–LIBYA BORDER CLASH 1977

After several years of strained relations, fighting broke out on the border between Egypt and Libya in July 1977. President Sadat of Egypt ordered a ceasefire on 24 July, which was observed by both sides.

CONFLICT IN ZAÏRE 1977–8

On 10 Mar 1977 Zaïre's Shaba province (formerly Katanga) was invaded from Angola by the Congolese Front de Libération Nationale. President Mobutu of Zaïre accused the Cubans of leading the invasion and suspended diplomatic relations with Cuba on 4 Apr. On 10 Apr 10 French transport aircraft airlifted 1500 Moroccan troops to Zaïre. They successfully aided the Zaïreans in repelling the invaders. In May 1978 a fresh invasion of Shaba by 2000 Katangan exiles took place. French and Belgian paratroopers were sent to Kolwezi to rescue white hostages on 19 May, and the invaders were dispersed.

GROWTH IN MANPOWER OF AFRICAN ARMED FORCES SINCE 1970

	1970	1975	1977	1980	1985	1987
Algeria	57 000	63 000	75 800	101 000	170 000	169 000
Angola	–	–	31 500	32 500	49 500	53 000
Benin	n.a.	n.a.	2 250	2 180	3 460	4 350
Botswana	n.a.	n.a.	n.a.	2 000	3 000	3 250
Burkina Faso	1 800	2 050	8 070	3 775	4 000	8 700
Burundi	n.a.	n.a.	n.a.	6 000	5 200	7 200
Cameroon	4 350	5 600	6 000	7 300	7 300	11 620
Central African Republic	n.a.	n.a.	1 200	1 860	2 300	4 300
Chad	2 650	4 200	5 200	3 200	12 200	17 000
Congo	2 200	5 500	7 000	5 525	8 700	8 750
Egypt	213 000	322 500	345 000	367 000	445 000	445 000
Ethiopia	45 400	44 800	53 500	229 000	217 000	320 000
Gabon	n.a.	n.a.	1 250	1 550	2 400	2 850
Ghana	15 900	15 450	17 700	17 450	15 100	10 600
Guinea	5 400	5 650	5 850	9 150	9 900	9 900
Ivory Coast	4 400	4 100	4 950	6 450	13 220	14 920
Kenya	5 400	7 550	7 700	14 750	13 650	13 350
Liberia	4 150	5 220	5 220	5 130	6 750	5 750
Libya	15 000	32 000	29 200	53 000	73 000	76 500
Madagascar	4 500	4 760	10 150	13 000	21 100	21 000
Malawi	1 150	1 600	2 400	3 600	5 250	5 250
Mali	3 650	4 200	4 200	4 950	4 950	7 350
Mauritania	1 530	1 250	7 450	7 970	8 470	14 870
Morocco	50 000	61 000	84 650	116 500	149 000	293 500
Mozambique	–	–	19 000	24 300	15 800	31 700
Niger	2 100	2 100	2 050	2 220	2 220	3 290
Nigeria	163 500	208 000	230 500	146 000	94 000	94 500
Rwanda	2 750	3 750	3 750	3 650	5 150	5 150

continued

	1970	1975	1977	1980	1985	1987
Senegal	5 850	5 900	5 950	9 420	9 700	9 700
Sierra Leone	1 600	2 125	2 200	2 700	3 100	3 100
Somalia	12 000	23 000	31 500	61 550	62 700	65 000
South Africa	43 800	50 500	55 000	86 050	106 400	97 000
Sudan	27 450	48 600	52 100	68 000	56 600	58 500
Tanzania	7 900	14 600	18 600	51 850	40 350	40 050
Togo	1 250	1 750	2 500	3 510	5 110	5 910
Tunisia	21 050	24 000	22 200	28 600	35 100	40 100
Uganda	6 700	21 000	21 000	7 000	18 000	20 000
Zaïre	38 250	43 400	33 400	20 500	48 000	51 000
Zambia	4 400	5 800	8 500	14 300	16 200	16 200
Zimbabwe	4 600	5 700	9 550	13 500	42 000	47 000

n.a. No figures available.
Source: *The Military Balance* (International Inst. Strategic Studies)

CIVIL WAR IN MOZAMBIQUE 1976–90

From 1976 Rhodesia fostered a military campaign by dissidents of the Mozambique National Resistance Movement, which carried out guerrilla raids and sabotage. After 1980 South Africa took over support of the NRM as part of its policy of 'destabilising' its neighbours. Mozambique and South Africa signed a non-aggression pact, the Nkomati accord, in 1984, but this had little effect on the levels of violence.

CIVIL WAR IN UGANDA 1981–8

Violence grew after the return of Dr Obote as the country's ruler between the armed forces and guerrillas of the National Resistance Army under the former defence minister, Yoweri Museveni. The turmoil in Uganda came to a head in July 1985 when dissension developed within the army between the Langi and Acholi tribes over sharing the burden of the campaign against the NRA. Dr Obote was ousted and a military council was formed under the army chief, General Tito Okello. In December 1985 General Okello and Mr Museveni reached agreement on a power-sharing government. But after continuing army violence the NRA occupied Kampala, General Okello was deposed and Mr Museveni became the new president in January 1986. Outbreaks of dissident activity were gradually brought under control by the new government.

COUPS, MUTINIES AND ASSASSINATIONS

1952	23 July	EGYPT. Coup by 'Free Officers' led by Gen. Neguib results in King Farouk's abdication. Neguib replaced by Nasser 14 Nov 1954.
1958	17 Nov	SUDAN. Military junta takes power, with Gen. Ibrahim Abboud as Prime Minister and Minister of Defence. Three further attempted military coups take place in 1959. Student demonstrations lead to the restoration of civilian rule 30 Oct 1964.
1960	13 Dec	ETHIOPIA. While Emperor Haile Selassie is in Brazil the Imperial Bodyguard under Brig. Gen. Mengistu Neway carries out a coup. It is suppressed by units of the regular army.
1962	21 Jan	TOGO. Unsuccessful attempt to assassinate President Olympio.
	1 Aug	GHANA. Unsuccessful attempt to assassinate President Nkrumah.

17 Dec   SENEGAL. Attempted coup by the Prime Minister, Mamadou Dia, to forestall a censure motion by the National Assembly. Paratroop commanders support President Senghor and Dia and his followers are arrested.

1963 13 Jan   TOGO. President Olympio assassinated during an army coup. The army installs a civilian government under Olympio's political rival, Nicholas Grunitzky.

15 Aug   CONGO (ex-French). President Youlou forced to resign and the army oversees handing over of power to Alphonse Massemba-Débat.

23 Oct   DAHOMEY. During a political crisis caused by the arrest of trade union leaders, President Maga stands down and Col. Soglo, army chief-of-staff, assumes power. He returns the country to civilian rule in Jan 1964.

1964 2 Jan   GHANA. Unsuccessful attempt to assassinate President Nkrumah.

12 Jan   ZANZIBAR. Popular armed insurrection drives the Sultan into exile and Sheikh Karume becomes President.

20 Jan   TANGANYIKA. Army mutiny over pay and conditions put down with the help of British troops.

23 Jan   UGANDA. Mutiny at army barracks at Jinja suppressed with the help of British troops.

23 Jan   KENYA. British troops restore order after a mutiny among Kenyan forces at Lanet.

18 Feb   GABON. Group of young lieutenants carry out a coup against President Léon M'Ba and begin to form a new government under the former Foreign Minister, Jean Aubame. Two days later the revolt is suppressed by the intervention of French troops.

1965 19 June   ALGERIA. President Ben Bella overthrown by Col. Boumédienne, army chief-of-staff.

18 Oct   BURUNDI. Army mutineers attack the King's palace and wound the Prime Minister, Léopold Biha. Martial law declared on 20 Oct 1965.

25 Nov   CONGO (ex-Belgian). Gen. Mobutu deposes President Kasavubu and becomes President in his place.

29 Nov   DAHOMEY. Col. Soglo forces the resignation of the Presi-

dent and Prime Minister. An interim government set up under Tahirou Congacou, but Col. Soglo again takes power on 22 Dec 1965, when politicians fail to agree on the composition of a new government.

1966	1 Jan	CENTRAL AFRICAN REPUBLIC. Col. Bokassa, army commander-in-chief, ousts President Dacko and takes power.
	4 Jan	UPPER VOLTA. Lt-Col. Lamizana deposes President Maurice Yameogo after conflict between political factions and installs a military government.
	15 Jan	NIGERIA. Young army officers led by Maj. Nzeogwu carry out a coup. The Nigerian cabinet requests Maj.-Gen. Ironsi, the army commander, to take over the government. In a fresh coup on 29 July 1966 Lt-Col. Gowon takes power.
	24 Feb	GHANA. Military coup overthrows President Nkrumah while he is in Peking. A government formed by Maj.-Gen. Ankrah and Police Commissioner Harlley.
	24 May	UGANDA. Armed expulsion of the Kabaka of Buganda by the Prime Minister.
	30 May	CONGO (ex-Belgian). Unsuccessful coup against Gen. Mobutu.
	June	CONGO (ex-French). Abortive coup by discontented army units.
	8 July	BURUNDI. King Mwambutsa IV, absent in Europe, is deposed by his son, Crown Prince Ndizeye, who becomes King Ntare V. He himself is deposed by his premier, Capt. Michel Micombero, on 28 Nov 1966 and a republic is proclaimed.
	26 Oct	CONGO (ex-Belgian). Prime Minister Gen. Mulamba ousted and President Mobutu assumes the office of Prime Minister as well as head of state.
1967	13 Jan	TOGO. Successful coup by Lt-Col. Eyadéma, army chief-of-staff, ousts President Grunitzky.
	8 Feb	SIERRA LEONE. Failure of attempted military coup.
	23 Mar	SIERRA LEONE. Following disputed elections, Sir Albert Margai's government overthrown by army under Lt-Col. Juxon-Smith.

17 Apr   GHANA. Abortive coup led by Lt. Arthur; leaders of coup publicly executed 9 May 1967.

5 July   CONGO (ex-Belgian). Rising by mercenaries against President Mobutu put down by Congolese army.

14 Dec   ALGERIA. Unsuccessful coup by Col. Zbiri, who had been dismissed as army chief-of-staff earlier in the week.

17 Dec   DAHOMEY. President Soglo overthrown by junior army officers. Government dissolved and a revolutionary military committee set up. On 18 Dec 1967 Maurice Kouandeté appointed President.

1968   18 Apr   SIERRA LEONE. Juxon-Smith's military junta overthrown in a 'sergeants' coup'. Civilian rule under Siaka Stevens restored 26 Apr 1968.

26 Aug   CHAD. At request of President Tombalbaye, French parachute troops flown in to help government put down rebellion.

4 Sep   CONGO (ex-French). President Massemba-Débat resigns, after fighting in Brazzaville. On 6 Sep a provisional government formed under Capt. Raoul, who is succeeded as President by Maj. N'Gouabi.

19 Nov   MALI. President Keita overthrown in a coup led by Lt. Moussa Traoré.

1969   5 Mar   EQUATORIAL GUINEA. Unsuccessful attempt to seize power by Foreign Minister, Atanasio Ndongo.

10 Mar   GUINEA. Unsuccessful attempt to overthrow President Sekou Touré.

25 May   SUDAN. Government overthrown in left-wing military coup and National Revolutionary Council formed under Col. Jaafar al-Nimeri.

1 Sep   LIBYA. King Idris deposed by military junta led by Col. Gaddafi, who proclaims a Socialist Arab Republic.

15 Oct   SOMALIA. President Abdelrashid Ali Shermarke assassinated; army and police commanders seize power and set up a Revolutionary Council.

Nov   CONGO (ex-French). Alleged coup attempt by supporters of ex-President Youlou.

10 Dec   DAHOMEY. President Zinsou overthrown in military coup.

19 Dec   UGANDA. President Obote wounded in assassination attempt.

1970   27 Mar   SUDAN. Unsuccessful attempt to assassinate President Nimeri.

1971   25 Jan   UGANDA. President Obote overthrown by Gen. Amin.

22 Mar   SIERRA LEONE. Abortive army coup, after which Prime Minister Stevens signs a mutual defence treaty with Guinea and Guinean forces enter Sierra Leone at his request on 28 Mar 1971.

5 May   SOMALIA. Revolutionary Council announces failure of coup.

31 May   MADAGASCAR. President Tsiranana announces failure of plot against his government.

5 July   BURUNDI. Unsuccessful attempt to overthrow government.

10 July   MOROCCO. Attempt to overthrow King Hassan fails.

11 July   UGANDA. Abortive coup against Gen. Amin by troops in north-east Uganda.

19 July   SUDAN. President Nemery overthrown in left-wing coup but restored in counter-coup on 22 July 1971.

1972   13 Jan   GHANA. Government of Dr Busia overthrown by Lt-Col. Acheampong, who establishes a military National Redemption Council to rule by decree.

22 Feb   CONGO (ex-French). Unsuccessful left-wing coup.

23 Feb   DAHOMEY. Abortive coup by mutinous army units from Ouidah.

7 Apr   TANZANIA. Sheikh Karume, First Vice-President, assassinated.

18 May   MADAGASCAR. Following fighting between students and security forces, President Tsirinana relinquishes executive power to army commander, Maj.-Gen. Ramanantsoa.

16 Aug   MOROCCO. In an attempted coup, rebel aircraft attack King Hassan's aircraft, Rabat airport and the royal palace; Gen. Oufkir, Minister of Defence and leader of coup, commits suicide.

26 Oct   DAHOMEY. Following military coup, Maj. Mathieu Kerekou, deputy commander of armed forces, becomes President and Defence Minister.

1973 5 July   RWANDA. Maj.-Gen. Habyarimana seizes power from President Kayibanda in a bloodless coup.

1974 7 Jan   LESOTHO. Failure of attempted coup.

8 Feb   UPPER VOLTA. Successful army coup.

28 Feb   ETHIOPIA. Dissident troops take over Asmara, and Emperor Haile Selassie's government resigns next day.

24 Mar   UGANDA. Attempted army mutiny fails.

15 Apr   NIGER. President Hamani Diori overthrown in military coup; Lt-Col. Seyni Kountché becomes head of state.

1975 11 Feb   MADAGASCAR. President Ratsimandrava assassinated after six days in office.

13 Apr   CHAD. President Tombalbaye killed in army coup, Gen. Félix Malloum takes power.

29 July   NIGERIA. Gen. Gowon ousted by Brig. Murtala Mohamed while attending OAU summit meeting.

18 Dec   MOZAMBIQUE. Revolt by dissident soldiers and police crushed by Frelimo government.

1976 13 Feb   NIGERIA. Gen. Mohamed killed in an unsuccessful coup. Army chief-of-staff, Lt-Gen. Obasanjo, takes power. Leader of coup, Col. Dumka, executed by firing squad 15 May 1976.

15 Mar   NIGER. Unsuccessful coup led by Maj. Bayere; eight leaders of coup executed in May.

11 June   UGANDA. Unsuccessful attempt to assassinate President Amin.

2 July   SUDAN. Unsuccessful attempt to assassinate President Nimeri.

2 Nov   BURUNDI. President Micombero's government overthrown by the army in a bloodless coup.

1977 16 Jan   BENIN. Unsuccessful coup attempt by group of mercenaries.

3 Feb   ETHIOPIA. Brig.-Gen. Teferi Benti, Chairman of Military

Council, killed and Lt-Col. Mengistu Haile Mariam succeeds him.

18 Mar   CONGO (ex-French). President N'Gouabi assassinated. Col. Yhombi-Opango elected head of state 3 Apr 1977. Former President Massemba-Débat executed as one of the assassins.

1 Apr   CHAD. Attempted coup crushed by security forces.

27 May   ANGOLA. Unsuccessful coup attempt by followers of pro-Soviet Nito Alves.

5 June   SEYCHELLES. President Mancham overthrown by ex-Premier Albert René in a bloodless coup.

1979 12 Feb   CHAD. Attempt by Prime Minister, Hissène Habré, to oust President Malloum leads to bitter fighting between their forces.

1980 12 Apr   LIBERIA. Successful coup against the government of President Tolbert led by Master-Sgt Doe. Tolbert and many of his cabinet killed.

14 Nov   GUINEA-BISSAU. Successful coup deposed Government of President Luis Cabral. A Revolutionary Council was established under Joâo Bernardo Viera.

25 Nov   UPPER VOLTA. President Lamizana overthrown in military coup by Col. Zerbo.

1981 16 Mar   MAURITANIA. Attempt by two exiled colonels to overthrow government failed.

30 July   GAMBIA. President Dawda Jawara ousted while in London but restored by Senegalese troops.

10 Aug   LIBERIA. Master-Sgt. Doe announced failure of attempted coup by his deputy, Weh Syen.

1 Sep   CENTRAL AFRICAN REPUBLIC. President Dacko overthrown and Gen. Golingba assumed power.

6 Oct   EGYPT. President Sadat assassinated by Muslim extremists during a military parade.

26 Nov   SEYCHELLES. Troops foiled coup attempt against President René by foreign mercenaries.

31 Dec   GHANA. President Hilla Limann overthrown by Flt.-Lt Gerry Rawlings.

1982   23 Feb   UGANDA. Coup attempt against Dr Obote failed.

       1 Aug   KENYA. Coup by junior air-force officers suppressed.

       17 Aug   SEYCHELLES. Coup attempt suppressed.

       7 Nov   UPPER VOLTA. Col. Zerbo ousted in military coup.

1983   2 Mar   GHANA. Coup attempt failed.

       17 May   SUDAN. Mutiny by southern troops refusing to transfer to
                 the north suppressed.

       19 June   GHANA. Further coup plot failed.

       4 Aug   UPPER VOLTA. Major Ouedraogo overthrown in coup led
                 by former prime minister, Captain Sankara.

       6 Oct   NIGER. Coup attempt failed.

       31 Dec   NIGERIA. President Shagari overthrown in bloodless coup
                 by Maj.-Gen. Buhari.

1984   3 Apr   GUINEA. Military seized power after death of President
                 Touré.

       6 Apr   CAMEROON. Rebels under Col. Saleh failed in coup at-
                 tempt against President Biya.

       12 Dec   MAURITANIA. Military coup led by former prime minis-
                 ter, Lt.-Col. Taya, overthrew President Haidalla while
                 he was attending a conference in Burundi.

1985   6 Apr   SUDAN. President Nimeri ousted in a bloodless coup by
                 Gen. al-Dahab.

       4 July   GUINEA. Coup attempt by former prime minister, Col.
                 Traore, suppressed.

       27 July   UGANDA. President Obote overthrown in military coup
                 by Brig. Okello.

       27 Aug   NIGERIA. Maj.-Gen. Buhari overthrown and Maj.-Gen.
                 Babangida became president and commander-in-chief.

       12 Nov   LIBERIA. Coup attempt by Thomas Quiwonkpa failed.

       20 Dec   NIGERIA. Government announced discovery of coup at-
                 tempt.

1986   20 Jan   LESOTHO. Premier Chief Jonathan overthrown and re-
                 placed by military regime under Maj.-Gen. Justin Lek-
                 hanya.

	25 Feb	EGYPT. Mutiny and riots by security police in Cairo suppressed by government troops.
	4 Sep	LIBERIA. Authorities announced that attempt to overthrow government from outside the country had failed.
	24 Sep	TOGO. Attempt by commandos crossing from Ghana to overthrow President Eyadema failed.
1987	23 Mar	SIERRA LEONE. Attempt to seize power by senior police and junior army officers suppressed; Francis Minah, First Vice-President, arrested.
	8 June	GHANA. Authorities announced that coup plot thwarted.
	3 Sep	BURUNDI. President Jean-Baptiste Bagaza overthrown by the military whilst attending summit meeting in Canada.
	24 Sep	TRANSKEI. Military coup by Bantu Holomisa.
	15 Oct	BURKINA FASO. Captain Sankara murdered and Captain Compaore became president.
	Oct	MAURITANIA. Coup attempt by dissident army officers failed.
	7 Nov	TUNISIA. President Bourguiba declared unfit to rule on grounds of senility and deposed by Prime Minister, Colonel Zine el-Abidine Ben Ali.
	30 Dec	TRANSKEI. Further coup in the 'bantustan'.
1988	9–10 Feb	BOPHUTHATSWANA. Attempted coup suppressed by South African forces.
	8 Mar	SÃO TOMÉ AND PRÍNCIPE. Coup attempt by dissident right-wingers failed.
1989	30 June	SUDAN. Military coup succeeds.
1989	Dec	LIBERIA. Rebel incursion from Ivory Coast developed into a civil war.
1990	4 Mar	CISKEI. Military coup toppled regime.
	22 Apr	NIGERIA. Abortive but bloody coup attempt in Lagos.
	23 Apr	SUDAN. Attempted coup.
	29 June	ZAMBIA. Attempted coup in Lusaka.

7 FOREIGN AFFAIRS AND TREATIES

1945	10 May	Arab League formed. Present members: Algeria, Bahrain, Djibouti, Egypt, Iraq, Jordan, Kuwait, Lebanon, Libya, Mauritania, Morocco, Oman, Palestine, Qatar, Saudi Arabia, Somalia, Sudan, Syria, Tunisia, United Arab Emirates, Yemen Arab Republic and People's Democratic Republic of the Yemen
1950	17 June	Collective Security Pact signed in Alexandria by EGYPT, SAUDI ARABIA, SYRIA, LEBANON and YEMEN
1951	9 Nov	Mutual defence assistance agreement between UNITED STATES and SOUTH AFRICA
1952	1, 3 July	Exchange of notes between ETHIOPIA and UNITED KINGDOM on provision of facilities for British military aircraft
1953	11, 13 Mar	Exchange of notes between ETHIOPIA and UNITED KINGDOM on provision of facilities for British military aircraft
	29 July	20-year agreement on military bases between LIBYA and UNITED KINGDOM
1954	14 May	Agreement between ETHIOPIA and UNITED STATES on military bases
	9 Sep	Agreement between LIBYA and UNITED STATES on air bases
	Oct	Treaty between EGYPT and UNITED KINGDOM for withdrawal of British forces from the Canal Zone
1955	4 July	Simonstown naval co-operation agreement between SOUTH AFRICA and UNITED KINGDOM (revised Jan 1967 and ended 17 June 1975)

	27 Sep	Armaments agreement between EGYPT and CZECHOSLO-VAKIA
1957	Jan	Treaty of friendship between TUNISIA and LIBYA
1958	1 Feb	EGYPT entered into a union with SYRIA, forming the United Arab Republic (dissolved in 1961)
1959	9 Apr	Treaty of friendship between ISRAEL and LIBERIA
	8 July	Defence agreement between LIBERIA and UNITED STATES
1960	22 June	Defence agreement between FRANCE and SENEGAL
	27 June	Defence agreement between FRANCE and MADAGASCAR
	13 Aug	Defence agreement between FRANCE and CENTRAL AFRICAN REPUBLIC
	15 Aug	Defence agreement between FRANCE and CHAD
	15 Aug	Defence agreement between FRANCE and CONGO (ex-French)
	17 Aug	Defence agreement between FRANCE and GABON
	13 Nov	Defence agreement between FRANCE and CAMEROON
	Nov	Defence agreement between UNITED KINGDOM and NIGERIA (abrogated 21 Jan 1962)
1961	24 Apr	Defence agreement between FRANCE and IVORY COAST
	24 Apr	Defence agreement between FRANCE and DAHOMEY
	24 Apr	Defence agreement between FRANCE and UPPER VOLTA
	24 Apr	Defence agreement between FRANCE and NIGER
	19 June	Defence agreement between FRANCE and MAURITANIA
	18 Aug	Treaty of friendship between GHANA and CHINA
	31 Aug	Treaty of friendship and mutual assistance between ISRAEL and MADAGASCAR
1962	18 Mar	Evian agreement between FRANCE and ALGERIA
1963	May	Organisation of African Unity formed in Addis Ababa
	10 July	Defence agreement between FRANCE and TOGO
	July	Defence agreement between KENYA and ETHIOPIA
1964	3 Mar	Defence agreement between UGANDA and UNITED KINGDOM

	6 Mar	Defence agreement between KENYA and UNITED KINGDOM
1965	20 Feb	Treaty of friendship between TANZANIA and CHINA
	24 Aug	Yemen ceasefire agreement signed by EGYPT and SAUDI ARABIA
1966	4 Nov	Defence agreement between EGYPT and SYRIA
1967	30 May	Defence pact between EGYPT and JORDAN (joined by IRAQ 4 June 1967)
	30 Aug	Agreement on the Yemen between EGYPT and SAUDI ARABIA
	28 Oct	Declaration of Arusha by KENYA and SOMALIA ending border war
1968	4 Feb	Union of Central African States formed by CHAD, CONGO (ex-French) and CENTRAL AFRICAN REPUBLIC
	12 Mar	Defence agreement between MAURITIUS and UNITED KINGDOM
	5 Sep	Agreement between ETHIOPIA and SOMALIA to end subversive activity
1969	15 Jan	Treaty of co-operation between ALGERIA and MOROCCO
	10 Apr	Treaty of solidarity between ALGERIA and LIBYA
	13 Dec	Agreement between LIBYA and UNITED KINGDOM for British withdrawal from Libyan bases
1970	6 May	Agreement on naval base at Dar es Salaam between CHINA and TANZANIA
	9 June	Treaty between KENYA and ETHIOPIA delimiting their border
	5 Nov	Agreement on political federation between EGYPT, LIBYA and SUDAN (joined by IRAQ 26 Nov 1970)
1971	16 Mar	Agreement for united military command between EGYPT and SYRIA
	26 May	Mutual defence treaty between SIERRA LEONE and GUINEA
	27 Mar	15-year treaty of friendship between EGYPT and SOVIET UNION (abrogated by Egypt 15 Mar 1976)
	20 Aug	Agreement for Federation of Arab Republics between EGYPT, SYRIA and LIBYA

	9 Oct	Aid agreement between ETHIOPIA and CHINA
1972	27 Mar	Peace agreement between SUDANESE GOVERNMENT and ANYANYA REBELS
	28 June	Mutual defence and trade agreements between UGANDA and SUDAN
	5 Oct	Peace treaty between UGANDA and TANZANIA
1973	3 Mar	Treaty of co-operation and mutual assistance between NIGERIA and MALI
	4 June	Agreement between FRANCE and MADAGASCAR ending French military presence
	11 Nov	Agreement on ceasefire line between ISRAEL and EGYPT
1974	14–18 Jan	Trade and economic and technical co-operation treaties between CHINA and MADAGASCAR
	18 Jan	Agreement between EGYPT and ISRAEL on disengagement of forces on Suez Canal
	13–15 Feb	Agreement on technical and economic co-operation between FRANCE and LIBYA
	Feb	Co-operation agreement between FRANCE and CAMEROON
	29 Mar	Co-operation agreement between FRANCE and SENEGAL
	12–14 June	Declaration of co-operation and friendship between EGYPT and UNITED STATES
	2–5 July	Aid pact between EGYPT and WEST GERMANY
	11 July	Friendship and co-operation treaty and technical agreement between SOMALIA and SOVIET UNION (renounced by the former Nov 1977)
	26 Aug	Independence agreement between PORTUGAL and PORTUGUESE GUINEA
	5 Sep	Economic and technical co-operation agreement between TOGO and CHINA
	7 Sep	Lusaka agreement between PORTUGAL and FRELIMO for independence of Mozambique
	27 Nov	Independence agreement between PORTUGAL and SÃO TOMÉ and PRIŃCIPE
1975	15 Jan	Agreement on Angolan independence between PORTUGAL and ANGOLAN LIBERATION MOVEMENTS

	4 Sep	Agreement between ISRAEL and EGYPT signed in Geneva for Israeli withdrawal in Sinai and establishment of buffer zone
	Dec	Defence agreement between ALGERIA and LIBYA
1976	20 Apr	Military aid protocol between EGYPT and CHINA
	19 July	Defence agreement between EGYPT and SUDAN
	10 Oct	Treaty of friendship between ANGOLA and SOVIET UNION
	21 Dec	Agreement of formation of unified political command between EGYPT and SYRIA
1977	Jan	Defence agreement between EGYPT and SUDAN
	31 Mar	Treaty of friendship between MOZAMBIQUE and SOVIET UNION
	6 May	Co-operation pacts between ETHIOPIA and SOVIET UNION
1978	26 June	Friendship and co-operation agreement between ANGOLA and PORTUGAL
	17 Sep	Camp David agreements between EGYPT and ISRAEL for conclusion of peace treaty and Middle East settlement.
	17 Oct	Agreements on co-operation and normalisation of relations between ANGOLA and ZAMBIA
	22 Oct	Treaty of friendship and co-operation between ANGOLA and BULGARIA
	20 Nov	Treaty of friendship and co-operation between ETHIOPIA and SOVIET UNION
	2 Dec	Treaty of friendship and co-operation between ETHIOPIA and CZECHOSLOVAKIA
1979	31 Jan	Treaty of friendship and co-operation between ETHIOPIA and KENYA
	19 Feb	Treaty of friendship and co-operation between ANGOLA and EAST GERMANY
	24 Feb	Treaty of friendship and co-operation between MOZAMBIQUE and EAST GERMANY
	26 Mar	Treaty of peace between EGYPT and ISRAEL
	11 Apr	Treaty of friendship and co-operation between GABON and ROMANIA

14 Apr	Treaty of friendship and co-operation between ANGOLA and ROMANIA
17 Apr	Treaty of friendship and co-operation between ZAMBIA and ROMANIA
20 Apr	Treaty of friendship and co-operation between MOZAMBIQUE and ROMANIA
23 Apr	Treaty of friendship and co-operation between BURUNDI and ROMANIA
25 Apr	Treaty of friendship and co-operation between SUDAN and ROMANIA
10 May	Agreement for creation of a joint security force between ANGOLA and ZAMBIA
12 Oct	Non-aggression pact between ANGOLA, ZAÏRE and ZAMBIA
9 Nov	Treaty of friendship and co-operation between GUINEA-BISSAU and NORTH KOREA
15 Nov	Treaty of friendship and co-operation between ETHIOPIA and EAST GERMANY
2 Dec	Treaty of friendship and co-operation between ETHIOPIA and SOUTH YEMEN
12 Dec	Treaty of friendship and co-operation between ETHIOPIA and POLAND
21 Dec	Lancaster House agreements between BRITAIN and representatives of the Popular Front and the Salisbury regime concerning the future of ZIMBABWE
1980 7 Feb	Technical military co-operation agreement between EGYPT and ZAÏRE
17 Mar	Defence pact between LIBYA and MALTA
19 Mar	Treaty of friendship and co-operation between ZAÏRE and ROMANIA
23 May	Military co-operation agreement between MOZAMBIQUE and ZIMBABWE
15 June	Treaty of friendship between LIBYA and CHAD
26 June	Military co-operation and aid agreement between KENYA and UNITED STATES
22 Aug	Military facilities agreement between SOMALIA and UNITED STATES

	17 Sep	Military co-operation agreement between SUDAN and FRANCE
	10 Oct	Formation by LIBYA and SYRIA of the 'Arab Masses State'
	12 Oct	Treaty of friendship and co-operation between GUINEA and NORTH KOREA
	12 Oct	Treaty of friendship and co-operation between ZIMBABWE and NORTH KOREA
	5 Dec	Treaty of friendship and co-operation between TANZANIA and ZIMBABWE
1981	21 Mar	Treaty of friendship and co-operation between ETHIOPIA and DJIBOUTI
	13 May	Treaty of friendship and co-operation between SOVIET UNION and the CONGO
	5 June	Co-operation agreement between SOMALIA and NIGERIA
	29 June	Co-operation agreement between SOMALIA and KENYA
	6 Aug	5-year defence agreement between EGYPT and UNITED STATES
	19 Aug	Treaty of friendship and co-operation between ETHIOPIA, LIBYA and SOUTH YEMEN
	13 Sep	Treaty of friendship and co-operation between ETHIOPIA and CZECHOSLOVAKIA
	16 Oct	Treaty of mutual military co-operation between TANZANIA and BULGARIA
	19 Oct	Treaty of friendship and co-operation between ANGOLA and NORTH KOREA
	21 Oct	Treaty of friendship between MOZAMBIQUE and CZECHOSLOVAKIA
1982	19 Jan	Agreement between EGYPT and ISRAEL on withdrawal from Sinai
	15 Feb	Military and economic co-operation agreement between TANZANIA and MOZAMBIQUE
	17 May	Co-operation agreement between ZAMBIA and CZECHOSLOVAKIA
	Sep	Treaty of friendship and co-operation between LIBYA and CZECHOSLOVAKIA

	12 Oct	Charter of political and economic integration between EGYPT and SUDAN
1983	5 Jan	Border demarcation agreement between NIGER and ALGERIA
	20 Jan	Military co-operation agreement between ISRAEL and ZAÏRE
	24 Jan	Treaty of friendship and co-operation between LIBYA and ROMANIA
	Jan	Treaty of friendship and co-operation between LIBYA and BULGARIA
	20 Mar	Treaty of friendship and concord between ALGERIA and TUNISIA (MAURITANIA acceded later in the year)
	27 Mar	Co-operation between ALGERIA and LIBYA
	8 May	Border demarcation agreement between ALGERIA and MALI
1984	16 Feb	Lusaka accord between ANGOLA and SOUTH AFRICA
	16 Mar	Nkomati accord between MOZAMBIQUE and SOUTH AFRICA
	13 Aug	Federation treaty between LIBYA and MOROCCO (abrogated by Morocco on 29 Aug 1986)
	17 Aug	Military training agreement between UGANDA and BRITAIN
	17 Sep	Agreement between LIBYA and FRANCE on mutual withdrawal of troops from Chad
	23 Oct	Defence and security co-operation agreement between MOZAMBIQUE and MALAWI
	24 Oct	Agreement between NIGERIA and NORTH KOREA on establishing joint defence programmes
	18 Nov	5-year treaty of security and economic co-operation between LIBYA and MALTA
	2 Dec	Border security agreement between SOMALIA and KENYA
	10 Dec	Co-operation agreement between GHANA, BENIN, NIGERIA and TOGO
	19 Dec	Military training agreement between GHANA and BRITAIN
1985	9 Feb	Agreement on defence and security between ANGOLA and ZAÏRE

	9 July	Military co-operation agreement between ZAÏRE and CHAD
1986	24 Nov	Treaty between SOUTH AFRICA and LESOTHO on the first phase of the Lesotho Highlands Water Project
1988	3 Apr	Agreement between ETHIOPIA and SOMALIA for the restoration of diplomatic relations and disengagement of troops in border areas

8 POPULATION AND ETHNIC GROUPS

The United Nations Population Division estimated the population of Africa in 1978 to be in the region of 435 millions while the World Bank gave a figure of 449 millions. Both figures are tentative owing to the lack of accurate population data for the continent. The United Nations estimate for 1985 had reached 550 millions. Many African states do not have a precise idea of their population size. Certain African states have never taken a census, a good many have only held a single count, and most official population figures are based on sample surveys. There have been fairly accurate, and therefore useful, census records for some states, for example, Mauritius and Ghana. However, many of the census returns that have been produced are of rudimentary value for purposes of social and economic planning. Political pressures sometimes have led to false census returns, a good example being the Nigerian census of 1962 and 1963 which produced highly questionable figures.

Africa's population is growing at a very rapid rate, well in excess of 2.5 per cent per annum. In some countries, for example Kenya, annual growth rates are as high as 4 per cent. A three per cent annual growth rate in population will result in a doubling in the number of people in thirty years and this inevitably means severe pressure being placed on Africa's limited resources. It is also a very young population, with about half the total below the age of 20 years. Eighty per cent of Africans live in rural areas, but urban growth is exceedingly rapid both as a result of natural growth and by movement from the rural areas to the towns. The largest city in Africa is Cairo, with about 10 million inhabitants; other large centres are Alexandria, Casablanca, Lagos, Algiers, and Johannesburg, the latter including the African 'township' of Soweto with a population estimated to be well in excess of one million.

Africa has a relatively low population density and an uneven distribution. Countries bordering desert or sahelian regions (e.g. Libya, Namibia, Mauritania, Somalia) have generally low population densities. The areas with the greatest density of population are some of the islands (Mauritius, Zanzibar) and the Nile Valley, Rwanda, Burundi, and regions of southern Nigeria.

Natural disasters, war and famine have resulted in more refugees in Africa, relative to the total population, than in any other continent. Since 1975 over

600 000 people have become refugees in Angola, largely as a result of war; in Mozambique war and drought-induced famine have driven over 250 000 people into exile in neighbouring countries. Hundreds of thousands of people (there is no accurate record) have become refugees in the Horn of Africa for similar reasons.

In the tables that follow, C = 'census'. Other figures are estimates.

AFRICA

Year	Total population (millions)		Growth rate	
1940	158		1925–50	45%
1950	175			
1960	260		1950–75	100%
1970	357			
1975	410		estimated annual rate	
1980	460		of increase	
1985	550		1975–85	2.7%
2000	800	(projection)		

ALGERIA

Year	Total population	Muslims	Non-Muslims	Urban (per cent)	Algiers
1948C	8 681 000	7 679 000	922 000		
1954C	9 529 000	8 449 000	984 000	26.9	449 299
1960C	10 853 000	9 760 000	1 093 000		
1966C	12 101 000[1]				897 352
1974	16 275 000			52	
1978	18 500 000				2 000 000
1981	19 230 000				
1985	20 900 000				

[1]Includes 268 800 registered Algerian migrants in France, although c. 70 000 Algerians were also resident there. The census of 1966 did not distinguish between Muslims and non-Muslims. Between 1960 and 1962 about 900 000 colons (i.e. European settlers) left Algeria.

ANGOLA

Year	Total population	Europeans		Urban	
1945	3 788 000				
1950	4 140 000	78 820			
1960C	4 840 000	172 000		11%	
1965	5 150 000		c.600 000 refugees		
1970C	5 646 100	300 000	in Zaïre.	400 000	
1975	6 761 000		Exodus of c.300 000		
1978	7 180 000		Europeans	700 000	Luanda
1985	8 573 000*			1 200 000	

* This figure is made even less reliable by the displacement of hundreds of thousands of people due to the civil war since 1975.

BENIN (formerly DAHOMEY)

Year	Total population	Urban (%)	Cotonou	Porto Novo
1945	1 458 000			
1950	1 538 000			
1960[1]	1 934 000	10		
1965	2 300 000	12		
1970	2 710 000	12.6		
1972			120 000	85 000
1974	3 029 000	13.5		
1977			175 000	100 000
1979C	3 331 000		383 000[2]	140 000[2]
1984	3 825 000			
1985	3 930 000	15		

Approximately 47 per cent of the population belong to the Fon ethnic group (1959 estimate).
[1] The 1961 census gave an inflated figure of 2 640 000.
[2] Figure for 1981.

BOTSWANA (formerly BECHUANALAND)

Year	Total population	
1946C	296 000	
1950	310 000	
1956C	320 675	
1964C	543 000	(Bamangwato ethnic group 199 700)
1971C	574 000[1]	
1976	693 000	
1978	749 000	(Gaborone 20 000)
1981C	941 000	(Gaborone 59 600)
1984	1 047 000	

80 per cent of the country's population live in the eastern strip of the country, the most developed area.
[1] The official figure understated the population which was c. 630 000.

BURKINA FASO (formerly UPPER VOLTA)

Year	Total population	Ouagadougou
1949	3 069 000	
1960	4 340 000	
1966		78 000
1970	5 380 000	
1975C	6 147 000	
1978	6 520 000	
1982		250 000
1985C	7 976 000	442 000

Annual rate of growth c. 2.3 per cent.
About 50 per cent of the population belong to the Mossi ethnic group.

BURUNDI

Year	Total population	Bujumbura
1959C	2 213 300	
1965C	3 210 000	71 000
1971	3 615 000	
1976	3 820 000	157 000
1979C	3 992 000	172 000
1985	4 718 000	

About 84 per cent of the population belongs to the Hutu, and 15 per cent to the Tutsi ethnic groups. It is estimated that 100 000 Hutu were killed in 1972.

CAMEROON

Year	Total population	French Cameroons	British Cameroons	Douala	Yaoundé
1950	3 558 000	2 500 000	797 000		
1955	3 955 000	3 073 000	1 084 000		
1960	4 700 000				
1970	5 836 000				
1975	6 539 000				
1976C	7 663 240			458 000	313 000
1984	9 542 000			850 000	650 000

CAPE VERDE ISLANDS

Year	Total population	Praia
1950C	147 328	
1960C	201 549	
1970C	272 071	
1978	330 000	
1980C	296 000	
1985	350 000	49 000

It is estimated that 600 000 Cape Verdeans live abroad, in Portugal, but 300 000 in the USA.

CENTRAL AFRICAN REPUBLIC (formerly UBANGI-CHARI)

Year	Total population	Bangui
1946	1 060 000	
1951	1 092 000	
1960	1 227 000	100 000
1965C	2 088 000	
1968	2 255 000	
1971	1 637 000	187 000
1975C	2 054 000	
1982		350 000
1985	2 608 000	

CHAD

Year	Total population	N'Djamena (formerly Ft Lamy)
1946	1 901 000	
1951	2 241 000	
1961	2 675 000	
1970	3 640 000	
1978	4 280 000	400 000
1985	5 061 000	

A large part of the population is concentrated in the south of the country.

COMORO ISLANDS

Year	Total population	Mayotte[1]
1945	150 000	
1950	168 890	
1958C	175 552	
1966C	248 517	
1970	275 227	
1978	330 000	40 000
1980C	356 000	
1985	395 000	67 167[2]

[1] Administered by France.
[2] Official census August 1985.

CONGO (formerly MIDDLE CONGO)

Year	Total population	Brazzaville
1946	651 000	
1951	684 000	
1961	773 000	
1970	900 000	
1974C	1 319 000	302 000
1978	1 450 000	
1983		456 000
1985C	1 912 000	

About 47 per cent of the population are Bakongo.

CÔTE D'IVOIRE see IVORY COAST

DAHOMEY see BENIN

DJIBOUTI (formerly FRENCH SOMALILAND, then FRENCH TERRITORY OF THE AFARS AND ISSAS)

Year	Total population	Djibouti town	
1952	61 000		
1963	88 000		
1967	125 000	60 000	
1976	220 000	100 000	
1986	456 000	200 000	(1981)

EGYPT

Year	Total population	Cairo
1947C	19 021 000	
1950	20 461 000	
1960C	25 832 000	3 346 000
1966C	30 075 000	
1976C	38 228 000	
1978	40 230 000	8 000 000
1981	43 470 000	
1984	47 100 000	
1987	49 280 000	12 000 000

Annual growth rate 2.3 per cent.

EQUATORIAL GUINEA

Year	Total population	Bioko (formerly Fernando Po) and Pagalu (formerly Annobon)
1950	170 580	33 980
1960C	245 980	62 600
1965C	246 940	48 850
1983C	300 000	60 000

In 1970–78 about one-third of the population of the mainland province of Rio Muni (80 per cent Fang ethnic group) fled into neighbouring countries.

ETHIOPIA

Year	Total population	Addis Ababa
1945		(Eritrea 6 000 000)
1950	12 000 000	
1961	21 800 000	
1971	25 248 000	
1975	27 946 000	
1978	30 000 000	1 000 000
1984C	42 180 000[1]	1 412 000
1985	43 350 000	

[1] Census estimated to have reached 85 per cent of the population
Drought and famine in the early 1970s are estimated to have killed 400 000 people.
About 40 per cent of the population are Oromo and 30 per cent Amhara–Tigre.

GABON

Year	Total population	Libreville
1946	382 000	
1951	407 300	
1961C	448 500	
1965	463 000	
1970C	500 000	
1975		251 000
1981	1 232 000[1]	
1985	1 150 000[2]	

[1] The census of 1980 was officially repudiated and the figure for 1981 was declared by decree.
[2] United Nations estimate. The World Bank estimates Gabon's mid-1985 population as 997 000.

THE GAMBIA

Year	Total population	
1944	241 135	
1951C	279 686	
1963C	315 486	
1973C	494 279	(Banjul 39 476)
1977	546 000	
1983C	695 800	
1986	698 817	

GHANA (formerly GOLD COAST)

Year	Total population	
1942	3 959 500	
1948C	4 412 000	(Ashanti 877 000, Northern Territories, 1 154 000)
1960C	6 727 000	(Accra 337 000–c. 10% of population foreign-born)
1970C	8 559 300	(Accra–Tema 738 000)
1978	10 970 000	
1984C	12 205 000	(Accra 964 000, Kumasi 348 000)

c.20 per cent of the population are Asante. In 1984 the urban population exceeded 30 per cent.

GUINEA

Year	Total population	Conakry
1945	2 125 000	
1950	2 250 000	
1955C	2 570 000	
1960	2 726 000	
1967C	3 780 000	167 000
1972	4 108 000[1]	
1978	4 760 000	600 000
1983C	5 781 000	

[1] Plus c. 1 000 000 refugees. 1972C 5 143 000.

About 500 000 people left the country between 1958 and 1968.

About 30 per cent of the population belong to the Malinke, and 28 per cent to the Fulani, ethnic group.

GUINEA-BISSAU

Year	Total population
1940	351 000
1950C	510 700
1960C	544 184
1970C	487 400
1978	553 500
1979C	767 000
1986	900 000

IVORY COAST (also known as CÔTE D'IVOIRE)

Year	Total population	Abidjan
1945	4 056 000	
1950	2 170 000	69 000
1961	3 300 000	180 000
1965	3 835 000	300 000
1970	4 310 000	
1975C	6 709 000	
1978	7 300 000	1 000 000
1984	9 742 000	

Annual growth rate 2.6 per cent.
About 19 per cent of the population belongs to the Baoulé ethnic group.

KENYA

Year	Total population	African	Asian	European	Nairobi
1946	4 055 000				
1948C	5 407 000	5 253 000	98 000	29 600	110 000
1962C	8 636 000	8 366 000	176 613	55 759	270 000
1969C	10 942 000	10 733 000	139 030	40 593	509 000
1973	12 482 000				
1978	14 650 000				650 000
1979C	15 327 000	15 112 000	59 000	50 000	827 700
1984	19 500 000				

Annual growth rate 1980–83 = 4.1 per cent. Seventy-five per cent of the population is largely confined to 10 per cent of the total area, giving densities as high as 4000 per sq. km.
Nineteen per cent of the population are Kikuyu, 14 per cent Luo, and 11 per cent Kamba.

LESOTHO (formerly BASUTOLAND)

Year	Total population	
1946C	563 850	
1956C	641 670	
1966C	969 630	(nearly 120 000 working in South Africa)
1976C	1 216 000	(Maseru 45 000)
1985[1]	1 528 000	

[1] Between 150 000 and 200 000 migrant workers were in South Africa, mostly as mine labour.

LIBERIA

Year	Total population	Monrovia
1950	under 1 000 000	42 000
1962C	1 016 400	81 000
1974C	1 501 400	172 000
1978	1 830 000	200 000
1985	2 189 000	425 000
1987	2 500 000	

Annual rate of growth 3.36 per cent (1962–74).
About 21 per cent of the population are Kpelle and 16 per cent Bassa.

LIBYA

Year	Total population	
1945	1 000 000	
1954C	1 091 800	
1964C	1 564 000	
1970	1 840 000	
1973C	2 259 000	
1978	2 620 000	(Tripoli 600 000)
1981	3 110 000	
1984	3 400 000	

Annual growth rate 3.1 per cent.

MADAGASCAR

Year	Total population	
1945	4 000 000	
1951	4 369 000	
1958	5 070 000	
1963	5 862 000	
1971	7 653 000	(incl. 50 000 French citizens)
1975C	7 603 000	(Antananarivo 406 000)
1981	8 995 000	
1985	9 985 000	(Antananarivo 662 000)

Annual growth rate 2.7 per cent.
About 25 per cent of the population are Merina (Hova).

MALAWI (formerly NYASALAND)

Year	Africans	Europeans	Asians
1945C	2 049 450	1 948	2 804
1954	2 494 830	5 128	7 795
1956C	2 900 000	8 900	12 200
1966C	4 039 000	7 395	11 299
1970	4 130 000[1]		
1977C	5 547 000	6 377	5 682
1985	7 058 000	(Blantyre 313 600; Lilongwe 158 500 in 1983)	

Annual growth rate 2.5 per cent.
Twenty-eight per cent are Chewa, 14 per cent Yao.
[1] Early 1970s 270 000 emigrant workers, mainly in South Africa.

MALI (formerly SOUDAN)

Year	Total population	Bamako
1945	3 480 000	
1959	4 200 000	130 000
1967	4 700 000	182 000
1976C	6 394 000	404 000
1985	8 206 000	

Annual rate of growth 2.5 per cent.
About 31 per cent of the population are Bambara.

MAURITANIA

Year	Total population	
1945	497 000	
1952	560 000	
1958C	655 650	(Nouakchott founded 1957)
1964	1 200 000	
1976C	1 420 000	(Nouakchott 134 380; nomadic population over 500 000)
1984	1 830 000	(Nouakchott 500 000)

Annual rate of growth 2.9 per cent.
About 82 per cent are Moors and 13 per cent Tukulor-Fulani.
Drought in the early 1970s and into the 1980s drove people in to the towns: urban population 1972 18 per cent, 1984 35 per cent.

MAURITIUS

Year	Total population	
1946	425 770	
1953C	540 700	(Indians 67%, Euro-Africans 29%, Chinese 3%)
1962C	700 269	
1972C	851 335	
1976	867 880	(Port Louis 141 343)
1983C	1 002 000	(Indo-Mauritians 664 480, Euro-Africans 264 530, Chinese 20 690)
1985	1 034 000	

Annual rate of growth 1.5 per cent.

MOROCCO

Year	Total population	
1950	8 953 000	(Tangiers 100 000; Jews 250 000; Europeans 590 000)
1955	10 113 000	
1960	11 626 000	(Jews 162 000, Europeans 170 000)
1965	13 325 000	
1971C	15 379 259	
1978	19 150 000	(Rabat 700 000, Casablanca 1 371 000; urban population 35%)
1981	19 871 000	
1984	21 562 000	

Annual growth rate 3 per cent.

MOZAMBIQUE

Year	Total population	Europeans	Maputo (formerly Lourenço Marques)
1945	5 000 000	31 221	
1950C	5 732 000	48 213	48 000
1955	6 117 000	67 798	
1960C	6 603 000	97 240	178 000
1970C	8 223 000	150 000	354 000
1973		200 000	
1975	9 320 000		
1978	9 890 000		
1980C	11 673 000		755 000
1984	13 426 000		903 000

Drought and famine 1981–4 killed over 100 000 people.
War and famine displaced hundreds of thousands of people 1972–90.

NAMIBIA (formerly SOUTH WEST AFRICA)

Year	Total population	Whites	
1946C	352 075	37 858	
1951C	417 768	49 524	
1960C	526 004	73 464	
1970C	746 328	90 658	(Ovambos 342 455)
1977	908 000	105 000	(Windhoek 70 000)
1981C	1 039 000	76 430	(Windhoek 70 000)
1986	1 184 000	78 000	(Windhoek 97 000)

Annual rate growth 1960–70 3.7 per cent.
Over half the population are Ovambo (587 000 estimate 1986).

NIGER

Year	Total population	Niamey
1946	2 000 000	
1951C	2 160 000	
1960C	2 500 000	30 000
1965	3 510 000	
1970	4 020 000	
1977C	5 098 000	225 300
1981	5 686 000	360 000
1984	5 800 000	

Annual growth rate 2.8 per cent.
About 46 per cent of the people are Hausa.

NIGERIA

Year	Total population	North	East	West	Lagos
1945	20 000 000				
1952–3C[1]	31 500 000	16 840 000	7 218 000	6 087 000	272 000
1962[2]	45 332 000	22 027 000	12 332 000	8 157 000	450 000
1963C[3]	55 670 000	29 808 000		10 265 000	665 000
1970	55 070 000				1 100 000
1973C[2]					
1978[4]	68 450 000				2 700 000
1982[5]	86 126 000				
1985[5]	95 198 000				
1988	105 000 000				

About 29 per cent of the population belongs to the Hausa–Fulani ethnic group, 20 per cent to the Yoruba and 17 per cent to the Igbo.

[1] Possibly 10 per cent in error.
[2] Census declared void.
[3] Figures not widely accepted; UN figure for 1963 46.3 million.
[4] UN Population Division estimate; the World Bank gave a figure for 1976 of 77.1 million.
[5] UN Population Division estimates.

RWANDA

Year	Total population	Kigali
1935	1 680 000	
1955	2 300 000	
1963	2 500 000	
1970	3 590 000	
1975	4 233 000	15 000
1978C	4 830 000	117 000
1981	5 350 000	156 650
1983	5 757 000	
1986	6 320 000	

Annual growth rate 2.9 per cent.
95 per cent of the population are Hutu and 4 per cent Tutsi.

ST HELENA, ASCENSION ISLAND, TRISTAN DA CUNHA

Year	St Helena	Ascension	Tristan
1945	4 700		
1951C	4 748	174	267 (1950C)
1961C	4 648	336	281 (1960C)[1]
1973C	5 159	1 231	271 (1969C)
1976C	5 147	1 058	314 (1977)
1985	6 258	1 075	310 (1986)

[1] Island evacuated 1961–3.

SÃO TOMÉ AND PRÍNCIPE

Year	Total population	Príncipe
1941	60 490	
1950C	60 159	
1960C	63 676	4 574
1970C	73 631	4 599
1978	83 000	
1981C	96 611	5 255
1983	102 500	5 600
1985	108 000	

Annual growth rate 1.2 per cent.

SENEGAL

Year	Total population	Dakar	
1945	1 895 000		
1949	1 992 000		
1951	2 093 000	250 000	
1960C	3 110 000	375 000	
1965	3 490 000		
1970	3 775 000	600 000	
1976C	5 085 300		
1978	5 350 000	800 000	(urban population 32%)
1980	5 703 000	980 000	
1984	6 397 000		
1986	6 700 000		

Annual growth rate 1970–78 2.2 per cent.
About 37 per cent of the population belongs to the Wolof ethnic group, 24 per cent to the Fulani–Tukulor and 16 per cent to the Serer.

SEYCHELLES

Year	Total population	
1945	34 419	
1950	36 000	
1955	39 000	
1960	42 000	
1966	46 700	
1971C	52 650	(Mahé 23 000)
1977C	61 898	(c. 28 000) Seychellois living abroad)
1985	65 244	

SIERRA LEONE

Year	Total population	Freetown
1948C	1 860 000	
1951	2 005 000	85 000
1963	2 183 000	127 000
1970	2 550 000	
1974C[1]	3 003 000	276 000
1978[2]	2 980 000	300 000
1985C	3 517 000[3]	470 000

Annual growth rate 2.5 per cent.
45 per cent of the population are Temne, and 36 per cent Mende.
[1] Census figure 2 735 000 which was believed to be understated; recalculated mid-1976 as 3 100 000.
[2] United Nations estimate.
[3] Adjustment upwards by 5 per cent to 3 700 000.

SOMALIA

Year	Total population	Mogadishu
1950	1 886 000	78 000
1960	2 010 000	
1970	2 790 000	
1972	2 941 000	
1975C	3 253 000	
1981		500 000
1985	4 653 000	

SOUTH AFRICA

Year	Total population	Black	'Coloured'	Asian	
1946C	11 415 925	7 830 559	2 372 044	928 062	285 260
1951C	12 671 452	8 560 083	2 641 689	1 103 016	366 604
1960C	16 002 797	10 927 922	3 088 492	1 509 258	477 125
1970C	21 448 169	15 057 952	3 751 328	2 018 453	620 436
1976	26 227 000	18 700 000	4 320 000	2 434 000	764 000
1980C	24 986 000[1]				
1985[2]	23 377 000	15 163 000	4 569 000	2 833 000	822 000
1985[3]	27 622 000	19 052 000	4 947 000	2 862 000	861 000
1985[4]	33 676 000	25 006 000	4 947 000	2 862 000	861 000

Annual growth rate for the black and 'Coloured' population, 3 per cent; for the white c. one per cent. Urban population: 'Coloured' and Asian well over 80 per cent; black, near to 40 per cent.
[1] The official census figure excluded blacks in the so-called independent 'homelands'.
[2] Official census count, 5 March 1985, which excluded the four 'homelands' of Transkei, Bophuthatswana, Venda and Ciskei.
[3] Census figure adjusted by Human Sciences Research Council (HSRC) of South Africa for estimated undernumeration.
[4] Census figure adjusted for net undernumeration by HSRC, plus Development Bank of Southern Africa estimates for 1985 black population for the four 'independent' homelands'.

POPULATION OF MAJOR CITIES IN 1970

	Black	White	Coloured	Asian
Cape Town	107 000	378 000	598 000	11 200
Johannesburg[1]	809 000	501 000	82 000	39 000
Durban	224 000	257 000	43 000	317 000

POPULATION OF MAJOR METROPOLITAN AREAS IN 1980

Cape Town	1 779 180	Pretoria	849 000
Johannesburg	1 729 130	Port Elizabeth	711 000
Durban	1 021 000		

SPANISH WEST SAHARA

SPANISH SAHARA

	Total	Saharans	Spaniards
1950	13 627	12 287[1]	1 340
1960	23 793	18 489[1]	5 304
1970	76 425	59 777	16 648[2]
1985	155 000		

[1] The figures for Saharans are very low estimates and in all probability inaccurate.
[2] The large increase in Spaniards is accounted for by the presence of Spanish troops.

IFNI

Year	Total population
1950	35 000
1960	49 889
1964	51 517
1971	46 000

SUDAN

Year	Total population	
1945	7 500 000	
1951	8 764 000	(Khartoum 71 000, Omdurman 130 000)
1956C	10 260 000	
1968	14 770 000	
1973C	14 819 000	
1978	16 720 000	(Khartoum 400 000)
1983C	20 564 000	(Khartoum 1 300 000)
1984	20 900 000	
1987	25 550 000	

Annual rate of growth 2.9 per cent.
Urban population 20 per cent.
About 51 per cent of the population are Arabic-speaking; 23 per cent belong to Nilotic ethnic groups.

SWAZILAND

Year	Total population	
1946	187 997	
1956	240 511	
1960	316 000	
1966C	395 264	
1976C	527 791[1]	
1986C	706 137	(Mbabane 35 000)

Annual growth rate 2.9 per cent.
[1] Includes c.30 000 migrant workers in South Africa.

TANZANIA (formerly TANGANYIKA, and including ZANZIBAR from 1964)

Year	Total population	Asians	
1948C	7 410 000	46 254	(Europeans 11 300)
1952C		59 739	
1957C	8 665 000	75 983	
1967C	12 313 000	75 015	(Europeans 16 884; Dar es Salaam 250 000)
1975	15 600 000		
1978C	17 551 900		(Zanzibar 271 000; Dar es Salaam 757 000)
1983	20 378 000		
1985	21 733 000		

Annual growth rate 3.1 per cent.

TOGO

Year	Total population	Lomé
1950	990 000	33 000
1960	1 440 000	
1970C	1 997 000	140 000
1978	2 440 000	230 000
1981	2 705 000	
1984	2 800 000	367 000
1987	3 158 000	

Annual growth rate 2.9 per cent.
About 44 per cent of the population are Ewé, 23 per cent Kabré.

TUNISIA

Year	Total population	Europeans	Tunis	
1946C	3 231 000	240 000	364 000	
1956	3 943 000	255 000		(urban population 30%)
1966C	4 533 000		469 000	
1975C	5 788 200			
1978	6 200 000		800 000	
1981	6 600 000			
1984	7 000 000		597 000	
1986	7 317 000			

UGANDA

Year	Total population	Asians	Kampala
1948C	4 958 000	35 215	
1959C	6 536 000	71 399	60 000
1963	7 200 000		
1970C	9 548 000	74 300	330 700
1974	11 171 000	88 000	
1978	12 430 000		
1980C	12 600 000		458 000
1982	13 300 000		
1987	16 790 000		

About 30 000 Asians were forced to leave 1972–3.
Annual growth rate 3.4 per cent, 1970–72.
About 16 per cent of the population belongs to the Ganda, and 15 per cent to the Nilotic, ethnic group.

UPPER VOLTA (see BURKINA FASO)

ZAÏRE (formerly BELGIAN CONGO, then REPUBLIC OF CONGO)

Year	Total population	Europeans	Kinshasa (formerly Leopoldville)	
1945	10 000 000	33 786	40 000	
1951	11 662 000	69 200	200 000	
1955			325 000	
1959	13 540 000	110 000		
1965			1 000 000	
1970C	21 637 800			
1978	26 460 000		2 000 000	(urban population 30%)
1981			2 338 000	
1984C	29 700 000		2 653 000	
1985	30 363 000			

Annual growth rate 2.6 per cent.
About 34 per cent of the population belongs to the Kongo, and 9 per cent to the Luba, ethnic group.

ZAMBIA (formerly NORTHERN RHODESIA)

Year	Total population	Europeans	Lusaka	
1941C	1 381 000		20 000	
1946C	1 656 800	21 919		
1951C	1 930 900	37 221	80 000	
1956C		66 000	170 000	
1961C	2 480 000	76 000		
1969C	4 056 000	58 000		
1972	4 515 000	58 000		
1978	5 510 000		430 000	(urban population 37%)
1980C	5 661 000		538 000	(urban population 41 per cent)
1985	6 650 000			

Annual growth rate 2.9 per cent 1969–74, 3.3 per cent 1974–80.
About 15 per cent of the population are Bemba, 12 per cent Tonga, and 3 per cent Lozi.

ZANZIBAR

Year	Total population	Asians/Arabs	
1948C	264 162	59 771	
1958C[1]	299 111	70 000	(urban population 37.9%)
1967C	354 360		
1978C	475 665		
1985	571 000		

[1] 1958C did not distinguish ethnic groups.

ZIMBABWE (formerly SOUTHERN RHODESIA: RHODESIA; ZIMBABWE-RHODESIA)

Year	Total population	Europeans	'Coloured'/Asian	Harare (Salisbury)	Bulawayo
1946C	1 777 000	82 382	7 501		
1951C	2 146 000	136 017	10 283		
1956C	3 640 000	178 000		183 000	
1958		207 000			
1961C	3 857 000	221 504	17 812		
1963				315 400	
1969C	5 090 000	228 580	24 118		
1977	6 820 000	263 000	33 300	600 000	
1980		223 000	37 000		
1982C	7 539 000			656 000	413 800
1985	8 174 000				

Annual growth rate 3.5 per cent.

About 60 per cent of the population belongs to the Shona, and 14 per cent to the Ndebele, ethnic group.

9 BIOGRAPHIES

Abbas, Ferhat (1899–1985), Born Constantine; educ. local *lycée* and Algiers Univ.; pharmacist. President of Algerian Muslim Students' Union. Involved in municipal politics; founded and edited weekly journal *L'Entente* 1933–9. Signatory of the Manifeste du Peuples Algériens 1943. Founded Union Démocratique du Manifeste Algérien 1945. Dèputy in French National Assembly 1946–7. Founder and editor of *La République Algérienne* 1954. Joined FLN 1955; based in Switzerland 1956–8. President of provisional government of Algeria in exile 1958–61. President of the National Assembly of independent Algeria 1962–4. Detained 1964–5.

Abboud, Ferik Ibrahim (1900–83), Sudanese army officer and politician. Educ. local schools and Gordon Memorial College, Khartoum. Commissioned in Egyptian army 1918–25 as military engineer; fought with British in North African campaign during Second World War. Principal Staff Officer, Sudan Defence Force 1952; C-in-C Sudanese army 1956. Led military coup against government and became Prime Minister 1958–64. Regime overthrown by a civilian coup 1964.

Acheampong, Ignatius Kutu (1931–79), Ghanaian soldier and head of state. Born Kumasi; educ. RC schools; teacher in commercial college 1949–52. Joined army 1953; commissioned 1959; military training in UK and USA; served in UN Congo operations 1962–3. Following 1966 coup served National Liberation Council as chairman of Western Regional administration. Acting head 1st Brigade Ghanaian army 1971; led coup overthrowing Busia government 1972. Chairman of National Redemption Council 1972; Chairman Supreme Military Council and head of state 1972–8. Deposed 1978; executed 1979.

Adoula, Cyril (1921–78), Zaïrean politician. Born Leopoldville; educ. RC Schools; employed in commerce and Banque Centrale as clerk. A trade-union activist in the 1950s and secretary of Fédération Générale du Travail du Congo. Founder-member of Patrice Lumumba's Mouvement National Congolais 1958. Elected senator for Equatorial Province in May 1960; Minister of Interior 1960; delegate to UN 1961; Prime Minister 1961–4. Ambassador to Belgium and the EEC and then the USA 1964–6.

Afrifa, Akwasi. A. (1936–79), Ghanaian soldier and politician. Born near Kumasi; educ. Adisadel College. Joined army 1956; trained Sandhurst 1957; commissioned 1960. Served twice with UN Congo operation 1961–2. One of the leaders of 1966 coup which overthrew President Nkrumah. Member National Liberation Council and Chairman 1969. In detention 1972–3. Executed for corrupt practices 1979.

Aguiyi-Ironsi, Johnson (1925–66), Nigerian soldier and head of state. Served in British colonial army in West Africa from 1942; officer-training in Britain 1948; commissioned 1949. Commander of Nigerian contingent in UN Congo operation 1960; C-in-C of UN forces in Congo 1963. Appointed C-in-C of Nigerian army 1965. Assumed power as head of state following coup of January 1966. Killed in the second coup, in July 1966.

Akuffo, Frederick William Kwasi (1937–79), Ghanaian soldier and head of state. Born Eastern Region, Ghana; educ. Presbyterian schools to 1955; civil servant 1955–7. In 1957 enlisted in army; selected for officer-training in UK 1958–60; commissioned 1960; served with UN emergency force in Congo 1962; Commander 2nd Infantry Brigade Group of Ghanaian army 1972; army commander and member of Supreme Military Council in Acheampong government, 1975; Chief of Defence Staff 1976–8. Head of state 1978–9. Overthrown in a junior officers coup led by Flight-Lt Rawlings and then executed for corrupt practices 1979.

Ahidjo, Ahmadou (1924–89), First President of Cameroon. Born Garona, Cameroon; educ. secondary school Yaoundé; radio operator in post office 1941. Member Cameroon territorial assembly 1947–58. Representative in Assembly of French Union 1953; Vice-Premier and Minister of Interior 1957–8; Prime Minister of autonomous French Cameroons 1958–60. President of Cameroon Republic from 1960 until his resignation in 1982.

Amin, Idi (1925–), Ugandan soldier and former head of state. Born a Kakwa, from West Nile province, Uganda. Joined King's African Rifles 1946; corporal 1949; fought with British in 'Mau Mau' campaign in Kenya; commissioned 1961; battalion commander 1963; deputy commander Uganda army 1965; commander 1968. Seized power in Uganda from Obote's civilian government Jan 1971. During his presidency, 1971–9, introduced a reign of terror and bloodshed resulting in deaths of several hundred thousand Ugandans. Overthrown following Tanzanian invasion 1979. Fled country and took refuge in Saudi Arabia.

Ankrah, Joseph Arthur (1925–), Ghanaian soldier. Educ. Wesleyan School, Accra. Military service in Second World War with Gold Coast Regiment; commissioned 1947; brigadier in Ghanaian army and in UN operations in

Congo 1960–61. Deputy Chief of Defence Staff but dismissed from army by President Nkrumah 1965. Chairman of National Liberation Council and Chief of Defence Staff following coup against Nkrumah 1966–9.

Awolowo, Chief Obafeni (1909–87), Nigerian nationalist leader and politician. A Yoruba, born Ijebu, southern Nigeria; educ. Protestant schools; teacher 1928–9; trader, trade-union organiser, and journalist 1934–44. Gained degree by private study 1944; studied law in London 1944–7; solicitor and advocate of Nigerian Supreme Court 1947–51. Helped found and led Action Group 1950; Minister of Local Government in Western Region 1951–4; Premier Western Region 1954–9. Leader of opposition in federal parliament 1960–62; imprisoned 1962–6. Released from prison after military coup of 1966. Federal Commissioner for finance 1967–71. Chancellor of Univ. of Ife 1967; returned to private legal practice 1971. Author of several books on politics. Leader of Unity Party of Nigeria and its unsuccessful candidate in presidential elections 1979.

Azikiwe, Benjamin Mhamdi (1904–), Nigerian nationalist leader and the country's first President. An Ibo, born Zenguru, northern Nigeria, son of an army clerk; educ. mission schools; government clerk 1921–5; studied at two univs in the USA, where he remained to teach 1925–34. Returned to West Africa 1934; active in nationalist politics and as founder and editor of various newspapers, including the *West African Pilot* 1934–47. Executive member of Nigerian Youth Movement 1934–41. President of National Council of Nigeria and Cameroon 1944; member Nigerian Legislative Council 1947–51. Elected member Western Region House of Assembly 1952–3, of Eastern Region House 1954–9; Premier Eastern Region 1954–9. Governor-General of Nigeria 1960–63 and President of the Republic 1963–6.

Babangida, Ibrahim (1941–), President of Nigeria since 1985. Born Niger State; joined Nigerian Military Academy 1963. Further military training in India 1962, United Kingdom 1966–7, and the United States 1972. During the civil war 1967–70 he commanded an infantry battalion. Served as Company Commander and Instructor at Nigerian Defence Academy 1970–72, and commander Armoured Corps 1975–81. He became Chief of Staff in 1984. The following year he became president having led a coup which overthrew the government of Maj.-Gen. Buhari.

Bakary, Djibo (1922–), Niger politician. Educ. William Ponty School, Dakar; teacher in Niger 1941. Founder secretary of Niger-section of the Rassemblement Démocratique Africain, the PPN. Split with RDA and formed the UDN 1951. Mayor of Niamey 1956. Opposed de Gaulle's proposals in the referendum of 1958. The UDN was crushingly defeated and then dissolved by the government in 1959. Bakary went into exile.

Balewa, Sir Abubakar Tafawa (1912–66), Nigerian politician. A Muslim born in Northern Nigeria; teacher and education officer 1930s–40s. Member Nigerian Legislative Council 1947. Helped found Northern People's Congress 1951. Federal Minister of Works 1952–4; Minister of Trade 1954; Chief Minister 1957–9; Federal Prime Minister 1959; knighted 1960. Federal Prime Minister of independent Nigeria 1960–66. Killed in first military coup 1966.

Banda, Hastings Kamazu (1906–), first President of Malawi. Born Kasungu district, Nyasaland; educ. in Nyasaland and South Africa; went to USA to study medicine 1927–37; medical practitioner in UK 1939–53 and Ghana 1954–8. Returned to Nyasaland as President-General of African National Congress 1958. Imprisoned 1959–60. Leader Malawi Congress Party 1961; Minister of Natural Resources and Local Government 1961–3; Prime Minister of Nyasaland 1963–4 and of independent Malawi 1964–6. President since 1966.

Bello, Sir Ahmadu (1910–66), one of the leaders of Northern Nigeria. Educ. Katsina College; teacher 1931; appointed Sardauna of Sokoto 1938. Leader of Northern People's Congress 1951. Minister in Northern Region government 1952; Prime Minister Northern Region 1954. Killed in first military coup Jan. 1966.

Ben Ali, Zine el-Abidine (1936–), second president of Tunisia. Army officer 1958–80 with post of Director General of National Security 1977–80. Ambassador to Poland 1980–84; Minister of National Security 1985, Minister of Interior 1986, Prime Minister 1987. When President Bourguiba was found to be medically unfit to continue in office, Ben Ali succeeded him as president of the republic.

Ben Bella, Ahmed (1919–). Born near Oran, son of a trader; served in French army during Second World War. Joined Parti Populaire Algérien 1945; member of its military wing, the Organisation Secrète, 1948. Imprisoned 1950; escaped 1952. One of the organisers of the Front de Libération Nationale 1954 and the armed revolt against French rule. Captured and imprisoned by French 1956–62. Prime Minister of Algeria 1962–6. Deposed by Boumédienne's military coup 1965 and placed under house arrest until 1979.

Benjeddid, Chadli (1929–), Algerian head of state. Educ. in Arab and French-speaking schools. Active in politics and a member of the Mouvement pour le Triomphe des Libertés Démocratiques. Joined war of independence 1955; became a battalion commander of the FLN; arrested by the French 1961. Commander of a military region in independent Algeria 1963. Took part in the coup of 1965 which removed Ben Bella from office; member of the Revolutionary Council which ruled Algeria. Co-ordinator of the armed forces 1978. President of Algeria 1979.

Biko, Steve (1947–77), South African nationalist leader. Born Eastern Cape, son of a government clerk; expelled from Lovedale College because of his brother's involvement in the illegal nationalist body Poqo, he studied at an RC boarding school, and then at Natal University. One of the founders of the Black Consciousness movement and President of the South African Students' Organisation established in 1969. An organiser of the Black Community Programme, he was banned by the South African government following the Durban strikes of 1973. He was arrested, and died as a result of police brutality.

Binaisa, Godfrey (1920–), Ugandan politician. A Buganda, born near Kampala; educ. King's College, Budo; studied law, London Univ. 1953–6. Member of Milton Obote's Uganda People's Congress. Appointed Attorney-General 1962; resigned office following disagreements with Obote over policies 1967. Chairman Uganda Law Society 1968. In exile during much of Amin regime. President of Uganda 1979–80.

Biya, Paul (1933–), President of Cameroon since 1982. Born in the southern part of the country he studied law in France. A close confidant of President Ahidjo he became a minister of state in 1968. In 1975 Biya was appointed Prime Minister. When Ahidjo retired in 1982 Biya became President.

Blundell, Sir Michael (1907–). Born London; emigrated to Kenya as farmer 1937. War service 1939–45. Member Legislative Council 1948–58, 1961–3. Minister of Agriculture 1955–9, 1961–2. Leader of New Kenya Party 1959–63.

Bokassa, Jean Bédel (1921–), army officer and former head of state of Central African Republic. Educ. mission schools in Bangui and Brazzaville. Joined French army 1939; became a sergeant and eventually commissioned in 1956; C-in-C army of Central African Republic 1963. Led coup to depose President Dacko. President 1966–76. Proclaimed himself Emperor of Central African Empire 1976. Deposed by coup 1979. Exiled in Ivory Coast and Paris and sentenced to death *in absentia*. Returned to Central African Republic, October 1986, publicly tried and sentenced to life imprisonment.

Bongo, Omar, formerly *Albert Bernard* (1935–), Gabonese politician. Educ. commercial college, Brazzaville. Civil servant in President's Office. Head, Ministry of Information and Tourism 1963; head, Ministry of National Defence 1964–5; Vice-President, Gabon 1967; President of Gabon since 1967 and Prime Minister 1968–76. Secretary-General of Parti Démocratique Gabonais 1968.

Botha, Pieter Willem (1916–), South African politician. Educ. Univ. of Orange Free State. Deputy Minister of Interior 1958–61; Minister of Community Development, Public Works and Coloured Affairs 1961–6; Minister of

Defence 1965 and of National Security 1978. Leader of National Party in Cape Province 1966; Prime Minister of South Africa 1978, and State President 1984-9.

Boumédienne, Houari (1925-78), Algerian nationalist leader and politician. Born near Bône; educ. in Tunis and Cairo. Served in French army. Joined Front de Libération Nationale in 1955 in war against French; FLN commander in Wilaya area 1955-7; Chief of Staff FLN 1960-62. Chief of Staff, Algerian army 1962-5; Minister of Defence 1962; and First Vice-Premier 1963-5. Led coup which overthrew President Ben Bella 1965. President of Algeria 1965-78.

Bourguiba, Habib Ben Ali (1903-), Tunisian politician and President. Educ. in Tunis; studied in France 1924-30. Member of Destour Party 1921, but split away from it to form the Neo-Destour Party, 1934; imprisoned by French 1934-6, 1938-43. Lived outside Tunisia 1946-9. Returned to Tunisia and again imprisoned by French 1952-4. Prime Minister of Tunisia 1956-7; President of republic of Tunisia from 1957 until he was deprived of office on grounds of ill-health in 1987.

Busia, Kofi (1913-78), Ghanaian politician and academic. Born Ashanti; educ. Oxford and London Univs; one of the first African assistant administrative officers appointed by British in Gold Coast 1942; lecturer, and later professor, Univ. College of Ghana 1948. Elected to Legislative Council 1951. A leader of the National Liberation Movement 1954-9; in exile 1959-66. Returned to Ghana as adviser to National Liberation Council after coup which deposed Nkrumah 1966. Founder and leader of Progress Party, which won general election 1969. Prime Minister of Ghana 1969-72. His government was overthrown by a military coup led by Lt-Col. Acheampong and he went into exile 1972. Held various academic posts; died in Oxford.

Buthelezi, Chief Mangosuthu Gatsha (1928-), South African politician. Born into Zulu royal family; educ. Fort Hare Univ. College. Government interpreter 1951-7; head of Buthelezi tribe 1953; elected leader Zulu Territorial Authority 1970. Rejected plan of South African Government to make Zululand into a 'bantustan'. Prime Minister of Kwazulu 1972; leader Black Unity Front 1976-7, and Inkatha Movement 1977.

Cabral, Amilcar (1924-73), Guinean nationalist leader. Born Bafatu, Portuguese Guinea; educ. in Bissau and at Lisbon Univ. as agronomist and hydraulic engineer. Civil servant in Portuguese Guinea and Angola 1956. Founded the nationalist PAIGC in Portuguese Guinea 1956; led war against the Portuguese from 1963 until his murder 10 years later.

Cabral, Luiz (1931-), Guinean nationalist leader. Born 1931, brother of

Amilcar Cabral; educ. in Portuguese Guinea; clerk, accountant and trade union organiser 1953–60. Member PAIGC; fled into exile 1960. Active in struggle for independence of Guinea. President of Republic of Guinea Bissau 1974–80 when he was overthrown in a coup.

Chipembere, Henry M. (1931–75), Malawian nationalist leader. Born Nyasaland; educ. there and at Fort Hare Univ. College. Secretary-General of the African National Congress (Nyasaland) and later the Malawi Congress Party. Elected to Legislative Council 1955. Detained for nationalist activity 1959–60. Minister of Local Government in Nyasaland government 1963; Minister of Education 1964. Resigned from the government of newly-independent Malawi in protest against the increasingly autocratic rule of Prime Minister Banda. Organised an abortive revolt in Malawi 1964–5. Exiled in Tanzania and the USA, where he worked mainly as a teacher 1965–75.

Chissano, Joaquim (1939–), President of Mozambique since 1986. Born Gaza province and attended local schools before matriculating from high school in Lourenço Marques (Maputo) in the 1950s. Went to Portugal to study medicine, involved in political activity and fled to France. A founder member of Frelimo 1962 and in charge of the party's Department of Security and Defence. Became foreign minister of independent Mozambique 1975. Negotiated the Nkomati agreement with South Africa 1984, becoming President of Mozambique on the death of Samora Machel in 1986.

Conté, Lansana (ca. 1945–   ), President of Guinea since April 1984. He was military commander of the Boké region. On the death of President Touré in March 1984 the army seized power. Colonel Conté became President and Colonel Traoré the Prime Minister. In July 1985 Traoré attempted to seize power while Conté was out of the country. The coup attempt failed, Traoré was probably executed, and Conté's position greatly strengthened. Thereafter he began to reform the economy of Guinea, and also to establish closer relations with France. A majority of civilians was brought into the government in December 1985.

Dacko, David (1930–), first President of the Central African Republic. Born Bouchia, Ubangi-Chari; educ. Brazzaville; teacher and leader of teachers' union. Elected to territorial assembly 1957; Minister of Agriculture 1957–8; Minister of Administrative Affairs 1958; Minister of Interior 1958–9; Prime Minister 1959–60. President of Central African Republic 1960–66. Deposed by military coup led by Bokassa 1966; imprisoned 1969–76. Appointed an adviser to President Bokassa 1976, but helped to overthrow him 1979. President 1979 but deposed by a military coup September 1981.

Daddah, Mohtar Ould (1924–), first President of Mauritania. Born into a prominent Berber family; educ. St Louis, Senegal, and Paris. Interpreter and lawyer. Elected to territorial assembly 1957; Vice-President to Executive Council 1957; Prime Minister 1959–61. President of Republic of Mauritania 1961–78. Deposed by coup 1978. Chairman OAU 1971–2.

Danquah, Joseph Boakye (1895–1965), Ghanaian nationalist leader and politician. Born Kwawu; educated locally and at London Univ.; lawyer. Returned to Ghana and founded *Times of West Africa* in 1931 and was active in the Gold Coast Youth Movement. One of the leaders of the United Gold Coast Convention (UGCC) 1947, which campaigned for self-government for the Gold Coast. The UGCC was eclipsed by Nkrumah's Convention People's Party, and with the introduction of self-government in 1951 Danquah led the opposition to the CPP. Imprisoned by Nkrumah's regime 1961–2, 1964–5. Died in prison.

Dia, Mamadou (1910–), Senegalese politician. Educ. William Ponty School, Dakar, and in Paris; teacher and journalist. Councillor for Senegal 1946–52; helped form Bloc Démocratique Sénégalaise 1948. Grand Councillor for French West Africa and deputy in French National Assembly 1952. Vice-President Senegalese Council of Ministers 1957; President of Senegal 1958–60. Vice-President of Mali Federation 1959–60. Prime Minister of Senegal 1960–62. Imprisoned 1963–74. Political rights restored 1976.

Diori, Hamani (1916–87), first President of the Republic of Niger. Born near Niamey; educ. locally, in Dahomey and at the William Ponty School, Dakar; teacher in Niger 1936–8; instructor in language school for colonial administrators 1938–46. Helped form Niger branch of Rassemblement Démocratique Africain 1946. Represented Niger in French National Assembly 1946–51, 1956–7. Head of Government Council in Niger 1958–60; President of Niger 1960–74. Chairman of West African Economic Community 1973. Ousted from presidency by coup in 1974 and placed under house arrest until 1987. He died in Morocco.

Diouf, Abdu (1935–), President of Senegal since 1981. Educated at the universities of Dakar and Paris he graduated as a lawyer. As President Senghor's protégé he was appointed secretary-general to the presidency in 1964. By 1970 Diouf was Prime Minister and he succeeded as President of Senegal when Senghor retired in 1981. Diouf revised many of the restrictions on political party activities. He was re-elected as President in 1983. Became head of the Organisation of African Unity in 1985.

Dlamani, Prince Makhosini J. (1914–76), Swazi politician. Educ. locally and in South Africa; teacher 1940–47. Active in local politics and as rural-development officer. Leader of royalist Imbokadvo party 1964. Prime Minister of Swaziland 1967–76.

Doe, Samuel K. (1951–), elected President of Liberia in 1985. Born in eastern Liberia; joined the army 1969 becoming a sergeant in 1975. In April 1980 Doe led an assault on the presidential palace in which President Tolbert was killed. This brought to an end the long rule of the Americo-Liberians. Other members and associates of the deposed government were publicly executed. Doe became head of state and in the presidential election of 1985 he won by a narrow margin.

Eyadéma, Gnassingbe, formerly *Étienne* (1937–), Togolese soldier and head of state. Born northern Togo. Served in French army 1953–61; commissioned in Togolese army 1963; Chief of Staff 1965. Led military coup 1967; President and Minister of Defence since 1967.

Gaddafi, Mu'ammar Mohamed al- (1938–), President of Libya since 1969 and staunch Muslim. Expelled from school for political activity but joined army and studied at Military Academy, Benghazi, 1965. Commissioned in Libyan army. Organised coup which overthrew King Idris 1969. Head of state, Chairman of Revolutionary Command Council and C-in-C armed forces since 1969.

Gizenga, Antoine (1925–), Zaïrean politician. Educ. RC mission schools. Helped found Parti Solidaire Africain in Kwango-Kwilu 1959. Deputy Prime Minister in Lumumba's coalition government 1960. Established breakaway pro-Lumumba regime in Stanleyville 1960–1. Resumed office as Vice-Premier of Congo 1960–62. Imprisoned 1962–5. Exile in USSR 1966.

Gowon, Yakubu (1934–), Nigerian army officer and former head of state. Born in what is now Benue-Plateau state; educ. Zaria and Royal Military Academy, Sandhurst. Commissioned into Nigerian army 1960; served with UN emergency force in Congo 1960–61; Adjutant-General Nigerian army 1963; Chief of Staff 1966. Head of Federal Military Government and C-in-C July 1966–75. Deposed 1975. Exile in UK, where he studied at Warwick Univ. 1976–80.

Graaf, Sir de Villiers, Bart (1913–69), South African politician. Educ. at univs in South Africa, UK and Netherlands. Military service in Second World War. Elected United Party MP 1948; party leader 1956–77. Member of New Republic Party 1977.

Grunitzky, Nicolas (1913–), Togolese politician. Born in central Togo; educ. in France as an engineer. Returned to Togo 1937. Deputy in French National Assembly 1951–6. Formed Parti Togolais du Progrès and was Prime Minister 1956–8. Exiled in Dahomey 1962–3. President of Togo 1963–7; overthrown by military coup and went into exile in France 1967.

Habré, Hissène (c. 1930–), Chad revolutionary and President of the republic since 1982. The son of a northern desert shepherd, he worked as a clerk for the French army and then became an administrator. Habré joined the FAN guerrillas in Tibesti fighting President Tombalbaye in the early 1970s. In 1978 he made peace with the new president Malloum and served as Prime Minister. He also briefly served as defence minister in the government of his former associate President Goukouni who had seized power in 1979. Habré, with support from the Central Intelligence Agency, fought against Goukouni's government and took power in June 1982. With French military assistance, and the diplomatic pressure of African states, he succeeded in forcing the Libyans to withdraw their armed occupation of northern Chad. This helped Habré to consolidate his control over the country.

Haile Selassie I (1892–1975), Emperor of Ethiopia. Born into royal family, a cousin of Emperor Memelik II. Governor of Harar province 1910; regent and head of government 1916–28. Became Emperor 1930. Exiled following Italian invasion of Ethiopia 1936–41. Leading figure in Organisation of African Unity which had its headquarters in Addis Ababa. Overthrown by a military coup 1974 and died the next year while in detention.

Hassan II (1924–), King of Morocco. Born Rabat, elder son of King Mohamed V. From 1945 adviser to his father, with whom he went into exile 1953–5. At Moroccan independence became C-in-C army 1956; Prime Minister and Minister of Defence 1960. Designated heir 1957; succeeded to throne on death of his father 1961. Chairman OAU 1972.

Houphouët-Boigny, Félix (1905–), President of Ivory Coast. Son of a Baoulé chief; educ. in Bingerville and Senegal; medical assistant and planter 1925–40. President of Syndicat Agricole Africain 1944. Founded Parti Démocratique de la Côte d'Ivoire 1945; deputy in French National Assembly 1946–59; Mayor of Abidjan 1956; minister of French governments 1956–9. Prime Minister of Ivory Coast 1959; President since 1960.

Huggins, Godfrey, later *Lord Malvern* (1883–1971), Southern Rhodesian politician. Born in UK; medical practitioner. Emigrated to Southern Rhodesia 1911; member of Legislative Council 1924. Leader of Reform Party 1931. Prime Minister and Minister of Native Affairs 1933–53. Advocate of Central African Federation and its Prime Minister 1953–6. Created Lord Malvern 1955.

Hussein, Abdirizak Hadji (1924–), Somali politician. Son of a poor trader; educ. Koranic school and Al-Azhar Univ. Cairo 1953. Joined Somali Youth League 1944; President of SYL 1956. Founded Greater Somalia League 1958. MP 1959; held various ministries in government 1960–64; Prime Minister 1964–7. Imprisoned 1969–73. Somali Permanent Representative at UN 1974.

Idris I (1890–83), former King of Libya. Succeeded to head of Senussi order in 1916. Recognised by Britain as Amir of Cyrenaica 1949. Became King of Libya on the territory's independence 1950. Deposed 1969 and later sentenced to death *in absentia*. Exiled in Egypt.

Ileo, Songoamba, formerly *Joseph* (1921–), Zaïrean politician. Educ. mission school; accountant. Co-founder with Patrice Lumumba of Mouvement National Congolais 1958, but joined Abako in 1959. Prime Minister 1960–61; Minister of Information and also in charge of Katangese affairs 1961–4. Member of Political Bureau of Zaïre government 1975.

Ironsi: see *Aguiyi-Ironsi*.

Jawara, Sir Dauda Kairaba (1924–), President of the Gambia. Born McCarthy Island; educ. locally and at Achimota School, Ghana and at Edinburgh Univ.; veterinary officer 1954–60. Leader of People's Progressive Party 1960; elected to Legislative Council and Minister of Education 1960–62; Chief Minister 1962 and Prime Minister 1963–70; President of the Gambia since 1970.

Jonathan, Chief Leabua (1914–), Lesotho politician. Educ. mission schools; worked in South African mines 1930s. Involved in Basutoland local politics from 1937 onwards; member Basutoland National Council 1956; founded Basutoland National Party 1959; member of Legislative Council 1960–64; Prime Minister of Lesotho since 1965. First black prime minister to make an official visit to South Africa. Overthrown by a military coup in January 1986.

Kapwepwe, Simon Mwanza (1922–80), Zambian nationalist leader and politician. Educ. mission schools; teacher 1945–51; helped found Northern Rhodesian African National Congress 1946; studied in India 1951–5. Treasurer of ANC 1956–8. Helped form Zambia National Independence Party (UNIP); treasurer UNIP 1960–67. Detained 1959. Held various ministries in Zambian governments 1964–71, including vice-presidency 1967–70. Resigned from UNIP government to form United Progress Party 1971; UPP banned and Kapwepwe detained 1972–3. Rejoined UNIP 1977.

Karume, Sheikh Abeid (1905–72), Zanzibari politician. Born on island of Zanzibar; sailor. Active in local politics 1940s–50s; town councillor 1954; founder-member Afro-Shirazi party 1957; Minister of Health and Administration 1959. Following coup which deposed the Sultan of Zanzibar became President of Revolutionary Council 1964. With union of Zanzibar and Tanganyika became First Vice-President of Tanzania 1964–72. Assassinated 1972.

Kasavubu, Joseph Ileo (1910–69), first President of Zaïre. Born Kongo region of Belgian Congo; educ. seminary 1928–39; teacher 1940; colonial civil service 1942. President of Abako 1955; Mayor of Leopoldville 1957. President of Republic of Congo 1960, 1961–5.

Kaunda, Kenneth David (1924–), Zambian nationalist leader and politician. Born Northern Rhodesia; educ. mission schools; teacher and welfare assistant; farmer. Secretary-General African National Congress 1953; formed Zambian National Congress 1958. Imprisoned for political activity 1959–60. Founder and leader of United National Independence Party 1960. Chief Minister Northern Rhodesia 1962–4; Prime Minister and then President of Zambia from 1964.

Kawawa, Rashidi M. (1929–), Tanzanian politician. Educ. at secondary school in Tabora. Founder member of TANU 1954; President of Tanganyika Federation of Labour 1950s; member of Legislative Council 1957. Various ministerial appointments 1960–62; Prime Minister 1962; Vice-President 1962–4; Second Vice-President 1964–72; Prime Minister and Second Vice-President 1972–7; Minister of Defence and National Service 1977.

Kayibanda, Grégoire (1924–), Rwandan politician. A Hutu; educ. RC mission schools; teacher 1949 and school inspector 1953; editor of a RC newspaper. Founded Mouvement Coopératif de Ruanda in 1952, and the Mouvement Social Hutu in 1957, which became Parmehutu. Head of provisional government 1960; Prime Minister 1961; President of Rwanda 1962–3. Deposed by military coup 1963.

Keita, Modibo (1915–77), Mali politician. Born near Bamako; educ. William Ponty School, Dakar. Helped found Rassemblement Démocratique Africain in Soudan 1946. Elected to territorial assembly 1948; deputy in French National Assembly 1956. President of Mali Federation 1959–60; President of Mali 1960–68. Imprisoned 1968–77.

Kenyatta, Jomo (1891–1978), first President of Kenya, Born in Kikuyuland; educ. mission school and London School of Economics; interpreter and employee of Nairobi municipal government 1920s. General Secretary of Kikuyu Central Association. Studied and worked mainly in the UK 1931–46; author of *Facing Mount Kenya* 1938. Returned to Kenya 1946; President of Kenya African Union 1947. Imprisoned and restricted during the 'Mau Mau' emergency 1952–61. President *in absentia* of Kenya African National Union 1960. Elected to Legislative Assembly 1962; Prime Minister 1963–4; President of Kenya 1964–78.

Kerekou, Mathieu (1933–), Benin soldier and politician. Born in northern Dahomey, son of a soldier; educ. army schools; served in French army.

Commissioned in Dahomey army 1961; Commander of army 1966. Took part in military coup 1967; Vice-President of Military Revolutionary Council 1967-8; led military coup 1972; President and Prime Minister from 1972.

Khama, Sir Seretse (1921-80), Botswana head of state. Educ. Fort Hare Univ. College, South Africa, and in the UK; lawyer. Heir of Ngwato chieftainship; banned from Bechuanaland 1950-56 because of his marriage to a white woman. Founded Bechuanaland Democratic Party 1962. Elected to Legislative Assembly 1965. President of Republic of Botswana 1966-80.

Kountché, Seyni (1931-87), Niger soldier and head of state. Joined French army 1947 and served in Indochina and Algeria; sergeant 1957; military training school in France 1957-9. Joined Niger army in 1961 and undertook further military training in France 1965-7. Chief of Staff Niger army 1973-4. Led coup against President Diori 1974. President of Niger, 1974-87.

Lamizana, Sangoulé (1916-), Upper Volta soldier and head of state. Joined French army 1936; served in Second World War and in Indochina. Chief of Staff army of Upper Volta 1961; led coup which deposed President Yameogo 1966. President of Upper Volta 1966-80.

Limann, Hilla (1934-), Ghanaian diplomat and head of state. Educ. Tamale, and univs in London and Paris; teacher and educationalist. Ghanaian diplomat to United Nations 1969-79. Leader of the People's National Party and successful presidential candidate in elections of 1979. President of Ghana 1979-81.

Lumumba, Patrice (1925-61), first Prime Minister of the Congo (now Zaïre). Born Kasai province; educ. RC and Protestant schools; post-office clerk; director of a brewery 1957. Helped form Mouvement National Congolais 1958; attended independence conference in Brussels 1960. Prime Minister of Congo Republic June–Sep. 1960; advocate of a centralised government for Congo. Arrested by army and handed over to Katanga secessionists, by whom he was murdered Feb 1961.

Luthuli, Chief Albert (1898-1967), nationalist leader in South Africa. Born in Southern Rhodesia of South African parents; educ. mission schools Natal; teacher. Inherited minor Zulu chieftainship 1935. Joined African National Congress 1946 and became president of Natal branch. Led passive resistance in Defiance Campaign against apartheid and as a result deposed from his chieftainship by South African government 1952. President ANC 1952 until it was declared an illegal organisation 1960. Repeatedly 'banned' by the government after 1952. Defendant in Treason Trial and imprisoned 1956-7. Awarded Nobel Prize for Peace 1961.

Machel, Samora M. (1933–86), Mozambique nationalist leader and politician. Born Southern Mozambique; trained as medical assistant. Joined Frelimo 1963; active in guerrilla war against Portuguese 1964–74. Leader of Frelimo after death of Mondlane in 1969. President of Republic of Mozambique from 1975 until his death in an air-crash October 1986.

Macias Nguema, Francisco (1922–79), first President of Equatorial Guinea. Educ. RC mission schools; coffee-planter and colonial civil servant 1944–63. Entered politics 1963. Vice-President Administrative Council 1964–8. President and Minister of Defence of Republic of Equatorial Guinea 1968. His 10 years of arbitrary and harsh rule were ended by a coup and his execution 1979.

Maga, Hubert (1916–), first President of Dahomey (now Benin). Born northern Dahomey; educ. locally and at the William Ponty School, Dakar. Deputy in French National Assembly 1951–8. Formed Groupe Ethnique du Nord and the Mouvement Démocratique Dahoméen 1956. Prime Minister of Dahomey 1959–60; President 1960–63. First leader of three-man Presidential Council 1970–72. Deposed by military in coup in 1972 and imprisoned until 1977.

Malan, Daniel François (1874–1959), South African politician. Born western Cape Colony; educ. South Africa and the Netherlands; minister in Dutch Reformed Church. Member of National Party 1914; editor *Die Burger* 1915; Minister of Interior 1924; helped re-form National Party 1933. Prime Minister 1948–54 and led government which introduced policy of apartheid in South Africa.

Malvern, Lord: see *Huggins*.

Mancham, James Richard (1929–), first President of the Seychelles. Educ. London and Paris; lawyer in Seychelles and member of Legislative Council 1961. Founded Seychelles Democratic Party 1964. Chief Minister 1970–75; President, Republic of the Seychelles 1976–7. Deposed by coup 1977.

Mandela, Nelson Rolihlahla (1918–), South African nationalist leader. Born in Transkei; educ. Fort Hare Univ. College 1938–40; lawyer 1942. Joined African National Congress and helped found Congress Youth League 1944. 'Banned' by South African government 1953–5; defendant in Treason Trial 1956–61. Leader of underground militant organisation Mkhonto we Sizwe 1961–4. Arrested and sentenced to life imprisonment in 1964, a sentence served mainly on Robben Island. Released from Victor Verster prison, Cape Town, 11 Feb 1990, elected Vice-President, ANC, March 1990.

Mangope, Chief Lucas L. M. (1927–), first President of Bophuthatswana 'bantustan'. Civil servant and teacher; succeeded his father as chief. Vice-Chairman Tswana Territorial Authority 1961–8. Chief Minister of Bophuthatswana 1972–7; President of 'independent' state since 1977.

Margai, Sir Albert Michael (1910–80), Sierra Leone politician, brother of Milton Margai. Son of a Mende trader; educ. RC schools; nurse and pharmacist; studied law in London 1944–7. Member Legislative Council 1951; Minister of Education, Welfare and Local Government 1951–7. Member of Sierra Leone People's Party 1951–8. Helped found People's National Party 1958. Minister of Finance 1962–4; Prime Minister 1964–7. Exile in London 1968.

Margai, Sir Milton A. S. (1895–1964), Sierra Leone nationalist leader and politician. Born in southern Sierra Leone, son of a Mende trader and brother of Albert Margai; educ. mission schools, Fourah Bay College and in UK; medical practitioner. Member Protectorate Assembly 1940; Elected to Legislative Council 1951. Helped found Sierra Leone People's Party 1951. Chief Minister 1954–8; Prime Minister 1958–64.

Mariam, Mengistu Haile (1937–), Ethiopian soldier and head of state. A Wolamo; educ. primary school and military academy; joined army and became major. Member of the Armed Forces Co-ordinating Committee (Dergue), which helped overthrow Emperor Haile Selassie 1974; head of Executive Committee of Dergue; head of state 1977.

Masire, Quett K. J. (1925–), President of Botswana since July 1980. Trained as a journalist; became a member of the Legislative Council 1961. Founder member and Secretary-General of the Botswana Democratic Party 1962. Appointed Deputy Prime Minister 1965, Minister of Finance 1966. Leading negotiator at the constitutional conference in London 1966, which led to Botswana's independence. Vice-President of independent Botswana, becoming President on the death of Seretse Khama in July 1980.

Massemba-Débat, Alphonse (1921–1977), Congo politician. Educ. locally; teacher in Chad 1940–47; secretary of Association of Chad évolués 1945–7. Returned to Middle Congo 1947. Member of Congo Assembly 1959–63; Minister of Planning 1961; Head of provisional government and Minister of Defence 1963. President of Republic of Congo 1963–8. Arrested 1969.

Matanzima, Chief Kaiser D. (1915–), South African politician. A Xhosa; educ. Lovedale Mission and Fort Hare Univ. College; lawyer. Member of United Transkeian Territorial Council 1942–56; Chief of Transkei Territorial Authority 1961, and Chief Minister 1963. President of the 'independent' bantustan Republic of Transkei from 1976 to his retirement in 1987.

Matthews, Zachariah K. (1901–68), South African academic and political leader. Born in Kimberley; educ. Fort Hare Univ. College, Yale, London School of Economics; lawyer. Principal of Adams College, Natal, 1925. Professor of African Studies and later Acting Principal of Fort Hare 1936 onwards. An organiser of the All-African Convention 1935. Joined African National Congress 1942. Defendant in the Treason Trial 1956–9; imprisoned 1960. Botswana ambassador to the United States in the 1960s and at the UN 1966–8.

M'Ba, Léon (1902–67), Gabon politician. Born Libreville; educ. RC school; accountant, journalist and administrator. Elected as Rassemblement Démocratique Africain member to Gabon Assembly 1952; Mayor of Libreville 1956; head of government 1957–60. First President of Gabon 1960–67.

Mboya, Thomas (Tom) Joseph (1930–69), Kenyan trade-union leader and politician. A Luo born in western Kenya; educ. RC mission school and Ruskin College, Oxford. Municipal employee 1951. Treasurer Kenya African Union 1953. Founder of Nairobi People's Convention; Secretary-General Kenya Federation of Labour 1955; Member of Legislative Council and then of Kenyan Parliament 1957–69. Founder member of Kenya African National Union and its Secretary-General 1960–69. Minister of Labour 1962; Minister of Justice and Constitutional Affairs 1963; Minister for Economic Planning and Development 1964. Assassinated 1969.

Messali, Hadj (Hadj Abd-el-Kadar) (1898–1974), Algerian nationalist leader. Soldier in French army in First World War; factory worker in France and an early member of the French Communist Party. Founded *Étoile Nord-Africaine* in Paris 1925, and also the nationalist newspaper *El Ouma* ('The National'). Imprisoned by French 1933–4, 1935, 1937–9, 1940–45. Founded Union Nationale de Musulmans Nord-Africains (1935), which was banned, and then the Parti du Peuple Algérien (1937). Imprisoned again 1945–7.

Micombero, Michel (1940–), Burundi army officer and former head of state. Educ. Bujumbura and at École Royale Militaire, Brussels, 1960–62. C-in-C Burundi army 1962; Minister of Defence 1965–6. Prime Minister 1966. Led coup which overthrew monarchy and in consequence became President 1966. Deposed and imprisoned by military coup 1976.

Mobutu, Sese Seko (1930–), Zaïrean soldier and politician. Born Equator province; educ. local primary and secondary schools. Sergeant-major in *Force publique* 1949–56. Member Mouvement National Congolais 1958; attended pre-independence talks in Brussels 1959–60; Chief of Staff Congolese army 1960. Took over government in name of army 1960; C-in-C army 1962; Prime Minister and Minister of Defence 1965–6; President of Congo, now Zaïre 1965. Founded Mouvement Populaire de la Revolution, 1967.

Mohamed V (1909–61), King of Morocco. Became Sultan of Morocco 1927. Supported Moroccan independence but deposed by French 1953; exile in Comoros and Madagascar 1954–5; returned to Morocco 1955. King of independent Morocco 1956; head of government 1960–61.

Mohamed, Murtala Ramal (1937–76), Nigerian soldier and head of state. A Muslim Hausa from northern Nigeria. Trained at Sandhurst and the Royal School of Signals in Britain. Commissioned in Nigerian army; served in UN Congo operations 1960; commander Nigerian 2nd Battalion at start of Biafra war. Inspector of Signals 1968; federal Commissioner of Communications 1974. Became head of state when General Gowon was deposed in 1975. Assassinated 1976.

Moi, Daniel T. Arap (1924–), Kenyan politician. Born north-west Kenya; educ. mission and government schools; teacher 1949–57. Member of Legislative Council 1957–63; Chairman Kenya African Democratic Union 1960–61; Minister of Education 1961–2; Minister of Local Government 1962–4; member of House of Representatives 1963; Minister of Home Affairs 1964–8; Vice-President of Kenya 1967–78; President 1978.

Momoh, Joseph Saidu (1937–), President of Sierra Leone since 1985. Attended secondary school in Freetown and studied at Nigerian Military Academy and the Mons Officer Training School in the United Kingdom. Commissioned in 1963; battalion commander 1969, and force commander 1972. Became a minister of state 1975. In preparation for his retirement President Siaka Stevens chose Momoh as his successor. This was endorsed in the presidential elections of October 1985 and Momoh, now a Major-General, succeeded to the presidency.

Mondlane, Eduardo (1920–69), Mozambiquan nationalist leader. Born Gaza district; educ. mission school and univs in South Africa, Lisbon and the USA. Sociologist with research post in USA and for UN. Returned to Mozambique 1961 and helped form Frelimo 1962. Launched guerrilla war against Portuguese 1964. Murdered in Dar es Salaam 1969.

Moshoeshoe II (Constantine Bereng Seciso) (1938–), King of Lesotho. Educ. Roma College and Oxford. King 1960; went into exile for nine months 1970. Head of state again 1970.

Mubarak, Hosni (1928–), President of Egypt since the assassination of Sadat in 1981. Son of a civil servant; graduated from military academy 1949 and then trained as a pilot; became air-force chief of staff 1969, and C-in-C 1972. He directed the forces that successfully repulsed Israeli forces from the east bank of the Suez Canal during the Arab–Israeli war of 1973. He became

Vice-President in 1975 and succeeded to the presidency on the murder of President Sadat.

Mugabe, Robert Gabriel (1928–), Zimbabwean politician. A Zezeru; educ. local RC mission schools; teacher in Southern Rhodesia 1952, Northern Rhodesia 1955, and Ghana 1958–60. Returned to Southern Rhodesia 1960 and became publicity secretary of the National Democratic Party 1960. Deputy Secretary-General Zimbabwe African People's Union 1961; helped form Zimbabwe African National Union 1963. Imprisoned 1962 and 1963 and detained by Smith regime 1964–74. Released 1974 and went into exile; leader of Zimbabwe Liberation Army. Joint leader with Joshua Nkomo of Patriotic Front in guerrilla war 1976–9. His Zimbabwe African National Union – Popular Front party won the pre-independence elections of 1980 and he became Prime Minister of Zimbabwe. Executive President since December 1987.

Museveni, Yoweri (1945–), President of Uganda since 1986. Studied at the University of Dar es Salaam. Assistant Secretary for Research in Presidential Office 1970–71; Head of Front for National Salvation against President Idi Amin 1971–9. Minister of Defence 1979–80 and vice-chairman of the ruling Military Commission. Chairman of High Command of National Resistance Movement since 1981.

Mutesa II (Edward Frederick; 'King Freddie') (1924–69), first President of Uganda. A member of Buganda royal family; educ. Makerere College and Cambridge Univ. Became Kabaka (king) of Buganda 1940. Opposed the development of Uganda as a centralised state and was deported by British authorities 1953–5. Co-operated with Obote's ruling party at independence and appointed President of Uganda 1963–6. Obote seized complete power 1966 and Mutesa went into exile in London, where he died.

Muzorewa, Abel T. (1925–), Zimbabwean churchman and politician. Educ. Methodist schools and at theological college USA 1958–63; ordained 1963; bishop of United Methodist Church in Southern Rhodesia 1968. Founder President African National Council 1971; mobilised African opinion against proposed Rhodesia settlement 1971–2; member of Executive Council of the transitional government in Zimbabwe–Rhodesia 1978–80.

Mwinyi, Ali Hassan (1925–), became President of Tanzania November 1985. A Zanzibari school teacher 1954–61; studied in the United Kingdom 1961–3, and then became a senior civil servant in the Ministry of Education, Zanzibar. In 1969 he became a Minister of State in the President's Office, Minister of

Health 1972, Minister of Home Affairs 1975–7. In April 1984 Mwinyi, a strong supporter of the union of Zanzibar with Tanzania, was elected President of Zanzibar. In October of the following year he was elected President of Tanzania.

Nasser, Gamal Abdul (1918–70), Egyptian army officer and nationalist leader. Born Alexandria, son of a postal official; educ. Cairo and Alexandria. Joined Egyptian army 1937; fought in Arab–Israeli war 1948–9. Member of 'Free Officers' movement 1948 and president of its executive committee 1950. A leader of the military coup which deposed King Farouk 1952. Member, Revolutionary Command Council 1952–4; Deputy Prime Minister and Minister of Interior 1953–4. Took over power from Gen. Neguib to become President of Egypt 1954–70.

Neguib, Mohamed (1901–79), Egyptian soldier and head of state. Joined Egyptian army; fought in Arab–Israeli war 1948–9. As a major-general he was the senior officer in the 'Free Officers' movement which overthrew the monarchy 1952. Prime Minister 1952–3; President and Prime Minister 1953–4. Under house arrest from 1954.

Neto, Antonio Agostinho (1922–79), Angolan nationalist leader. Son of a Methodist pastor; educ. Methodist school Luanda and studied medicine at univs in Portugal. Returned to Angola to work in colonial medical service. Joined MPLA; imprisoned four times 1952–60 and in Cape Verde Islands 1960–62. Escaped to Congo (ex-Belgian). President of MPLA and its leader in guerrilla war against Portuguese 1962–74. First President of Republic of Angola 1974–9.

N'Gouabi, Marien (1938–77), Congolese soldier and head of state. Joined army 1962; commander Brazzaville paratroop battalion; Chief of General Staff 1968. Seized power from President Massamba-Débat and became head of National Revolutionary Council 1968. President until assassinated 1977.

Nimeri, Jaafar Mohamed al- (1930–), Sudanese army officer and head of state. Born Omdurman; educated at the Sudan Military College. Army service in Southern Sudan 1959–63; in charge Shendi district 1966–9; led military coup 1969. Chairman of the Revolutionary Command Council and Prime Minister 1969–71. President 1971 until overthrown by a coup in 1985.

Nkomo, Joshua M. N. (1917–) Zimbabwean nationalist leader. Educ. Adams College, Natal, and Univ. of South Africa. General Secretary of Rhodesian Railway African Employees Association 1951. Chairman Bulawayo branch, African National Congress 1951; President ANC 1957–60. In exile 1959–60. President National Democratic Party 1960. When NDP was banned helped form and became President of Zimbabwe African People's Union; imprisoned 1964–74; joint leader of African National Council 1976; joint leader, with Robert Mugabe, of Patriotic Front in guerrilla war 1976–9. His Zimbabwe African People's Union–Popular Front party won 20 seats in the pre-independence elections; Minister of Home Affairs 1980–81.

Nkrumah, Kwame (1909–71), nationalist leader and first President of Ghana. Born Western Gold Coast; educ. local RC school, Achimota College, Lincoln and Pennsylvania Univs USA 1935–45; studied law London 1945–7. Cochairman Fifth Pan-African Congress, Manchester 1945. Returned to Gold Coast as General Secretary of United Gold Coast Convention. Broke with UGCC and formed Convention People's Party 1949. Imprisoned 1950–51; elected to parliament and released from prison to become 'leader of government business' 1951; Prime Minister 1952–7. Prime Minister of Republic of Ghana 1957–60; President 1960–66. Deposed by military coup while on visit to Peking 1966. Exile in Guinea, where Sekou Touré made him titular co-President.

Nkumbula, Harry M. (1916–83), Zambian nationalist leader. Educ. local schools; teacher 1934; studied at Makerere College and London School of Economics 1946–50. President of Northern Rhodesia African National Congress 1951; imprisoned 1955. Supported a moderate constitution but lost support of Kaunda, who left the ANC to form UNIP 1958. Member of coalition government with Kaunda 1962–4. A leader of opposition to UNIP 1965–72; restricted 1970 but rejoined UNIP 1973.

Nujoma, Sam (1929–), Namibian nationalist leader. Educ. mission schools; railway worker and clerk to 1959. Founder SWAPO 1959; arrested same year. Went into exile 1960; presented Namibian case at UN; returned to Namibia but expelled from country 1966. Leader of SWAPO's armed struggle against South Africa's continued occupation of Namibia from 1966. Returned to Namibia for pre-independence elections 1989. First President of independent Namibia, March 1990.

Nyerere, Julius K. (1922–), Tanzanian nationalist leader and politician. Born north-west Tanganyika; educ. Tabora, Makerere College 1943–5 and Edinburgh Univ. 1949–52; secondary-school teacher 1945–49, 1952–3. Secretary of Tanganyika African Association 1953; temporary nominated member of Tanganyika Legislative Council. Founder member and President of TANU 1954; full-time organiser of TANU 1955. Nominated member Legislative Council 1957, but resigned. Elected to Legislative Council 1958; Chief Minister 1960–61; Prime Minister 1961–2; President of Tanzania 1964. Introduced Arusha Declaration 1967. Resigned as President 1985.

Obasanjo, Olusegun (1937–), Nigerian army officer and former head of state. A Yoruba, born Abeokuta. Joined army 1958; trained at military colleges in

UK and India; a military engineer. Served with Nigerian unit in UN Congo peacekeeping force 1960; military commander in Federal forces during Biafran war 1967–70. Federal Commissioner of Works and Housing 1975; Chief of Staff 1975; head of state 1975–9.

Obote, A. Milton (1924–), Ugandan nationalist leader. Born Lango district, north-east Uganda; educ. mission schools and Makerere College; worked as labourer, clerk and salesman in Kenya 1950–57. Founder member of Kenya African Union. Member Uganda National Congress 1952–60; elected to Legislative Council 1957. Helped form Uganda People's Congress 1960; leader of opposition in Ugandan parliament 1961–2; Prime Minister 1962–71; President of Uganda 1966–71. Deposed by military coup led by Gen. Amin. Exile in Tanzania 1971–9. Regained presidency 1980. Toppled from power by General Tito Okello July 1985, and fled into exile in Zambia.

Odinga, Ajuma Oginga (1911–), Kenyan politician. A Luo; educ. Alliance High School, Kenya, and Makerere College; schoolteacher; active in local politics 1947–57. Elected Legislative Council 1957; Vice-President Kenya African National Union 1960–66; Minister of Home Affairs 1963–4; Vice-President of Kenya 1964–6; resigned office to form Kenya People's Union 1966, which was banned by government 1969. Imprisoned 1969–71, 1977. Rejoined KANU 1971.

Ojukwu, Chukwenmeka O. (1933–), Nigerian army officer and politician. An Ibo; educ. Lagos and Oxford Univ. Joined Nigerian army 1957; attended military college UK; served in UN peacekeeping force in Congo 1962; Lieutenant-colonel 1963. Military governor Eastern Nigeria 1966; proclaimed Eastern Region the independent Republic of Biafra 1967; President of Biafra and leader in war with federal Nigeria 1967–70. On collapse of Biafra fled to Ivory Coast 1970.

Olympio, Sylvanus (1902–63), Togolese politician and head of state. Born Lomé; studied at London School of Economics; district manager of United Africa Company. President of Togolese Assembly 1946; leader Togolese government 1958–60; President of Republic of Togo 1960–63. Killed in military coup 1963.

Pereira, Aristides Maria (1924–), Cape Verde politician. Educ. Senegal; radio telegraphist. Founded PAIGC with Amilcar Cabral (q.v.) 1956; exile in Guinea 1960. Leader of PAIGC war council in guerrilla war with Portugal 1965–74. President of Republic of Cape Verde 1975.

Ramanantsoa, Gabriel (1906–), Malagasy soldier and politician. Educ. Antananarivo, at military colleges in Madagascar and France. Joined French army

1931; served North Africa, Paris, Indochina 1931–55. C-in-C Malagasy army 1960–72. President 1972–5.

Ramgoolam, Sir Seewoosagur (1906–86), Mauritian politician. Educ. Mauritius and London Univ.; practised as medical doctor in Mauritius. Member Legislative Council 1940–48, and Executive Council 1948. Ministerial Secretary to the Treasury 1958–60; Chief Minister and Minister of Finance 1961. Prime Minister 1965; Chairman OAU 1977–8. Governor-General of Mauritius 1984–6.

Ratsiraka, Didier (1936–), Malagasy naval officer and former head of state. Educ. in Madagascar and at French naval college; naval posts 1963–70. Minister of Foreign Affairs 1972–5; President Supreme Revolutionary Council 1975; President of Republic 1976.

Rawlings, Jerry (1948–), Ghanaian air-force officer and former head of state. Educ. Achimota College and Univ. of Ghana; commissioned in air-force. Led abortive coup and imprisoned 1979; escaped from prison and staged successful coup a few months later. Headed Armed Forces Revolutionary Council. Head of state but returned power to an elected president in 1979. Retired from air-force 1979. Seized power again in a coup December 1982.

René, France Albert (1935–), Second President of Seychelles. Educ. Switzerland and UK; lawyer 1957. Founded and led Seychelles People's United Party 1964; member of Legislative and National Assembly 1965–77; Minister of Works 1975–7 and Prime Minister 1976–7. Seized power and became President 1977.

Roberto, Holden (1925–), Angolan nationalist leader. Born São Salvador, northern Angola; educ. at mission schools in Belgian Congo. Formed União das Populaçoes de Angola (1954), which joined other nationalist groups in 1963 to become the Frente Nacional de Libertação de Angola (FNLA). Led FNLA in guerrilla war with Portugal 1963–74. Continued war against the government of Angola following the withdrawal of Portuguese forces in 1975.

Sadat, Mohamed Anwar El (1918–81), Egyptian head of state. Educ. military college; joined army 1938. Member of 'Free Officers' movement 1948, and the Revolutionary Command Council after army coup 1952. Minister of State 1955–6; Vice-Chairman National Assembly 1957–61; Speaker United Arab Republic Assembly 1961–9; Vice-President 1964–6, 1969–70. Interim President 1969–70; President of Egypt 1970–81. Negotiated peace terms with Israel 1977–9. Assassinated 1981.

Sankara, Thomas (1950–87), army officer and President of Burkina Faso

1983–7. Military cadet at the age of 19 in Ouagadougou, then in Madagascar and the Parachute Training Centre in France, 1971–4. Lieutenant during brief border war with Mali 1974, which increased the radical ideas he had acquired in Paris. Held ministerial post in the Saye Zerbo government, but increasingly his Marxist revolutionary views looked to a 'popular revolution' to help solve the social injustice which he believed had been caused by French colonialism. Following 1983 coup he became Prime Minister and head of state. His radical policies, over women's equality, economics, and towards the large Mossi community earned him enemies. He was deposed and shot in a coup led by his close associate Blaise Compaoré in October 1987.

Santos, José Eduardo dos (1942–), second President of Angola. Born Luanda; educ. Moscow (petroleum engineering) and Lisbon (medicine). An early member of the MPLA and organiser of its medical services during the guerrilla war against the Portuguese 1964–74. At independence became Foreign Minister and First Deputy Prime Minister, Planning Minister and head of the National Planning Commission 1976–7. President on death of Agostinho Neto (q.v.) 1979.

Sassou-Ngeusso, Denis (1943–), army officer and President of the People's Republic of Congo since 1979. Attended secondary school, joined the army and did military training in France. Active in the Parti Congolais du Travail from 1961; became Minister of Defence 1975. Designated head of state 1979 and sworn in as President later that year.

Savimbi, Jonas (1934–), Angolan politician. Born Central Angola; educ. Angola and Switzerland. Leader of Popular Union of Angola (UPA) and Foreign Minister in the Angolan government-in-exile 1962–4. Formed Union for the Total Independence of Angola (UNITA) 1966 and fought against the Portuguese until 1974. When Angola became independent the UNITA forces continued a civil war from bases in the south-east of the country supported by South Africa.

Senghor, Léopold Sédar (1906–), poet and first President of Senegal. Born Joal, Senegal; educ. RC schools Dakar, and Univ. of Paris; teacher in France 1935–9. Joined French army 1939; prisoner-of-war 1940–42; member of Resistance 1942–4. Helped found Bloc Africain 1945 and the journal *La Présence Africaine* in Paris 1947. Deputy for Senegal in French National Assembly 1946–58; formed Bloc Démocratique Sénégalaise 1948. University teacher 1948–58. Formed Union Progressiste Sénégalaise 1958. President of Federal Assembly, Mali Federation 1959; President of Senegal 1960–81. A distinguished poet in French.

Shagari, Alhaji Shehu Usman A. (1925–), Nigerian head of state. Born in northern Nigeria; educ. there and became schoolteacher. Member of the federal parliament 1954–8; Federal Minister of Economic Development 1959–60; Minister of Establishments 1960–62, of Internal Affairs 1962–5, of Works 1965–6. State Commissioner for Education, Sokoto province, 1968–70; Federal Commissioner for Economic Development and Reconstruction 1968–70, and Finance 1971–5. Member of the Constituent Assembly 1977. Successful presidential candidate for the National Party of Nigeria in the elections of 1979. President of Nigeria 1979, but overthrown by a military coup in December 1983.

Siad Barre, Mohamed (1919–), Somali soldier and head of state. Educ. locally and at military academy in Italy. Police officer in British and Italian trust administrations 1941–50. Joined Somali army as colonel 1960. President following army coup 1969.

Sisulu, Walter M. U. (1912–), South African nationalist leader. Born Transkei; educ. mission schools. Joined African National Congress Youth League 1944; organised Defiance Campaign to oppose apartheid 1952; restricted by government 1952–6; defendant in Treason Trial 1956–61. Imprisoned 1962; escaped to Bechuanaland but returned to South Africa; recaptured and sentenced to life imprisonment on Robben Island 1964; transferred to mainland, 1982, released 1989.

Sithole, Ndabaningi (1920–). Zimbabwean nationalist leader. Educ. Waddilove Institute, Southern Rhodesia; teacher 1941–53; studied theology in USA 1953–6 and ordained as Congregational clergyman 1958. Wrote *African Nationalism* 1959. President African Teachers' Association 1959–60; treasurer National Democratic Party 1960. With Joshua Nkomo founded Zimbabwe African People's Union 1962; split with Nkomo and helped form Zimbabwe African National Union 1963; imprisoned by Smith regime 1964–75; exile in Zambia 1975–7 as leader of African National Council; formed his own faction of the ANC; negotiated with Smith regime and became a member of the Executive Council of the transitional government in Zimbabwe–Rhodesia 1978–80.

Smith, Ian Douglas (1919–), white Rhodesian politician. Born Southern Rhodesia; educ. Gwelo and Rhodes Univ., South Africa. Served with Royal Air Force in Second World War; farmer. Member of Southern Rhodesian Legislative Assembly 1948; member of Federal Parliament, 1953, becoming Chief Whip for United Federal Party. Helped found Rhodesia Front 1962. Prime Minister 1964–78. Declared Southern Rhodesia independent of UK 1965 (UDI). Forced by guerrilla war and external pressure to negotiate an internal settlement with certain African nationalists 1978. Member of Executive Council of the transitional government in Zimbabwe–Rhodesia 1978–80.

Smuts, Jan Christian (1870–1950), South African politician. Born Western Cape Colony; educ. Stellenbosch and Cambridge Univs 1889–94; lawyer 1895. Moved to Transvaal 1896; State Attorney of Transvaal 1898–1900. General commanding Boer troops in Cape 1901–2. Helped form an Afrikaner party, Het Volk, in Transvaal 1906; Minister of Interior and Education in Transvaal Colony 1907–9; Transvaal delegate to National Convention 1909. South African Minister for Mines, Interior, Defence, Finance 1910–19. Commanded forces in South West African campaign 1914–15; East Africa 1916–17. Member Imperial War Cabinet in UK 1917–18. Prime Minister, Minister of Defence, Native Affairs 1919–24; leader of white opposition in South African parliament 1924–33; Deputy Prime Minister, Minister of Justice in United Party government 1933–9; Prime Minister, Minister of Defence, External Affairs 1939–48. Defeated by National Party in general election 1948.

Sobhuza II (1899–1982), King of Swaziland. Educ. Lovedale College, South Africa. Installed as King 1921. Head of state of independent Swaziland 1968; assumed full executive and legislative powers 1973.

Sobukwe, Robert M. (1924–77), South African nationalist leader. Born Cape Province; educ. mission schools, Fort Hare Univ. College. President Students' Representative Council 1949; member African National Congress Youth League. Became teacher but dismissed for his part in the Defiance Campaign against apartheid 1952. Univ. teacher 1953–60. Helped found Pan-African Congress and became its president 1959. An organiser of anti-'pass-law' demonstrations 1960. Banned and imprisoned 1960–69. Released from prison but restricted to Kimberley 1969–77.

Stevens, Siaka Probyn (1905–   ), Sierra Leone head of state. Born in northern Sierra Leone; educ. Freetown; railwayman and miner. Founded Mine-workers Union 1943; appointed representative in Protectorate Assembly 1943. Studied at Ruskin College, Oxford, 1945. Helped found Sierra Leone People's Party 1951. Member of Protectorate Assembly; Minister of Lands, Labour, Mines; member Government Executive Council 1953. Attended independence conference London 1960. Founded All People's Congress Party 1960; Mayor of Freetown. Invited to be Prime Minister but forced into exile by army 1967; returned to Sierra Leone as Prime Minister 1968. President 1971–85.

Strijdom, Johannes Gerhardus (1893–1958), South African politician. Born Cape Province; educ. South African univs; lawyer and farmer. Elected to South African parliament 1929; Minister of Lands and Irrigation 1948; Prime Minister 1954–8.

Tambo, Oliver (1917–), South African nationalist leader. Born Pondoland; educ. mission schools and Fort Hare Univ. College; teacher 1942–7; lawyer 1952. Joined African National Congress Youth League 1944; member of ANC executive 1949; Secretary-General 1955. Defendant in Treason Trial 1956–7. Deputy President ANC 1959; went into exile from South Africa 1960; President of ANC in exile 1977. Returned from exile, 1989, in readiness for Namibian independence in 1990.

Todd, Reginald Stephen Garfield (1908–), white Rhodesian politician. Born in New Zealand; educ. New Zealand and South Africa. Came to Southern Rhodesia as a missionary 1934. Member Southern Rhodesian Legislative Assembly 1946. President United Rhodesia Party and Prime Minister of Federation of Rhodesia and Nyasaland 1953–8. Helped form multi-racial Central Africa Party 1959 and then the New Africa Party 1961. Returned to farming 1962. Opponent of Smith regime; restricted and imprisoned 1965–6, 1972–6. Associated with Joshua Nkomo in the elections of 1980.

Toiva Ja Toiva, Andimba (1924–), Namibian nationalist leader. Born Ovamboland; educ. mission school. Served in South African forces in Second World War. Miner of Rand; moved to Cape Town and involved in nationalist politics; expelled from South Africa 1957. Founder member of South West Africa People's Organization (SWAPO) 1959 and its Northern Region secretary. Arrested 1966; sentenced to life imprisonment 1968. Released 1984.

Tolbert, William Richard (1913–80), President of Liberia. Educ. Liberia College, Monrovia; civil servant 1935–43. Member House of Representatives 1943–51; Vice-President 1951–71; President 1971–80. President of Baptist World Alliance 1965–6. Assassinated in the 1980 army coup.

Tombalbaye, N'Garta, formerly *François*, (1918–75), Chad politician. Born in Chad and educ. locally; teacher; trade-union organiser. Helped organise the Chad branch of the Rassemblement Démocratique Africain (RDA) in 1947. Member of the territorial assembly 1952, and also of the General Council of West Africa 1957. Prime Minister of Chad 1959–62; President 1962–75. Killed in a military coup in Apr 1975.

Touré, Ahmad Sekou (1922–84), first President of Guinea. Educ. koranic school and Conakry 1936–40. Commercial worker and trade-union organiser 1945–7. Helped form Union Cégétiste des Syndicats de Guinée; attended the Confédération Générale des Travailleurs (CGT) Congress in Paris 1947; imprisoned by French 1947. Helped found Rassemblement Démocratique Africain in Guinea 1946 and Secretary-General of that branch 1952;

Secretary-General CGT in Guinea 1952; organised general strike 1953. Member Territorial Assembly 1953; Mayor of Conakry 1955. Deputy in French National Assembly 1956. Founded Union Générale des Travailleurs d'Afrique Noir 1957. Vice-President Governor's Council 1957. Secured overwhelming *non* vote in de Gaulle's referendum 1958 and Guinea became independent. President 1958–84.

Traoré, Moussa (1936–   ), Mali politician. Born Kayes; educ. cadets' college, Kati, and in France. Non-commissioned officer in French army. Senior officer in Mali army 1964. President of Mali following coup 1968.

Tshombe, Moïse (1919–69), Congolese politician. Born Katanga (Shaba) province, had close links with Lunda royal family; educ. mission schools; businessman. Helped found Confédération des Associations du Katanga (Conakat) 1957. President of secessionist Katanga province 1960–63. Exile from Congo 1963–4 but returned as President 1964–5. Went into exile a year after Mobutu's coup, 1966, and sentenced to death *in absentia* by Kinshasa high court 1967. In same year he was kidnapped to Algiers, where he died in prison.

Tsirinana, Philibert (1912–   ), first President of Madagascar. Born northern Madagascar; educ. locally and in France 1946–50. Organised Social Democratic Party. Member of Representative Assembly 1956; deputy to French National Assembly 1957. Deputy President of Madagascar 1958; President 1959–72. Overthrown by military coup 1972.

Tubman, William V. S. (1895–1971), Liberian President. Born Maryland, south-east Liberia, a member of the Americo-Liberian elite; educ. Methodist seminary; teacher 1913–17; lawyer and Methodist preacher. True Whig Party member of Senate 1922–30; Deputy President Supreme Court 1937–44. President of Liberia 1944–71.

Tutu, Desmond (1931–   ), Anglican Archbishop of Cape Town since 1986. Son of a schoolteacher, born in the Western Transvaal, attended school in Sophiatown and was greatly influenced by Trevor Huddleston. Graduating from the University of South Africa in 1955 he became a teacher and was then ordained in 1960. Studied and worked in Britain and Lesotho. As Dean of Johannesburg and secretary of the South African Council of Churches he increasingly took a lead in opposing apartheid. Awarded the Nobel Peace prize 1984; in the same year he became Bishop of Johannesburg. In 1986 Tutu became the first black African Archbishop of Cape Town.

Verwoerd, Hendrik Frensch (1901–66), South African politician. Born

Netherlands but taken as a baby to South Africa; educ. South Africa, Netherlands and Germany; Professor of Psychology and later Sociology, Stellenbosch Univ. 1927. Founder and editor of *Die Transvaaler* 1937. Appointed to Senate by National Party after its victory in general elections 1948. As Minister of Bantu Affairs he introduced the apartheid legislation 1950–58. Prime Minister 1958–66. Strong advocate of a South African republic and withdrawal from Commonwealth – both achieved in 1961. Crushed African opposition 1960–64. Assassinated in parliament by a mentally deranged man 1966.

Vorster, Balthazar Johannes (1915–83), South African politician. Born Cape Province; educ. Stellenbosch Univ.; lawyer. Interned for pro-Nazi sympathies during Second World War. National Party MP 1953; Deputy Minister of Education 1958; Minister of Justice 1961–66; Prime Minister 1966–78. President of South Africa 1978, but resigned following 'Muldergate' scandal 1979.

Welensky, Sir Roland (Roy) (1907–   ), white Rhodesian politician. Born Southern Rhodesia; educ. locally; railway worker from age 14; boxing champion. Leader, Railway Workers' Union in Northern Rhodesia 1933. Member Northern Rhodesian Legislative Council 1938–53; founded Northern Rhodesia Labour Party 1941; chairman unofficial opposition in Legislative Council 1947–53. A strong advocate of a federation in Central Africa, he attended the Victoria Falls Conference in 1951. Elected to Federal Parliament; Deputy Prime Minister 1953; Prime Minister and Minister of External Affairs of Federation of Rhodesia and Nyasaland 1956–63. Retired from politics 1964.

Whitehead, Edgar C. F. (1905–71), Southern Rhodesian politician. Born and educ. UK; emigrated to Southern Rhodesia 1928; civil servant 1928–30; farmer 1930–39; elected to parliament 1939; war service 1940–45. Southern Rhodesian High Commissioner in London 1945–6; Minister of Finance 1946–53. Retired to farming 1953–7. Representative of Federation of Rhodesia and Nyasaland in USA 1957–8; Prime Minister of Southern Rhodesia 1958–62.

Yameogo, Maurice (1921–   ), first President of Upper Volta. A Mossi; educ. locally; civil servant and trade-union leader. Elected to territorial assembly 1946; member Grand Council of French West Africa 1948. Vice-President Upper Volta section of Confédération Français du Travailleurs Chrétiens and activist in the local branch of the Rassemblement Démocratique Africain 1954. Founded the Mouvement Démocratique Voltaique 1957. Minister of Agriculture in coalition government 1957–8; Minister of the Interior 1958;

President of Upper Volta 1958–66. Deposed by military coup 1966; imprisoned 1966–70; went into exile in Ivory Coast.

Youlou, Abbé Fulbert (1917–72), first President of the Congo Republic. Born near Brazzaville; educ. at seminaries in Cameroon and Gabon; ordained an RC priest in 1946. Mayor of Brazzaville 1957. Formed Union Démocratique de la Défence du Interêts Africains, opposed to the local socialist party, the MSA. Elected to territorial assembly 1957; Minister of Agriculture 1957–8; Prime Minister 1958–9; President of Congo 1959–63. A general strike and widespread unrest in the country forced him to resign and to go into exile in Spain in 1963.

BIBLIOGRAPHY

The Africa Review (Saffron Walden: World of Information, annually from 1976).
Africa South of the Sahara (London: Europa Publications, annually from 1971).
Africa Year Book and Who's Who (London: Africa Journal, annually from 1976).
African Historical Dictionaries series. Series ed. John Woronoff. (Metuchen, NJ, Scarecrow Press, 1975–). Forty vols on individual countries to date.
Baum, Edward, and Felix Gagliano, *Chief Executives in Black Africa and South East Asia* (Athens, Ohio University Center for International Studies, 1976).
Caldwell, John C., and Chukua Okonjo, *The Population of Tropical Africa* (London: Longman, 1968).
Colonial Office Lists (London: annually from 1945).
Constitutions of African States, 2 vols, prepared by the Secretariat of the Asian–African Legal Consultative Committee, New Delhi (Dobbs Ferry, NY: Oceana, 1972).
Cook, Chris, and John Paxton, *Commonwealth Political Facts* (London: Macmillan, 1979).
Delury, George E. *World Encyclopedia of Political Systems*, 2 vols. (London: Longman, 1983)
Dickie, John, and Alan Rake, *Who's Who in Africa. The political and business leaders of Africa*. (London: African Development, 1973).
Domschke, E. and D. S. Goyer, *The Handbook of National Population Censuses: Africa and Asia* (New York: Greenwood, 1986).
Graça, John V. da., *Heads of State and Government* (London: Macmillan 1985).
Griffith, Ieuan Ll., *An Atlas of African Affairs* (London, Methuen, 1984).
Hailey, Lord, *An African Survey* (Oxford: Oxford University Press, 1938; rev. edn. 1956).
Henige, David P., *Colonial Governors from the Fifteenth Century to the Present* (Madison, WI: University of Wisconsin Press, 1971).
Hodd, Michael, *African Economic Handbook* (London: Euromonitor, 1986).
Kurian, George T. (ed.), *Encyclopaedia of the Third World*, 3 vols (New York: Facts on File, 1987).
Legum, Colin (ed.), *African Handbook*, rev. edn. (Harmondsworth: Penguin, 1969).
Legum, Colin, and John Drysdale (eds.), *Africa Contemporary Record. Annual Survey and Documents* (London: Rex Collings, vol. 1, 1968–9, published annually).
Lipschutz, Mark R., and R. Kent Rasmussen, *Dictionary of African Historical Biography*, 2nd ed. (London: Heinemann, 1986).
Makers of Modern Africa. Profiles in History (London: Africa Journal Ltd, 1981).
Martin, Phyllis M. and Patrick O'Meara (eds), *Africa* (Bloomington, IN, 2nd edn, 1986).
Middle East and North Africa (London: Europa Publications, annual).
Morony, Sean (ed), *Africa, 2 vols. Handbooks to the Modern World* (New York: Facts on File, New York, 1989).
Morrison, D. G., et al., *Black Africa: A Contemporary Handbook* (New York: Free Press, 1972).

Morrison, D. G., et al., *Black Africa. A Comparative Handbook* (London: Macmillan, 1989).

New African Yearbook (London: IPC, 1988, 7th edn).

Oliver, Roland, and Michael Crowder (eds), *The Cambridge Encyclopedia of Africa* (Cambridge: Cambridge University Press, 1981).

Ominde, S. H. and C. N. Ejiogu (eds), *Population Growth and Economic Development in Africa* (London: Heinemann, 1972).

Paxton, John (ed.), *The Statesman's Yearbook* (London: Macmillan, annually from 1945).

Potgieter, D. J. (chief ed.), *Standard Encyclopaedia of Southern Africa* (Cape Town, 1971).

Stewart, John, *African States and Rulers* (Jefferson, NC., 1989).

UN Economic Commission for Africa, *Economic Bulletin for Africa*. 1961–. (Addis Ababa: irregular).

UN Demographic Yearbook (New York: United Nations, annually).

UN Statistical Yearbook (Paris: UNESCO, annually from 1963).

Whitaker's Almanack (London, annually from 1945).

World Statistics in Brief: UN Statistical Pocketbook (New York: United Nations, 1977).

INDEX

Anglo-Egyptian Sudan, *see* sub entries
  for Sudan
Armed Forces, 201–2
Ascension Island, *see* St Helena

Biographies of leaders, 244–72
Bophuthatswana, *see* sub-entries for
  South Africa
Border disputes
  Algeria–Morocco, 197
  Egypt–Libya, 200
  France–Tunisia, 195
  Kenya–Somalia, 197
  Somalia–Ethiopia, 197–8

Chronology of major events 1945–89,
  1–11
Colonial governors, *see* Governors
Constitutions
  Algeria, 103
  Angola, 104
  Basutoland, 124
  Bechuanaland, 105–6
  Belgian Congo, 150–1
  Benin, 104–5
  Botswana, 105–6
  British Somaliland, 140–1
  Burkina Faso, 106–7
  Burundi, 107–8
  Cameroon, 108–9
  Cape Verde Islands, 109
  Central African Republic, 109–110
  Chad, 110–11
  Comoro Islands, 111–2
  Congo People's Republic, 112
  Côte d'Ivoire *see* under Ivory Coast
  Djibouti, 113
  Egypt, 113–4
  Equatorial Guinea, 114–5
  Eritrea, *see* Ethiopia
  Ethiopia, 115
  French Congo, 112

French Equatorial Africa, 116
French Guinea, 121
French Somaliland, 113
French Soudan, 127–8
French West Africa, 116–7
Gabon, 117–8
Gambia, The, 118–9
Ghana, 119–20
Gold Coast, 119–20
Guinea, 121
Guinea-Bissau, 121–2
Italian Somaliland, 140–1
Ivory Coast, 122
Kenya, 122–4
Lesotho, 124
Liberia, 125
Libya, 125–6
Madagascar, 126
Malawi, 126–7
Mali, 127–8
Mauritania, 128–9
Mauritius, 129
Mayotte, *see* Comoro Islands
Morocco, 129–30
Mozambique, 130–1
Namibia, 131–2
Niger, 133
Nigeria, 133–4
Northern Rhodesia, 151–2
Nyasaland, 126–7
Portuguese Guinea, 121–2
Rhodesia, 153–4
Rhodesia and Nyasaland, 135–6
Ruanda-Urundi, 136
Rwanda, 136
St Helena, 137
São Tomé and Príncipe, 137
Senegal, 138
Seychelles, 138–9
Sierra Leone, 139–40
Somalia, 140–41
South Africa, 141–2

South West Africa, *see* Namibia
Spanish Guinea, 114–5
Spanish Sahara, 143–4
Sudan, 144
Swaziland, 145–6
Tanganyika, 146–7
Tanzania, 146–7
Togo, 147–8
Tunisia, 148
Ubangi-Chari, 109–10
Uganda, 149
Upper Volta, 106–7
Zaïre, 150–1
Zambia, 151–2
Zanzibar, 129, 152
Zimbabwe, 153–4

Eritrea, *see also* sub-entries for Ethiopia

Foreign affairs, 212–20

Governors
  Algeria, 12
  Angola, 13
  Basutoland, 25–6
  Bechuanaland, 14
  Belgian Congo, 41
  British Somaliland, 35–6
  Cameroon, 15–16
  Cape Verde Islands, 16
  Chad, 17–18
  Comoro Islands, 18
  Dahomey, 13
  Eritrea, 20–1
  French Congo, 18–19
  French Equatorial Africa, 21
  French Guinea, 24
  French Somaliland, 35–6
  French Soudan, 27–8
  French West Africa, 21–2
  Gabon, 22
  Gambia, The, 22–3
  Gold Coast, 23
  Italian Somaliland, 35–6
  Ivory Coast, 25
  Kenya, 25
  Libya, 26
  Madagascar, 27
  Mauritania, 28
  Mauritius, 28–9
  Morocco, 29
  Mozambique, 29–30

Namibia, 30
Niger, 31
Nigeria, 32
Northern Rhodesia, 41
Nyasaland, 27
Portuguese Guinea, 24
Rhodesia and Nyasaland, 32–3
Ruanda-Urundi, 33
St Helena, 33
São Tomé and Príncipe, 34
Senegal, 34
Seychelles, 34–5
Sierra Leone, 35
Southern Rhodesia, 42
Spanish Guinea, 20
Spanish Sahara, 37–8
Sudan, 38
Swaziland, 38
Tanganyika, 39
Togo, 39–40
Tunisia, 40
Ubangi-Chari, 16–17
Uganda, 40–41
Upper Volta, 14–15
Zanzibar, 42

Heads of state
  Algeria, 12
  Angola, 13
  Benin, 13–14
  Botswana, 14
  Burkina Faso, 14–15
  Burundi, 15
  Cameroon, 15–16
  Cape Verde Islands, 16
  Central African Republic, 16–17
  Chad, 17–18
  Comoro Islands, 18
  Congo People's Republic, 18–19
  Djibouti, 19–20
  Egypt, 20
  Equatorial Guinea, 20
  Ethiopia, 21
  Gabon, 22
  Gambia, The, 22
  Ghana, 23–4
  Guinea, 24
  Guinea-Bissau, 24
  Ivory Coast, 25
  Kenya, 25
  Lesotho, 25–6
  Liberia, 26

Libya, 26
Madagascar, 27
Malawi, 27
Mali, 27–8
Mauritania, 28
Mauritius, 28–9
Morocco, 29
Mozambique, 29–30
Namibia, 30
Niger, 31
Nigeria, 31–2
Rhodesia, 42–3
Rwanda, 33
São Tomé and Príncipe, 34
Senegal, 34
Seychelles, 34–5
Sierra Leone, 35
Somalia, 35–6
South Africa, 36–7
Sudan, 38
Swaziland, 38–9
Tanzania, 39
Togo, 39–40
Tunisia, 40
Uganda, 40–41
Upper Volta, 14–15
Zaïre, 41
Zambia, 41
Zanzibar, 42
Zimbabwe, 42–3

Ifni, *see* sub-entries for Spanish Sahara

Malagasy Republic, *see* sub-entries for
 Madagascar
Military coups, 203–11
Ministers
 Algeria, 44–5
 Angola, 45–6
 Benin, 46–7
 Botswana, 48
 Burkina Faso, 48–9
 Burundi, 49–50
 Cameroon, 51
 Cape Verde Islands, 52
 Central African Republic, 52–3
 Chad, 54–5
 Comoro Islands, 55–6
 Congo People's Republic, 56–8
 Djibouti, 58
 Egypt, 58–62
 Equatorial Guinea, 62

Ethiopia, 63–4
Gabon, 64
Gambia, The, 65
Ghana, 65–7
Guinea, 67–8
Guinea-Bissau, 68
Ivory Coast, 68
Kenya, 69
Lesotho, 69–70
Liberia, 70–71
Libya, 71–3
Madagascar, 73–4
Malawi, 74
Mali, 75
Mauritania, 76–7
Mauritius, 77–8
Morocco, 78–9
Mozambique, 80
Namibia, 80
Niger, 80–81
Nigeria, 81–2
Rhodesia and Nyasaland, 82
Rhodesia/Southern Rhodesia, 83–4
Rwanda, 84
São Tomé and Príncipe, 84–5
Senegal, 85–6
Seychelles, 86
Sierra Leone, 86–8
Somalia, 88
South Africa, 89–90
Sudan, 90–92
Swaziland, 92–3
Tanganyika, 93
Tanzania, 93–4
Togo, 94–5
Tunisia, 95–7
Uganda, 97–8
Upper Volta, 48–9
Zaïre, 98–100
Zambia, 101–102
Zanzibar, 102
Zimbabwe, 102

Parliaments
 Algeria, 103
 Angola, 104
 Basutoland, 124
 Bechuanaland, 105–6
 Belgian Congo, 150–1
 Benin, 104–5
 Botswana, 105–6
 British Somaliland, 140–1

Burundi, 107–8
Cameroon, 108–9
Cape Verde Islands, 109
Central African Republic, 109–10
Chad, 110–11
Comoro Islands, 93, 111–2
Congo People's Republic, 112
Djibouti, 113
Egypt, 113–4
Equatorial Guinea, 114–5
Ethiopia, 115
French Congo, 112
French Equatorial Africa, 116
French Guinea, 121
French Somaliland, 113
French Soudan, 127–8
French West Africa, 116–7
Gabon, 117–8
Gambia, The, 118–9
Ghana, 119–20
Gold Coast, 119–20
Guinea, 121
Guinea-Bissau, 121–2
Italian Somaliland, 140–1
Ivory Coast, 122
Kenya, 122–4
Lesotho, 124
Liberia, 125
Libya, 125–6
Madagascar, 126
Malawi, 126–7
Mali, 127–8
Mauritania, 128–9
Mauritius, 129
Mayotte, see Comoro Islands
Morocco, 129–30
Mozambique, 130–1
Namibia, 131–2
Niger, 133
Nigeria, 133–4
Northern Rhodesia, 151–2
Nyasaland, 126–7
Portuguese Guinea, 121–2
Rhodesia, 153–4
Rhodesia and Nyasaland, 135–6
Ruanda-Urundi, 136
Rwanda, 136
St Helena, 137
São Tomé and Príncipe, 137
Senegal, 138
Seychelles, 138–9

Sierra Leone, 139–40
Somalia, 140–41
South Africa, 141–2
Spanish Guinea, 114–5
Spanish Sahara, 143–4
Sudan, 144
Swaziland, 145–6
Tanganyika, 146–7
Tanzania, 146–7
Togo, 147–8
Ubangi-Chari, 109–10
Uganda, 149
Upper Volta, 106–7
Zaïre, 150–1
Zambia, 151–2
Zanzibar, 152
Zimbabwe, 153–4
Political parties
Algeria, 155–6
Angola, 156
Basutoland, 169–70
Bechuanaland, 157
Belgian Congo, 188–9
Benin, 156–7
Botswana, 157
Burkina Faso, 157–8
Burundi, 158
Cameroon, 158–9
Cape Verde Islands, 159
Central African Republic, 159–60
Chad, 160
Comoro Islands, 161
Congo People's Republic, 161
Dahomey, 156–7
Djibouti, 161–2
Egypt, 162–3
Equatorial Guinea, 163
Eritrea, 164
Ethiopia, 164
French Congo, 161
French Guinea, 168
French Somaliland, 180–1
French Soudan, 172
Gabon, 165–6
Gambia, The, 166
Ghana, 166–8
Gold Coast, 166–8
Guinea, 142, 168
Guinea-Bissau, 168
Ivory Coast, 169
Kenya, 169

Lesotho, 169–70
Liberia, 170
Libya, 170
Madagascar, 171
Malawi, 171–2
Mali, 172
Mauritania, 172
Mauritius, 173
Morocco, 173–4
Mozambique, 175
Namibia, 175–6
Niger, 176
Nigeria, 177
Northern Rhodesia, 189–192
Nyasaland, 171–2
Rhodesia, 189–192
Rwanda, 178
St Helena, 178
São Tomé and Príncipe, 178
Senegal, 178–9
Seychelles, 179–80
Sierra Leone, 180
Somalia, 180–1
South Africa, 181–4
Spanish Guinea, 163
Sudan, 184–5
Swaziland, 185
Tanganyika, 186
Tanzania, 186
Togo, 186
Tunisia, 187
Uganda, 187–8
Upper Volta, 157–8
Zaïre, 188–9
Zambia, 189
Zimbabwe, 189–192
Population
Africa, 222
Algeria, 222
Angola, 223
Benin, 223
Botswana, 224
Burkina Faso, 224
Burundi, 224
Cameroon, 225
Cape Verde Islands, 225
Central African Republic, 225
Chad, 226
Comoro Islands, 226
Congo People's Republic, 226
Djibouti, 227

Egypt, 227
Equatorial Guinea, 227
Ethiopia, 228
Gabon, 228
Gambia, The, 228
Ghana, 229
Guinea, 229
Guinea-Bissau, 229
Ivory Coast, 230
Kenya, 230
Lesotho, 230
Liberia, 231
Libya, 231
Madagascar, 231
Malawi, 232
Mali, 232
Mauritania, 232
Mauritius, 233
Morocco, 233
Mozambique, 233
Namibia, 234
Niger, 234
Nigeria, 235
Rwanda, 235
St Helena, 236
São Tomé and Príncipe, 236
Senegal, 236
Seychelles, 237
Sierra Leone, 237
Somalia, 237
South Africa, 238
Spanish Sahara, 239
Sudan, 239
Swaziland, 240
Tanzania, 240
Togo, 240
Tunisia, 241
Uganda, 241
Upper Volta, 224
Zaïre, 242
Zambia, 242
Zanzibar, 243
Zimbabwe, 243

Revolts
Algeria, 194
Angola, 195
Belgian Congo, 195–6
Kenya, 194
Madagascar, 193
Morocco, 194

Mozambique, 195
Portuguese Guinea, 195
Tunisia, 195
Rhodesia, *see also* sub-entries for
    Zimbabwe

South West Africa, *see* sub-entries for
    Namibia

Transkei, *see* sub-entries for South Africa
Treaties, 212–20
Tristan da Cunha, *see* sub-entries for
    St Helena

United Arab Republic, *see* sub-entries
    for Egypt

Venda, *see* sub-entries for South Africa

Wars, *see also* Revolts
    Algeria, 194

Burundi, 199
Chad Civil War, 198–9
Egypt, 193
Eritrea, 196–7
Ethiopia, 196–7
Mozambique Civil War, 203
Nigerian Civil War, 199
Rwanda, 199
Somalia–Ethiopia, 197–8
Southern Africa, 198
Southern Sudan, 197
Uganda Civil War, 203
Uganda–Tanzania, 199–200
Western Sahara, 200
Zaïre, 200
Western Sahara, 200; *see also*
    sub-entries for Morocco and
    Mauritania